The Accountability of Conduct

Conduct

A Social Psychological Analysis

This is a volume in
EUROPEAN MONGRAPHS IN SOCIAL PSYCHOLOGY

Series Editor: Henri Tajfel

EUROPEAN MONOGRAPHS IN SOCIAL PSYCHOLOGY 33
Series Editor: HENRI TAJFEL

The Accountability of Conduct

A Social Psychological Analysis

G.R. SEMIN
School of Social Sciences
University of Sussex, Brighton, U.K.

A.S.R. MANSTEAD
Department of Psychology
University of Manchester, Manchester, U.K.

1983

Published in cooperation with
EUROPEAN ASSOCIATION OF EXPERIMENTAL
SOCIAL PSYCHOLOGY
by
ACADEMIC PRESS
A Subsidiary of Harcourt Brace Jovanovich, Publishers
London   New York
Paris   San Diego   San Francisco   São Paulo
Sydney   Tokyo   Toronto

ACADEMIC PRESS INC. (LONDON) LTD.
24/28 Oval Road
London NW1

United States Edition published by
ACADEMIC PRESS INC.
111 Fifth Avenue
New York, New York 10003

British Library Cataloguing in Publication Data
Semin, G.R.
  The accountability of conduct.—(European monographs in social psychology;
33)
  1. Interpersonal relations   2. Psychology
  3. Series
  I. Title   II. Manstead, A.S.R.
  158'.2   HM132

  ISBN 0-12-636650-0
  LCCCN 82-73803

Printed in Great Britain at
the Alden Press, Oxford.

European Monographs in Social Psychology

Series Editor: HENRI TAJFEL

E. A. CARSWELL and R. ROMMETVEIT (*eds*)
Social Contexts of Messages, 1971

J. ISRAEL and H. TAJFEL (*eds*)
The Context of Social Psychology: A Critical Assessment, 1972

J. R. EISER and W. STROEBE
Categorization and Social Judgement, 1972

M. VON CRANACH and I. VINE (*eds*)
Social Communication and Movement: Studies of Interaction and Expression in Man
    and Chimpanzee, 1973

C. HERZLICH
Health and Illness: A Social Psychological Analysis, 1973

J. M. NUTTIN, JR
The Illusion of Attitude Change: Towards a Response Contagion Theory of Persuasion,
    1975

H. GILES and P. F. POWESLAND
Speech Style and Social Evaluation, 1975

J. K. CHADWICK-JONES
Social Exchange Theory: Its Structure and Influence in Social Psychology, 1976

M. BILLIG
Social Psychology and Intergroup Relations, 1976

S. MOSCOVICI
Social Influence and Social Change, 1976

R. SANDELL
Linguistic Style and Persuasion, 1977

A. HEENWOLD
Decoding Oral Language, 1978

H. GILES (*ed*)
Language, Ethnicity and Intergroup Relations, 1977

H. TAJFEL(*ed*)
Differentiation between Social Groups: Studies in the Social Psychology of Intergroup
    Relations, 1978

M. BILLIG
Fascists: A Social Psychological View of the National Front, 1978

C. P. WILSON
Jokes, Form, Content, Use and Function, 1979

J. P. FORGAS
Social Episodes: The Study of Interaction Routines, 1979

R. A. HINDE
Towards Understanding Relationships, 1979

A-N. PERRET-CLERMONT
Social Interaction and Cognitive Development in Children, 1980

B. A. GEBER and S. P. NEWMAN
Soweto's Children: The Development of Attitudes, 1980

S. H. NG
The Social Psychology of Power, 1980

P. SCHÖNBACH, P. GOLLWITZER, G. STIEPEL and U. WAGNER
Education and Intergroup Attitudes, 1981

C. ANTAKI (*ed*)
The Psychology of Ordinary Explanations of Social Behaviour, 1981

W. P. ROBINSON (*ed*)
Communication in Development, 1981

H. BRANDSTÄTTER, J. H. DAVIS and G. STOCK-KREICHGAUER (*eds*)
Group Decision Making, 1981

J. P. FORGAS (*ed*)
Social Cognition: Perspectives in Everyday Understanding, 1981

H. T. HIMMELWEIT, P. HUMPHREYS, M. JAEGER and M. KATZ
How Voters Decide: A Longitudinal Study of Political Attitudes extending over Fifteen
    Years, 1981

P. STRINGER (*ed*)
Confronting Social Issues: Applications of Social Psychology, Vol. 1, 1982

P. STRINGER (*ed*)
Confronting Social Issues: Applications of Social Psychology, Vol. 2, 1982

M. VON CRANACH
Goal-Directed Action, 1982

G. MUGNY
The Power of Minorities, 1982

In preparation
J. JASPERS, F. FINCHAM and M. HEWSTONE
Attribution Theory and Research: Conceptual, Developmental and Social Dimensions

P. HELMERSON
Family Interaction and Communication in Psychopathology

Preface

The monitoring and regulation of everyday activities and the maintenance of social order in daily life are problems which have not been
addressed in an integrated manner by social psychologists. There are
many facets to the regulation of everyday activities and the maintenance of social order, besides the clearly psychological. Other social
scientific disciplines, such as sociology, political theory, anthropology
and law, have treated social regulation and social control as key issues.
Within social psychology these issues have not been accorded such an
important status — but this is not to say that they have not been
addressed at all. For example, conformity research, which reached its
zenith in the late 1950s and early 1960s (cf. Allen, 1965, for a review), is
without doubt a field of investigation which addresses the issues of
social regulation and social control from a distinctly social psychological perspective. However, this research tradition has not drawn
out the relationship between the 'psychological processes' involved in
conformity and the possibility of an orderly society, largely because of
the lack of consideration by experimental social psychologists of the
role played by the social and cultural context of everyday activity.
There are other research traditions which also have a bearing on the
issues of social regulation and social control. Within 'psychological'
social psychology there is for example work on the attribution of
responsibility (e.g. Fincham & Jaspars, 1980), on the relationship
between mood states and helping behaviour, and on prosocial
behaviour in general (e.g. Staub, 1978, 1979). Within 'sociological'
social psychology there is work on the role played by emotion in
self-monitored social control (e.g. Shott, 1979), on accounts and other
forms of motive talk (e.g. Scott & Lyman, 1968), and on the management of social identity (Goffman, 1959). In sum, there has been a
widespread but poorly integrated concern within social psychology
with just those *aspects* of social life which involve social regulation and
social control, and through which social order is maintained. The
central purpose of the present volume is to establish the points of
contact between some of these diverse lines of theory and research, and
to provide an epistemological foundation and an integrative
framework within which future research can develop.

Having established the breadth of our aims in writing this book, it would be as well to outline some of the ways in which our pursuit of these aims is necessarily limited. As noted above, the regulation of social activity in everyday life is a topic which has been addressed within a variety of disciplines other than social psychology. We have drawn on concepts and findings from these other disciplines in the course of this book, but it is clearly impossible to do justice to all the various approaches in this type of book. Indeed, even within the context of the social psychological research that is relevant to social regulation and social control we have been selective, focusing on what may be termed the *social-cognitive* approach, as opposed to what may be termed the *social-emotional* approach. The meaning of this distinction is best conveyed in the course of a brief description of the subject-matter of this volume.

In this book we shall examine the social practices which are employed in everyday life in order to repair 'fractured' social interaction, that is social interaction which has been disrupted by the fact that one or more parties to the interaction have (or are thought to have) committed a social transgression. The practices involved in repairing fractured interaction include the means by which breaches of shared rules, conventions and standards are identified, explained, understood, and normalized. These practices we refer to collectively as 'the accountability of conduct', because they together reflect the fact that individuals are held to be responsible for their actions, and when these actions are thought to be questionable the individual concerned feels obliged or is obliged by others to provide an account — an explanation of the actions which mitigates either the actor's responsibility for the action or the questionability of the action — or to apologize for the action. The medium for these accounting practices is *talk*, and talk therefore constitues the central object of our inquiry. It is this emphasis which we term the *social-cognitive* approach to social regulation and social control.

A rather different and currently re-emerging approach to these same issues emphasizes *social-emotional* processes. Indeed, this approach has a rather longer (but more discontinuous) history in the social scientific literature than the social-cognitive approach outlined above. For example, the longstanding debate in the anthropological and cross-cultural psychology literature about 'shame and guilt' cultures (e.g. Ausubel, 1955), the psychoanalytic work on civilization and society (e.g. Badcock, 1981; Bocock, 1976; Freud, 1930, 1974), and the more recent work on 'emotion rules' (e.g. Hochschild, 1979; Shott, 1979) can all be seen as contributions to the understanding of social order and social control. The distinctive characteristic of these lines of research is their emphasis on the role played by emotional processes in socializing individuals to monitor and control their own conduct in everyday life. The present volume does not attempt to incorporate this social-emotional approach, and is therefore quite selective in focusing on those aspects of social regulation which are manifested in everyday talk.

The first chapter of this volume serves two main purposes. The first is to provide the reader with an idea of the theoretical framework which we believe should guide thinking and research in this field of inquiry, together with our reasons for rejecting the better established and ostensibly suitable framework provided by attribution theory. The second purpose of Chapter 1 is to specify the generic conditions under which conduct becomes questionable. It is as well at this point to explain our use of the term *conduct*. This term is used in preference to 'behaviour' on the grounds that all judgments pertaining to social action are evaluative, whether the judgments are made about one's own actions or those of another person. Even when action does not appear to have evaluative implications because it accords with cultural standards, it is not evaluatively neutral. 'Behaviour' is a term used in psychology to refer to action in an ostensibly neutral fashion, so we have preferred to use the term 'conduct'.

called into question from a variety of perspectives. Chapter 2 examines this issue from the perspective of self-presentation. Drawing heavily on the concepts and observations of Erving Goffman, it is argued that a fundamental feature of social interaction is the presentation of selves that are acceptable to the other parties to the interaction. Because each individual has a vested interest in maintaining the acceptability of his or her 'face', or self-presentation, he or she will engage in presentational strategies and tactics intended to minimize threats to the encounter and/or to restore social equilibrium when it is threatened by an action or occurrence that does call into question an individual's self-presentation. These strategies and tactics are given the generic term 'facework' by Goffman, and the chief purpose of this chapter is to describe systematically the typology of facework practices developed by Goffman, and to review immediately relevant empirical work in terms of this typology.

Chapter 3 consists of a finer-grained examination of those facework practices which manifest themselves in talk. These practices are referred to collectively as *motive talk*, following Mills (1940), insofar as they seek to ward off or revise potential or actual questioning of the motives underlying certain actions. Four types of motive talk are distinguished: apologies, requests, disclaimers, and accounts. The properties and functions of each type are considered both in isolation and in relation to other types of motive talk. Empirical work directly relevant to motive talk is then reviewed in the light of the resulting typologies.

In Chapter 4 we examine the antecedents and consequences of the ascription of responsibility for conduct. This is an area which has been the subject of intensive inquiry within experimental social psychology, but which has also been studied within other social scientific disciplines such as social anthropology and legal philosophy. Identifying the conditions under which individuals are held responsible for their actions provides a perspective on accounting practices that relates intimately to the most obviously institutionalized aspect of accounting, namely the judicial process.

Finally, in Chapter 5 we examine the accountability of conduct from a societal perspective. Here we consider the functions served by the accountability of conduct for the human species and thereby seek to delineate the role it plays in human societies in general. Examining the ontological and epistemological foundations of the accountability of conduct enables us to consider the more concrete issues raised in earlier chapters in a different light. Specifically, this final chapter deals with the degree to which the concepts and findings described and discussed in earlier chapters are bound by cultural and historical constraints, and commensurately with the degree to which these concepts and findings have transcultural and transhistorical validity.

March 1983   G.R.Semin and A.S.R.Manstead

Acknowledgements

As with any book of this kind, there are some individuals whose help we would like to acknowledge. Several colleagues were kind enough to read one or more of the chapters in draft form and have given us the benefit of their comments. They are: Rod Bond, Barbara Lloyd, Thomas Leithaeuser, Caroline McCulloch, Brian Parkinson, Rex Rogers, Claudius Sauer, Wes Sharrock, and Neil Warren. Special thanks are due to Marie Jahoda for her insightful comments on several of the chapters. We have not always followed their advice but we are confident that the book has benefitted as a result of their suggestions. We would also like to thank the staff of Academic Press for their help, especially Ruth Gadsby and Deborah Macaulay.

We would particularly like to take this opportunity to acknowledge the encouragement given to us by Henri Tajfel, who kindly invited us to have this volume published as part of the *European Monographs in social Psychology* series. We were greatly saddened by Henri's death during the preparation of this book, not simply because it meant that he never saw the completed manuscript, but also because it robbed British social psychology of one of its most inspirational figures. We hope that he would have been pleased with the final version of the book.

Finally, we would like to acknowledge the help and support given to us by Annette Woodroffe and Caroline McCulloch, who have seen this project to develop from a hazy but (to us) exciting idea, through several drafts and occasional bouts of self-doubt, to its completion. Without their patience, advice and encouragement, it would have been a more difficult book to write.

Credit is also due to the following for permission to reprint or adapt material: Tables 3.1, 3.2, 3.3 and 3.4 are adapted from P. Schönbach, A category system for account phases. *European Journal of Social Psychology,* 1980, **10,** 195-200, by permission of the author and John Wiley & Sons Ltd. Tables 3.5 and 3.6 are adapted from J. T. Tedeschi & M. Riess, Predicaments and impression management. In C. Antaki (Ed.), *Ordinary Explanations of Behaviour.* Academic Press, 1981, by permission of Academic Press.

To our parents

Contents

1

The explanation of social behaviour in everyday life

1.1. Introduction

This book is concerned with the social practices employed by people in coping with everyday situations that are problematic in the sense that they do not fit into the flawless progress of social interaction. In large part, our everyday social life moves within tacitly 'accounted' boundaries; that is, the behaviours we engage in are implicitly taken to be rational, warrantable and intelligible. However, there are also numerous incidents in our everyday lives when such routine execution of social behaviour is disrupted, such as intentional or unintentional breaches of social conventions and rules; the challenging of another person's reputation; the threatening of identities; various types of *faux pas;* the uncovering or disclosure of private intentions or motives.

In addressing the social psychology of such problematic incidents, the general themes that will be pursued in this book are (i) the perception and interpretation of such incidents, and (ii) the social practices that are employed, both by actors experiencing such problematic situations and by observers who witness or participate in such incidents, to explain and normalize these disruptions of social interaction. It should be noted in advance that an important aspect of these situations is that they occur, and are perceived and recognized as such, against the backdrop of routine activities.

The central purpose of the chapters that follow will be to analyse disruptions of social interaction, by examining their genesis, the interpretative processes guiding actors and observers, and the types of strategies employed to explain, understand, and normalize disruptions. However, before attempting such an analysis of 'fractured social interaction' it is necessary to examine one broad theoretical approach, namely attribution theory, which would appear to be a potential theoretical framework for the analysis of fractured social interaction and to discuss its features with regard to the potential it offers for such an analysis.

The themes addressed in the present volume clearly belong to a broader set of issues which stem from the question of how we understand, interpret and explain others and ourselves, and thereby manage to interact with each other in everyday life. These themes are also concerned with how we monitor the ongoing aspects of social interaction and negotiate their realities. A well-established theoretical approach that offers itself readily for this general type of problematic is attribution theory (cf. Heider, 1958; Jones & Davis, 1965; Kelley, 1967, 1972; *inter alia*). We shall consider the merits and demerits of attribution theory, stimulated by the fact that it is currently a popular vehicle for a considerable number of social psychological inquiries and it explicitly attempts to address the issue of how people arrive at explanations in the course of everyday life. After this examination of attribution theory we shall consider an alternative theoretical approach, which we have called interpretative social psychology, which seems to us to embody a potentially more fruitful, if less well articulated, framework for the understanding of fractured social interaction. By 'interpretative social psychology' is meant those social psychological treatments of interpretation and understanding in everyday life that have been influenced by sociological considerations, as exemplified by symbolic interactionism (e.g. Blumer, 1962, 1966; Hewitt, 1976; Mead, 1932; *inter alia*), ordinary language analysis (cf. Antaki, 1981), and the ethnomethodological tradition (e.g. Mehan & Wood, 1975). A third section will deal with the analysis of disruptive social incidents, from their perception to their normalization.

1.2. Attribution theory; a critical precis*

The highly influential writings of Heider (e.g. 1958) have led to the formulation of models which are concerned with the psychological

---

* This section is based in part on Semin (1980).

'premises' underlying everyday epistemology, and the ensuing works of Jones & Davis (1965) and Kelley (e.g. 1967, 1972a,b, 1973) have laid the necessary foundations for what is probably the most influential framework in present day social psychology: attribution theory. This presently burgeoning area certainly contains the promise that most previous social psychological theories have lacked, namely the possible integration of hitherto disparate fields under a common theoretical umbrella (cf. Harvey & Smith, 1977).

Several reviews of attribution models already exist (e.g. Harvey & Weary, 1981; Kelley & Michaela, 1980; Schneider, Hastorf & Ellsworth, 1979; Shaver, 1975), so no attempt will be made to present a review here; instead, we shall develop a critical assessment of the main models of attribution (i.e. Jones & Davis, 1965; Jones & McGillis, 1976; Kelley 1967, 1972a; 1972b) and some of their implications. Before proceeding with this critique, however, it is as well to remind ourselves of the principal features of the main attribution models. We shall confine ourselves to a skeletal recapitulation of three models: Jones and Davis' (1965) theory of correspondent inferences, Kelley's (1967) covariation model, and Kelley's (1972b) causal schemata model. Our recapitulation is intended to be no more than a memorandum addressed to those who already have some knowledge of attribution models. Those without such knowledge are referred to one of the aforementioned reviews.

Jones and Davis' (1965) model is primarily concerned with inferences about internal causality. The model assumes that any given action represents a choice, in that the actor could have opted to behave differently. Each action is regarded as having a number of effects, and actors are assumed to be aware of the effects resulting from their action. The perceiver is seen as attempting to infer which effects were intended by the actor. *Correspondence* refers to the extent to which an action could be caused by an intention, the extent to which that intention could be caused by a disposition and, therefore, the extent to which the action is a reflection of an underlying disposition. Under conditions of high correspondence the perceiver's inferences about the actor's intentions result in further inferences about the actor's dispositional properties: the inferred personality traits *correspond* to the observed behaviour.

Two factors in particular are held to determine the degree of correspondence that obtains for a given action. First, the extent to which the action is *socially desirable;* and secondly, the number of *noncommon effects* produced by the action. Social desirability is regarded by Jones and Davis as helping the perceiver to infer the actor's intentions, but hindering the perceiver's ability to make dispositional inferences. In other words, the model assumes that actors intend to produce those effects of their actions which are desirable. However, socially desirable effects tell the perceiver little about the actor's personality, since it would be 'normal' to want to produce such effects and the intention to produce them simply indicates that the actor is similar to many other persons. Thus when the apparently intended effects of an observed action depart from what most actors would have intended, correspondence increases, and the perceiver is therefore likely to make more confident and stronger inferences about the actor's dispositions. Noncommon effects are those which are unique to the observed action, in the sense that they would not also have been produced had the actor opted to take alternative courses of action. As the number of noncommon effects diminishes, so correspondence increases, because effects which are unique to the chosen action will be inferred to be the intended effects.

Kelley's (1967) covariation model has as its central tenet the notion that "An effect is attributed to one of its possible causes with which, over time, it covaries" (1967, p. 108). This model therefore assumes that the perceiver has observed the actor's behaviour on a number of occasions, in order that such covariance can be judged. The perceiver is also assumed to have some knowledge of how *others* would behave under similar circumstances. The 'possible causes' of an effect are seen as the *actor*, the *entities* present in the setting of the action, and the *contextual features* of the setting. Information about the extent to which the observed effect covaries with these three classes of possible cause will enable the perceiver to make an internal or external attribution. The degree to which the effect covaries with the actor is said to provide *consensus* information, concerning its generality across different actors. When consensus is high (i.e., most actors would behave/react in the same way as the target actor), perceivers should make external attributions (e.g. to prevailing social norms). The degree to which the effect covaries with the entity in question is said to provide *distinctiveness* information, concerning its generality across different entities. When distinctiveness is high (i.e., the effect is specific to this particular entity), perceivers should again make external attributions (e.g. to the compelling appeal of the entity). The degree to which the effect covaries with the context in question is said to provide *consistency* information, concerning its stability across different times and/or modalities. When consistency is low (i.e., the effect occurs only in a certain context), perceivers should once again make external attributions (e.g. to the drunkenness of the actor). Thus internal attributions should result from a pattern of covariation incorporationg low consensus, low distinctiveness and high consistency.

Kelley's (1972b) causal schemata model seeks to account for attributions based on single observations of behaviour. This model assumes that perceivers possess a store of knowledge concerning causal relations between outcomes and causes, and that this knowledge is implemented when a perceiver wants to or has to make an inference about causality on the basis of limited information. Knowledge of causal relations takes the form of different *causal schemata*. Properties of the action and its setting determine which causal schema is activated in making a given inference. Some effects are 'known' to be produced by any of a variety of causes. Charitable donations, for example, may be made because of altruistic or self-presentational motivations. Either cause is sufficient. If we know that an actor has made a charitable donation, and we also know something about one of the possible causes (e.g. that self-presentational concerns are unlikely to have caused the action because the donation was anonymous and we have discovered the donor's identity by accident), then something can be inferred in relation to the other cause (i.e., that the donation resulted from altruistic concerns). In making such an inference, we are using what Kelley terms the *multiple sufficient causes* schema. The inferential processes associated with this schema are summarized by Schneider et al. (1979) in the following way: "...given that the effect has occurred, perceivers make stronger inferences that A was the effective cause when B is absent than when B is present. When B is present, A *could be* the effective cause; when B *is absent*, though, A *must* be the cause. When an effect has occurred and one cause is known to be present, the second cause will be *discounted* as an effective element in the causal picture" (p.57). Contrast this with a different causal schema, referred to by Kelley as the *multiple necessary causes* schema. This will tend to be activated where the effect about which inferences are made is 'known' to be produced by a conjunction of causal factors. The classic example here is the achievement of a difficult task, such as passing an examination, which would be regarded by many persons as requiring the joint presence of ability and effort. The logic of such a schema is that if the effect (passing an examination) is present, then both the necessary causes must also be present. If the effect is absent, however, then *either or both* of the necessary causes might be absent. Kelley also considers a variety of other causal schemata which we shall not mention here, but the general principle of the causal schema model should be apparent: the application of a schema entails a perceiver to arrive at conclusions about causation on the basis of limited information.

While the three attribution models that we have briefly summarized differ in some important respects, they nevertheless share certain assumptions and have many similarities. Together they are generally regarded as comprising 'attribution theory'. We shall now proceed to our evaluation of attribution theory.

Four critical arguments can be directed at attribution theory. The first argument concerns the status of the model of man employed in attribution theory. With the advent of attribution theory the 'naive psychologist' has acquired "...a status equal to that of the scientist who investigates him" (Ross, 1977, p. 174). Hence, it is deemed to be "...not inappropriate for attribution theorists to use the formal procedural rules of science as a model for Everyman's inferential processes" (Harvey & Smith, 1977, p.14). This approach, it will be suggested, disregards the role played by the complex heritage of centuries of preinterpreted experiences distilled by human beings and constantly handed down to their offspring. This preinterpreted experience, generally subsumed under the terms 'culture' or 'custom', provides us in our everyday life with intersubjective guidelines for interpreting events, and thus provides the social context of our existence (cf. Semin & Manstead, 1979), a context which is disregarded by attribution theory. The second argument examines the ideological status of attribution theory and proposes that attribution theory adopts a *prescriptive* stance to the evaluation of self-knowledge and the knowledge of others and is therefore ideological. The third argument addresses a central theme in attribution theory, namely the classification of social causation into situational (external) and dispositional (internal) causes. This 'dichotomy' has already elicited some critical comment from attribution theorists themselves (e.g. Buss, 1978; Kruglanski, 1975; Ross, 1977). The argument to be presented here is that, despite its potential heuristic value, this classification does not afford a fuller understanding of the social context within which attributions are made, and all too often remains an ambiguous distinction that leads to prescriptive statements. The fourth and last argument centres on the conditions under which we do and do not make attributions in everyday life, that is the conditions under which we invest attributional effort.

1.2.1. THE MODEL OF MAN AS STATISTICIAN

If one starts with George Kelly's extrapolation of the notion of 'man as scientist' (Kelly, 1955, chs. 1-3) and his view that human behaviour can be seen in terms of human attempts to understand, predict and control the environment, then the question is: how does the individual engage in this 'science'? Indeed this is precisely the question attribution theorists have asked themselves (e.g. Heider, 1958; Jones & Davis, 1965; Kelley, 1967, 1972a,b, 1973). In answering this question, however, attribution theorists have projected a statistician into their model of man and, further, both central attribution theories have regarded the 'scientific' interpretation of 'cause-effect relationships' as being the criterion against which all other interpretations of cause-effect relationships should be evaluated. The model of the statistician is clearly central to Kelley's writings: "It is convenient to conceptualize the process under discussion, the inference of cause from the observation of covariance, in terms of the analysis of variance employed in psychology to interpret experimental results" (1973, p. 109). If the 'naive psychologist' has a single datum instead of data he/she is assumed to employ a 'causal schema': "More specifically (and this is the link between the analysis of variance and the schemata ideals), the causal schema can be viewed as 'an *assumed pattern of data* in a complete analysis of variance framework'. It is within this assumed configuration of data that the single observation is fitted and interpreted. 'Given information about a certain effect and two or more possible causes, the individual tends to assimilate it to a specific assumed analysis of variance pattern, and from that to make a causal attribution' (Kelley, 1972, p.2)" (Kelley, 1973, p. 115, emphasis in the original).

However, the meaningful conduct of everyday life is based on the possession of common, known-to-all rule systems with multifarious referents (i.e. to specific events, behaviours, human nature, the ego and the alter), as well as rules which enable the interlinking of such reference points. A hypothetical story illustrates the point. A Brazilian aborigine visits Rio by invitation of the Ministry of Aboriginal Affairs. On returning to his tribe he gives his friends an account of a bizarre 'religious orgy' to which he was taken. "On particular days more people than all those you have seen in your whole lifetime roam to this huge place of worship, an open hut the size of which you will never imagine. They come, chanting, singing, with symbols of their Gods, and once everybody is gathered the chanting drives away all alien spirits. Then, at the appointed time the priests arrive wearing colourful garments, and the chanting rises to war cries until three high priests, wearing black, arrive. All priests who were running around with sacred round objects leave them and at the order of the high priests prepare to begin the religious ceremony. Then, when the chief high priest gives a shrill sound from himself they all run after the single sacred round object that is left, only to kick it away when they get hold of it. Whenever the sacred object goes through one of two doors and hits the sacred net the religious followers start to chant, piercing the heavens, and most of the priests embark on a most ecstatic orgy until the chief high priest makes more shrill sounds". If aborigines wished to understand this social reality and the causes of this odd behaviour, to make sense of it they would at least have to know the rules of soccer: no analysis of variance is going to help them, however scientifically or naively applied. Furthermore, the attribution theorist would need to know something of the social reality of the aborigine if he/she wished to understand the aborigines' attributions.

The conduct of our everyday life presupposes distinct rule structures with their distinctive types of 'languages' (cf. Peters, 1969) for a variety of settings and behaviours in such settings. The 'social' in social behaviour refers to a collection of 'conventions' created and adopted by a collectivity and as such is objectivated and anonymous (Semin & Manstead, 1979). This common stock of knowledge at hand enables individuals belonging to the collectivity jointly to construct and maintain a mutual social reality. From this viewpoint it follows that the rule-following, social and cultural dimensions of everyday social existence are central to the pursuit of the question of how we interpret our social reality and engage in meaningful social action and interaction. If the aim is to understand how social explanation takes place, then the examination of the nature and organization of this common stock of knowledge which is culture-bound and historical (Elias, 1977; Schutz, 1953) is inevitable.

However, it is precisely these rules, conventions, and metaphors, central as they are to our everyday existence, that attribution theory neglects in regarding the interpretation of everyday reality as a type of calculator which follows statistical rules and into which 'raw data' need to be fed.

A further and related point arises from the assumption made in attribution theory that the criterion by which everyday interpretations of social reality must be 'evaluated' is the 'scientific' interpretation of 'cause-effect relationships' (cf. Jones & Davis, 1965, p. 220; Kelley, 1973, p. 109). By applying this criterion attribution theorists have established the foundations of what Ross (1977) has aptly described as "...two distinct but complementary goals. One goal has been the demonstration that, by and large, social perceivers follow the dictates of logical or rational models in assessing causes, making inferences about actors and situations, and forming expectations and predictions. The other goal has been the illustration and explication of the sources of imperfection, bias, or error that distort such judgements" (1977. p. 179). The latter goal has indeed proved to be attractive to researchers (cf. Nisbett & Wilson, 1977; Nisbett & Ross, 1980; Ross, 1977, 1978).

The implication is that the most rational attribution of causality is that proposed by scientific research. Attribution theorists' definition of the domain for research (i.e., how do we make causal attributions?) is unproblematic, since we generally take for granted the 'fact' that we make causal attributions and it is often the case that we cannot explicity state how we have been able to do so. What *is* problematic is the assumption in attribution theory that the 'naive psychologist's' phenomenology contains a conception of rationality that is similar to, if not identical with, the 'rationality' of analysis of variance. The next section deals with the elaboration and implications of this problem.

1.2.2. THE PRESCRIPTIVE ELEMENT IN ATTRIBUTION THEORY

If 'science' is regarded within attribution theory as interchangeable with 'analysis of variance', and 'rationality' is regarded as synonymous with 'science', then the inescapable conclusion is that such a view can only be prescriptive, and that attribution models are normative, containing prescriptions as to how people 'should' understand themselves and others. By following the three tricks which Smith (1974) regards as the 'recipe' for making ideological representations of what people think, it can be shown (as will be illustrated later) that attribution theory, particularly as developed by Kelley, does precisely this. The ambiguity of the twofold cause classification, as we shall see later on, is the loophole which enables the attribution theorist to achieve an 'intuitive leap', by fitting what people *say* into what attribution theory suggests that they *mean*.

In comparison with Jones & Davis's (1965) model, Kelley's model is more broadly conceived, encompassing not only personal dispositional attributions, but also self and situational attributions. Further, it attempts to be more precise in specifying how the attribution process continues should no personal attribution be made. Jones & Davis (1965) do not provide any specifications on this issue, although they do imply that other actions and their effects have to be considered, as well as the action observed. In effect, Kelley suggests that, in order to solve the uncertainty that enters Jones & Davis's model when the attribution of personal disposition cannot be confirmed, the actor's environment has to be subdivided into 'actors', 'entities' and 'contexts', so that the three criteria of consensus, distinctiveness, and consistency can be applied in determining the particular aspect of the environment to which the action can be attributed. These three criteria are the constituents of the 'covariation principle', which applies when the attributor has multiple observations available. In the case where only a single datum is available, causal schemata are supposedly employed by the attributor. It is clear from the quotations provided above that Kelley regards the covariation principle and causal schemata as being related, for an analysis of variance pattern of 'data' is striven for in both cases.

The application of these principles is precisely the point at which there is vagueness in Kelley's model, for it does not specify how an attributor identifies which part of the environment constitutes 'entities', 'contexts', or 'actors', or how an attributor knows the dimensions to which the criteria of distinctiveness, consistency, and consensus should be applied. In fact, Kelley's model implicitly assumes that the individual is operating in a 'social vacuum' (Tajfel, 1972, with Moscovici's 1973 proviso), processing something which resembles 'raw data'. This impression is strengthened in Ross's writings (cf. 1977, p. 174), where socially preinterpreted input is regarded as 'raw data' and its validity is judged by statistical principles. This leaves attribution theorists with an awesome burden, in that they have to impute the social content and meaning in each instance themselves, constantly plugging the gaps of the model with 'intuitive leaps' from their implicit assumptions about the nature of social reality.

The main issue here is that the 'fundamental enterprise' (Jones, 1977) which is singled out for attention by attribution theorists and which is regarded by them as a fundamental enterprise of 'the man in the street' is 'finding the causes for behaviour' (Jones, 1977, p.317). The weak link is that the attribution theorist takes as his point of departure end-products of explanation in everyday life and imputes processes of a supposedly psychological nature to explain how these products are achieved.

In an earlier paper we have argued that such inference is generally impossible, and that the sources which can potentially account for the regularities in the dependent-independent variable relationship are manifold as long as the distinction between the social and the psychological properties of social behaviour is not clearly made (Semin & Manstead, 1979). The social properties of social behaviour are regarded as those rules, conventions and norms that are potent guides for behavioural regularities. The psychological properties of social behaviour are regarded as those processes which enable the identification, elicitation and monitoring of such social codes.

Since both attribution theorist and experimental subject share the same language and cultural background they both have access to the same shared knowledge about the rules that govern the relationship between specific 'stimuli' and their 'responses'. However, if theorists elect to ignore the social knowledge within which behaviour is made meaningful, they have taken the first step in Smith's (1974) recipe for making an ideological representation of what people think, namely: "Separate what people say they think from the actual circumstances in which it is said, from *the actual empirical conditions of their lives and from the actual individuals who said it*" (p. 41, emphasis added). The next step involves regarding attribution theory, particularly with the imputed ANOVA model, in precisely the manner suggested by Kelley himself: "If I repeatedly refer to attribution *theory*, it should not lead the reader to expect too much in the way of a systematized set of assumptions, propositions and deductions. 'Theory' is used here in a broad and, I would insist, *entirely appropriate sense*, to refer to a more or less *plausible set of general principles offered to explain certain observed phenomena*" (Kelley, 1973, p.108, emphasis added). Such an approach to theory accords precisely with Harré's (1974) characterization of the neo-positivistic stance: "The neo-positivistic idea of science was that the compilation of a catalogue of laws describing such regularities completely exhausted the content of a science" (p.241). The aim of theories which take such a stance is to bring order into data, and it is not clear whether or not such a theory corresponds to a real state of the mind, i.e. whether the suggested processes do in fact have any phenomenological reality.

Thus, in postulating an analysis of variance model to account for regularities in observed phenomena, the second step of Smith's recipe is fulfilled, namely: "Having detached the ideas, they must now be arranged. *Prove then an order among them which accounts for what is observed*" (1974, p. 41, emphasis added).

The crucial criterion that attribution theorists adhere to when re-attributing their models to 'reality' is that of consistency, for: "consistency is ... a *criterion* for understanding, a criterion for when the causal explanation is thought to be sufficient" (Jones et al., 1972, p. xi). Thus attribution theorists make the crucial assumption that each individual constructs his or her causal attributions in a systematic manner, but because such theorists take the possibility of causes and effects for granted (i.e. unquestioningly accept that 'causes' and 'effects' are readily identifiable, discrete entities in everyday life), this systematic nature of causal attributions is not considered by them to be indicative of a cultural rule-system guiding the perception of actions and events. Rather, the systematization is assumed to be a part of each individual's cognition, and the attribution theorists' models clearly claim to represent this cognition. Thus, every attribution, if it is to achieve 'true understanding', must *consistently* follow the models, and it is at this point that the models reveal a prescriptive, rather than explanatory nature, for it follows that if any attribution 'deviates' from this consistency, it must be deemed 'irrational': this is clearly a value-judgement.

This prescription is apparent in Shaver (1975), for in considering the 'category mistake' he states that "attribution is a *psychological* process that may or may not be entirely rational, and it is clear that perceivers do attribute some behaviour to enduring personal dispositions presumed to exist apart from the overt actions that can be observed" (p. 70, emphasis in original). Now, it may be true that, according to formal logic, the ascription of causality to a 'personal disposition' is an unwarranted extrapolation but it is not valid for Shaver to conclude that, because attributors do not perceive their 'mistake', this must be due to a universal *cognitive* process. Indeed, it could be said that attribution theorists exhibit one of their own 'irrational attributions' — namely, "too little account is taken of external causes (contextual factors) in judgements of other persons' behaviours" (Kelley, 1972, p. 18) — when they claim that their models are representations of cognitive processes. That is, they attribute agency to their models even though these models may simply be representative of the external cultural context within which these models were constructed, a context in which 'cause-effect' terminology is taken for granted as a part of everyday life. This constitutes the third ingredient of Smith's (1974) recipe: "The ideas are then changed 'into a person', that is, they are constituted as distinct entities to which agency (or possible cause efficacy) may be attributed. And they may be re-attributed to 'reality' by attributing them to actors who now represent the ideas" (p.41).

Thus, Shaver makes the same mistake as all other attribution theorists in assuming that the ability to know when, where, and how to use the very notion of a 'cause' is unproblematic, for 'suspending our certainty' in having that ability is precisely the standpoint of 'radical doubt' that constitutes the starting-point of a truly phenomenological analysis of causal attribution. Such an analysis would therefore not set out to decide whether or not an attribution is 'right' or 'wrong' (i.e. whether or not it is consistent with an actual state of affairs to which it is supposed to correspond), but rather would seek to describe what people do to make the concept of 'causality' something *that can be said*. When such an analysis is complete, then it will have reflexively explained how it is that it was possible to theorize about causal attribution in the first place.

1.2.3. THE TWOFOLD CAUSE CLASSIFICATION

A key means by which the dubious translation of what is said into what is meant is achieved is the twofold cause classification, i.e. the attribution of cause either to an enduring, stable property of the actor (dispositional attribution) or to an environmental contingency (situational attribution). The problematic nature of this cause classification should already be evident from the preceding discussion. The twofold classification is crucial for attribution theoretical inquiry at each of the three major points of dependent variable assessment, namely assignment of cause, social inference, and prediction of some future act or outcome from some observed event (cf. Jones et al., 1972; Monson & Snyder, 1977; Ross, 1977). Together these three tasks constitute the locus of ambiguity, as well as constituting the origin of an 'intuitive leap' that is made from 'data bases' to interpretative statements by the attribution theorist.

The problem with the twofold cause classification lies primarily in the 'subjective interpretation of meaning' (Weber, 1947). In the preceding section it was argued that attribution theory neglects this process, insofar as it invokes *post hoc* explanations of attributions with disregard for the social context in which these attributions are made. The difficulty also lies in part with the point that the twofold classification *is not* a dichotomy (cf. Monson & Snyder, 1977, p.90; Ross, 1977). As Ross (1977) points out, attribution theorists very often ask a subject to explain why a particular act occurred, and then code the answer into 'situational' or 'dispositional' attributions. The ambiguity is brought out in his example of 'Jack bought the house because it was so secluded'.The cause of Jack's house purchasing behaviour can be regarded as either dispositional (he likes seclusion) or situational (the house was secluded). Using closed-ended rather than open-ended questions to elicit attributions does not help to avoid this problem, for the same interpretational ambiguity will prevail. As Monson & Snyder (1977) have noted, we are nevertheless recommended to retain this twofold classification, albeit with the proviso that the attributions "imply or state" (p.90) one or other type of explanation. Despite the possibility that a twofold classification may have some merits we are left with no clear criteria for classifying subjects' answers, and can only conclude that Kruglanski's (1975) more radical criticism has to be accepted under such circumstances, namely that "...the use of the external-internal distinction in reference to attributional findings has typically lacked explicit rationale. Rather it seems to have been grounded in an arbitrary semantic decision to characterize some purposes in a 'motive' language (that has an 'internal' feel to it), and other purposes in a 'goal' or object language (that feels 'external')" (1975, p. 390).

1.2.4. THE NOTION OF 'ATTRIBUTIONAL EFFORT'

Attribution theory's disregard for the social context in which attributions are made and the prescriptive nature of the theory give rise to a further serious shortcoming, namely that it makes the person in the street a continuous 'reality constructor'. It is obvious that we do not construct social reality from scratch every morning when we get up; however, attribution theory does not specify the circumstances in which attributions are or are not made. If it were the case that we had constantly to explain the causes of behaviour the cognitive load involved would be intolerable, and the individual would literally be lost in thought (cf. Langer, 1976). As argued above, our everyday life consists of rules, conventions and guidelines, both for behaviour and its interpretation. In the flow of everyday life we do not constantly ask the question 'why?'. Only when there is a temporary 'breakdown' of the rules, only when social reality has slipped temporarily through our fingers, do we need to invest some effort in reconstructing that reality (cf. Pyszczynski & Greenberg, 1981). As Mills (1940) has pointed out: "...Men live in immediate acts of experience and their attentions are directed outside themselves until acts are in some way frustrated. It is then that awareness of self and of motive occur. The 'question' is a lingual index of such conditions. The avowal and imputation of motives are features of such conversations as arise in 'question' situations" (p. 905). However, because attribution theory does not make any statements about the nature of social reality, or the social context within which actions are designed and acts executed, it also fails to specify when we ask ourselves the question 'why?'. That we ask the question 'why?' is taken for granted, but its aetiology is not examined at all. The least one has to do is to specify (as Mills does) those minimal conditions under which the question 'why?' is asked, in other words identify the conditions under which attributional effort is invested.

Generally rule systems themselves contain explanations or accounts for the people acting 'in rule', such that interlocutors have their socially defined 'invariant motives' (cf. Schutz, 1953; Semin & Manstead, 1979). These rule systems enable the invariant attribution of motives, and posing the question 'why?' in such contexts becomes somewhat tautological (e.g. 'Why is he delivering the mail?' - 'Because he is the postman'). Only when there is a 'violation' of the unquestioningly taken-for-granted reality of everyday life does the 'why?' question become relevant, and only then is attributional effort invested. (The conditions under which this question is posed will be examined in detail in section 1.4. below). In order to specify this question, the theory must contain some recognition of, or statement about, the content of social reality. If such statements are not forthcoming, as is the case in attribution theory, then one is left in the rather awkward position of having to explain every single occurrence in everyday life as if it were an unprecedented act. What is more, if the rules which govern the running of everyday life are not clearly identified, together with their properties, then one runs the danger of *imputing 'processes' to regularities which are historical* (cf. Gergen, 1973).

The 'why?' question is a question about reflection, i.e. regarding one's self or one's acts, or the alter and its acts, posed retrospectively as a detached observer. That is also why the agent in attribution theory has not really achieved its required status of 'emancipation', for it is never able to reflect properly and its answers will always be those which are of a raw data processor and not of a 'scientist' in G. Kelly's sense. (This issue is central to our elaborations in section 1.3. below). This failure to acknowledge the reflexivity of human actions is no small matter, for as Giddens (1976) points out, "... nothing is more central to, and distinctive of, human life than the reflexive monitoring of behaviour, which is expected by all 'competent' members of society of others. In the writings of those social thinkers who do not acknowledge this as central, there is an odd paradox, often pointed to by their critics: for recognition of their very 'competence' as authors involves just what is obliterated in the accounts they offer of the behaviour of others" (Giddens, 1976,p.114).

1.2.5. CONCLUSIONS

Attribution theory's chief shortcoming, according to the argument developed above, is its disregard for the social context of everyday existence, and this shortcoming is manifest in the model of man implicit in the theory. This may be due mainly to the tradition within which attribution theory evolved. In this tradition social psychology has been regarded as a 'science', no different in principle from any 'natural science', and the question of the ontological relationship between social psychologists and their subjects (cf. Holzkamp, 1973) has been accorded little attention, apart from a research concern labelled 'the social psychology of the psychological experiment' (cf. Orne, 1962, 1970; Riecken, 1962; Rosenthal & Rosnow, 1969; *inter alia*). This research endeavour has now become a self-contained and rather dormant field, and has had little impact, if any, on the nature of theorizing in social psychology. However, "any scientific understanding of human action, at whatever level of ordering or generality, must begin with and be built upon an understanding of the everyday life of the members performing those actions" (Douglas, 1971, p. 11). The use of formal ('scientific') categories defined in advance of their examination (cf. Douglas, 1971, p. 13) leads, in the case of attribution theory, to a clearly prescriptive position which is difficult to dist-inguish from ideology. Furthermore, the unwillingness to consider the specific role the 'scientist' occupies in his/her investigatory activities as an integral part of the theory being constructed makes attribution theory an undesirable candidate for our present purpose, which is to develop a theory capable of coping with the problem of how we explain, interpret and understand our social reality. In our view the major problems encountered by attribution models stem from their disregard of the distinctive status of social psychology as a *social* science. Thus, attribution theorists ignore the fact that their own theoretical and research practices rely and draw upon precisely those resources that are implicitly taken for granted not only in the course of everyday life, but tacitly and thus unreflectingly by themselves (cf. for the general case, Douglas, 1971; Winch, 1958). As Giddens (1976) argues, "a grasp of those resources used by members of a society to generate social interaction is a condition of the social scientist's understanding of their conduct in just the same way as it is for those members themselves" (Giddens, 1976, p. 16). This *pre*condition (rather than condition) and its implications are precisely what is disregarded by attribution models, because the resources involved are only tacitly acknowledged.

One consequence of the attribution theoretical approach in this connection is its failure to distinguish between action descriptions and attributions, to which Tedeschi and Riess (1981) have drawn atten-tion. Following Langford (1971), they distinguish between descrip-tions of behaviour concerned with *actions*, which include the purposes or aims of the acting agent, as well as the connection between the action and social rules; and *activities*, which are performed for intrinsic reasons and are not goal directed (e.g. jogging, sailing a boat). Although this distinction is not particularly powerful or convincing, the main point made by Tedeschi and Riess with respect to action descriptions is very important. This is that action descrip-tions typically include purposes, motives, goals, and intentions and that they are learned with a particular language. Tedeschi and Riess (1981) note in this connection the following: "The lack of recognition of action descriptions by prominent attribution theorists is illustrated by an example from the theory of correspondent inferences proposed by Jones and Davis (1965). An observer watches two people, labelled A and B, working together on a task. A gives orders to B, monitors his performance , and indicates that the quality and quantity of B's work are inferior. According to the theory, presuming that no environmental causes for A's behaviour appear to exist, the observer will tend to regard A's dominating behaviour as indicative of his personal qualities or dispositions to be domineering. As Jones and Davis (1965) stated, 'the most correspondent inference is that which assumes with high confidence that domineering behaviour is a direct reflection of the person's intention to dominate, which in turn reflects a disposition to be dominant'(p.223). Our point is that describing the behaviour as domineering already includes the notion of intent and does not require any further inference. Once the observer chooses the action description which describes the behaviour as dominating,... the inference that A intended to be domineering has already been made. It is true that from a description of a particular behaviour an observer might draw the inference that the actor is prone to engage in a class of actions which have some common characteristics, such as a disposition to control and evaluate the behaviour of others, but this prediction based on inference is different from the initial disposition inference itself'(pp.274-275).

This criticism, which is consistent with our earlier observations about the shortcomings of attribution theory, raises an issue which is central to understanding how we afford explanations of others' behaviours, define the situations in which we find ourselves, and monitor and negotiate our everyday social interaction. This issue concerns the role played by language in such explanations, definitions, and monitoring, and will be considered in more detail in the course of our examination of interpretative social psychology. In conclusion, attribution models do not, in view of the above considerations, provide an adequate vehicle for the analyses that are attempted in this book. This is mainly due to the fact that they do not regard language as a social practice, or as a repository of common sense knowledge. Attribution theories also contain deficiencies with respect to other central features of explanation and interpretation in everyday life which make them an unsuitable vehicle for our present purposes. Among such shortcomings are the lack of attention to reflexivity, the absence of any specifications of the conditions of under which attributions are made, the disregard for the social context within which attributions are made, and finally, its prescriptive stance.

1.3. Interpretative social psychology

An examination and a theoretical outline of how disruptions of social interaction are recognized, interpreted, negotiated and normalized can only be made against the background of a theoretical conception of the properties of social interaction and the processes through which social reality is constituted and maintained. However, the elaboration of such a conception would in itself require a complete project, and consume a whole volume. In what follows we shall therefore confine ourselves to an *outline* of the conception of social interaction and the social psychology of the construction of social reality that guides the present work, rather than providing a detailed exposition. The shape of the outline we shall present is obviously influenced by those aspects of social interaction that are especially pertinent to the accountability of conduct. The central feature of the accountability of conduct is that it operates perforce through communication. "Through talk, values and norms may be expressly stated, and consequences of departure from them spelled out. Through word, gesture and expression potentially disruptive conduct may be prevented or diverted and warnings conveyed" (Roberts, 1979, p. 43). Thus, the central medium through which the accountability of conduct takes place is *talk*, and Chapters 2, 3 and 4 consist in the main of work which has explicitly or implicitly evolved around considerations pertaining to talk. Our examination of interpretative social psychology will therefore emphasize those properties of social interaction that are relevant to interpersonal communication.

First, we shall consider the most important aspect of social interaction, i.e., that it involves continual *interpretation* of the actions and the setting involved, as well as the broader social context within which it takes place. So we shall first of all deal with social interaction as interpretation. The notion of reflexivity will be considered as it relates to the conception of the interpretative processes guiding social interaction. This conception originates in Mead's social psychology (cf. McHugh, 1968; Mead, 1932, 1934). Second, the notion of temporality will be discussed, since accountability of conduct is an ongoing process in which a past event is negotiated with respect to its meaning. The communicative processes involved in the accountability of conduct consist of interpretations which unfold as a part of the ongoing negotiations of meanings between participants. The meaning of the present is consistently shifted as a consequence of its changing temporal references to the past and the future. The relevance of these considerations will become particularly apparent in the discussion of the ascription of responsibility in Chapter 4, and in the examination of the epistemological status of accountability of conduct in Chapter 5. Third, the concept of 'rule' as it is used here will be discussed briefly. Fourth, the status of explanatory constructs for conduct will be examined. Fifth, the resource that social interpretation relies upon, namely social knowledge, will be considered. This provides us with a general frame of reference about the foundations of social knowledge in everyday life upon which the accountability of conduct relies.Our treatment of social knowledge derives mainly from Alfred Schutz's (1964) sociology of knowledge, which "may be understood as the sociological critique of consciousness, concerning itself with the construction of social reality in general" (Berger, 1966, p. 106). Having examined the theoretical approach offered by interpretative social psychology, we shall return to the main theme of the present volume, namely disruptions of routine social interaction and the ways in which individuals recognize, interpret, negotiate and normalize such disruptions.

1.3.1. SOCIAL INTERACTION AS INTERPRETATION AND REFLEXIVITY

Social interaction is a continual flow of conduct that involves interpretation. It is, in other words, a *process* in which the meaning of another person's actions is continually assessed and defined, indicating to the agent how to act in that particular context. Thus, human sociality consists of continual interpretations through which persons mutually adjust their actions and in doing so give guidance to each other. "Human beings interpret or 'define' each other's actions instead of merely reacting to each other's actions. Their 'response' is not made directly to the actions of one another but instead is based on the meaning which they attach to some actions. Thus, human interaction is mediated by the use of symbols, by interpretation, or by ascertaining the meaning of one another's actions" (Blumer, 1962, p.157). In this conceptual context actors acquire a status that is different to the one they have in attribution theory: they can not only monitor others' actions, but also their own. This is precisely what Mead means when he refers to the unique character of the actor, i.e. the possession of a *self.* For Mead, possession of self entails the possibility of an actor being an object to him- or herself; thus the actor may perceive his or her self, have varying conceptions of self,interact with his or her self, and introduce self-corrective action (cf. Blumer, 1966, p. 535). This reflexive monitoring enables the actor not only to interpret and monitor his/her world, but also design and shape his/her conduct within it. The reflexive monitoring of action, one's own and that of others, is a continual process and the self is therefore regarded within symbolic interactionist theorizing as a *process* rather than the *static entity* that is prevalent in much psychological theorizing about persons. This point will be dealt with in greater detail below. In the context of our inquiry this conception of the self is central to an understanding of human motives and motivation; it is fundamental to the description and explanation of social interaction both as a general process and as one which operates in specific contexts (cf. Hewitt, 1976, p. 61).

Reflexive monitoring of conduct is a routine feature of everyday life. A prominent feature of this reflexive monitoring of human actors is the accountability of it (cf. Garfinkel, 1967; Giddens, 1979). The accounts that agents are able to present for their conduct rely on a stock of knowledge (Schutz, 1964) from which they also derive their actions. The practical translation of this knowledge both into action and, if and when necessary, into accounts of action is routinely available. Indeed, in our view, the main condition for the accountability of conduct becoming a feature of social interaction is the violation of common sense expectations of rationality and/or a lack of correspondence between conduct and those social expectations pertaining to the setting (cf. Mills, 1940; Peters, 1969; *inter alia*). Thus, reflexive monitoring in this context refers to a process which is followed routinely. The reflexive propensity of monitoring becomes particularly manifest when conduct is out of line with expectations, and is therefore called into question (cf. section 1.4).

1.3.2. THE TEMPORAL DIMENSION OF INTERPRETATION

The temporal dimension of activity can be analytically distinguished into past, present and future. This distinction remains a purely analytical one, because all three mutually affect action. It is, however, impossible to explain or understand social interaction without reference to this analytical distinction (cf. McHugh, 1968; Mead, 1932). This is best captured in an observation attributed to Whitehead by Giddens (1979, p.55): "What we perceive as the present is the vivid fringe of memory tinged with anticipation." Thus, in social interaction, interpretation of ongoing action in the present is shaped continually by our reconstructed pasts and our future projects. The present is a continual process. For Mead, "... that which marks the present is its becoming and its disappearing"(p.1)."Durations are a continual sliding of presents into each other. The present is a passage constituted by processes whose earlier phases determine in certain respects their later phases" (Mead,1932, p. 28). This continual process is what Mead refers to as *emergence*. This of course means that the definition of a situation is progressively open to transformation over time because its temporal references to the past and the future change continually. Obviously, the temporal dimension of social action and interpretation is a parameter which has not featured strongly in experimentally orientated social psychologies. For example, attribution models do not make any reference to this aspect of social interpretation and explanation in everyday life. In the case of accountability of conduct the temporal perspective acquires particular relevance because the interpretations that are involved concern an event which has occurred in the past and has to be negotiated with respect to its meaning in social interaction. The negotiation itself is however an unfolding process with the meanings of the event shifting through the process itself.

1.3.3. RULES

The concept of 'rule' enables one to specify the conditions under which both routine and disrupted social interaction are reflexively monitored and to identify the potential routes which the normalization of disruptions can take. As a working basis, let us take as a general definition of rule that which is offered by Black (1962). He argues that a rule is "an instruction to a certain class of actors to produce (or not to produce) a certain class of performances on a certain class of occasions" (p. 108). In contrast to other types of instructions, rules have no unique referents, otherwise they would not be generic. We shall not elaborate upon the concept of rule beyond specifying the general way in which we shall use it, since the concept of rule is not central to the concerns of this book.

However, what is relevant here is that, together with Cheal (1980), we regard rules for action as instructions, their important characteristic being that behaviour which is governed by rules has a form of patterned indeterminacy. That is, there are limits to the possibilities of correct actions, but within those limits behaviour is unlimited. This indeterminacy poses problems both to the social scientist who is interested in defining rules and finding their boundaries, and to actors who routinely follow the meaning of specific acts and gestures of others and interpret them as falling inside or outside the boundaries of what is appropriate practice for a given social situation. Clearly, it is impossible to monitor *all* aspects of social interaction exhaustively. This means that when an agent is asked 'Why did you do that?', he/she may on occasion be unable to provide a 'good' reason for it, and may simply resort to 'I don't know'. However,this applies mainly to realms of behaviour in everyday life which are generally regarded as trivial or unimportant. Competence in terms of social interaction entails accountability of conduct, i.e. the provision of reasons for action. When an individual's behaviour violates the boundaries of appropriate practice, others can typically introduce sanctions for rule violation, and the search for motives for the behaviour in question is invoked (cf. Mills, 1940). This point will be discussed in detail in section 1.4. below.

The argument thus far can be summarized as follows. In the course of social interaction the respective participants construct their conduct through constant interpretation of each other's actions. In registering the other's acts the actor must assess his/her own conduct, adjust it to the requirements of the situation, and judge the fitness of both his/her own actions and the other's actions in terms of their correspondence to the rules that are appropriate for the particular setting.

1.3.4. THE STATUS OF EXPLANATORY TERMS FOR CONDUCT

It is important to note that the present volume is *not* concerned with uncovering the psychological dimensions or properties which *underlie* the way in which people cope with disruptions in social interaction, but rather with the systematic examination of *social practices* that arise in such situations, and with the interface between such practices and the possibility of society as produced by such practices. Thus, the psychological reality that concerns us here refers to the ways in which participants apprehend themselves, and others, and their processes of consciousness. This psychological reality is contained in the social practice of *talk* which is the main vehicle through which accountability of conduct takes place. Such an approach makes it unnecessary and indeed unsatisfactory to develop psychological or sociological models which rely on explanatory factors such as dispositions, motives, traits, social class, and so on that are temporally and situationally invariant (or nearly so), and are assumed to be 'hidden' parameters, or motivators of action. The importance of the notions of reflexive monitoring of action and the temporal dimension of interpretation is that together with the concept of the self, they lend a different complexion to considerations about properties of persons and explanations of conduct. Such psychological and sociological properties as may be involved are regarded as admissible only to the extent that they are employed in the interpretative processes of everyday social situations. However, current social psychological thinking often adopts the opposite practice, in that social interaction is typically explained by resorting to such concepts as motives, feelings, attitudes, and personality organization.

It is worth noting in passing that a variety of domains of psychological theorizing may involve a paradoxical analysis of social behaviour, due to the failure to distinguish between the social and the psychological properties of social interaction (Semin & Manstead, 1979) and a lack of interest in examining the phenomena of everyday life in their own terms (Douglas, 1971; Semin, 1980). The paradox is rather a disturbing one because it represents a prototypical instance of circular thinking and the consequent development of tautological models. Psychological properties which are taken to be enduring properties of individuals are themselves defined by the ongoing action and interaction and are thus consequences of the interpretation of the situation. These properties are nevertheless taken in their own right as 'explanations' of the genesis of the action. Lack of reflection about the status of such concepts and their emergence both in everyday life and in psychological theory tends to result in tautological reasoning. A similar critique is made by Blumer (1966), who objects to accounts of human behaviour which resort to elements of psychological equipment as fundamental explanatory concepts.

Psychological properties are regarded here as admissible to the extent that they are employed in everyday usage to explain and understand conduct. Such properties are used to make action socially intelligible, in that they enable the assignment of 'identity' to the behaviours in question (cf. Blum & McHugh, 1971; Mills, 1940). For example, to speak of a type of person (i.e. in terms of traits, dispositions, moods, characteristics) is regarded here as a listing of the features of a persons which only acquire their relevance with reference to potential courses of action. Alternatively, "... motives are imputed by others before they are avowed by self. The mother controls the child: 'Do not do that, it is greedy.' Not only does the child learn what to do, but he is given standardized motives which promote ascribed actions and dissuade those proscribed. Along with the rules and norms of action for various situations, we learn vocabularies of motive appropriate to them. These are the motives we shall use, since they are part of our language and components of our behaviour" (Mills, 1940, p. 909). This view also provides a different perspective on the relationship between psychological properties as employed in every-day life, the individual, his/her actions, and society. This is best captured in Berger's (1966, p. 107) elaboration of this issue:

> Self and society are inextricably interwoven entities. Their relationship is dialectical because the self, once formed, may act back in its turn upon society that shaped it ... The self exists by virtue of society, but society is only possible as many selves continue to apprehend themselves and each other with reference to it.
>
> Every society contains a repertoire of identities that is part of the 'objective knowledge' of its members. It is 'known' as a matter 'of course' that there are men and women, that they have such-and-such psychological traits and that they will have such-and-such psychological reactions in typical circumstances. As the individual is socialized these identities are 'internalized'. They are then not only taken for granted as constituents of an objective reality 'out there' but as inevitable structures of the individual's own consciousness. The objective reality, as defined by society, is subjectively appropriated. In other words, socialization brings about symmetry between objective and subjective reality, objective and subjective identity. The degree of this symmetry provides the criterion of the successfulness of socialization. The psychological reality of the successfully socialized individual thus *verifies* subjectively what his society has objectively defined as real. He is then no longer required to turn outside himself for 'knowledge' concerning the nature proper of men and women. He can obtain that result by simple introspection. He 'knows who he is'. He feels accordingly. He can conduct himself 'spontaneously', because the firmly internalized cognitive and emotive structures make it unnecessary or even impossible for him to reflect upon alternative possibilities of conduct.

From this perspective concepts representing the psychological properties of the individual, such as traits, dispositions, attitudes, and values become rather dubious theoretical constructs. This is so because their epistemological status in relation to the psychological reality of these conceptions in everyday life is generally not clarified in social psychology (cf. Semin, Rosch & Chassein, 1981; Semin, Rosch & Krolage, 1982; Semin, Rosch, Krolage & Chassein, 1981). Generally, psychological thinking disregards the resources available in common sense knowledge and implicitly takes them for granted. However, an understanding of precisely those resources (and particularly in this context, those which refer to psychological properties) is central to the understanding of conduct. "Every socially constructed world contains a psychological model. If this model is to retain its plausibility, it must have some empirical relationship to the psychological reality objectivated in society" (Berger, 1966, p. 114).

Established forms of cultural life and social interaction exist simply because of the continued use of the same schemata of interpretation, which are maintained through continued use and confirmation by others. These interpretative schemata constitute a stock of knowledge, which contains recipes for handling situations, solving practical problems, etc. The social psychological analysis offered here refers to psychological reality as apprehended in everyday life and contained in our everyday knowledge about the world. We shall now consider the properties and characteristics of this social knowledge (Schutz, 1953, 1964), together with an analysis of how intersubjectivity is possible.

1.3.5. THE REALITY OF EVERYDAY LIFE, SOCIAL KNOWLEDGE, AND INTERSUBJECTIVITY

In this final section of our examination of interpretative social psychology, three interrelated features of everyday knowledge are considered in turn. First, the central characteristic of social knowledge, namely that it is represented in idealized abstractions, is examined by means of an illustration of how this knowledge is employed in devising everyday action plans. The second feature is the general attitude that is taken towards everyday life and that governs routine social practices, namely that we take the reality of everyday life unquestioningly for granted. Finally, the intersubjective nature of everyday life is briefly considered, along with an argument about the interrelationship between intersubjectivity and sociality.

Social knowledge as idealized abstractions

In order to achieve an understanding of how people devise action plans, explain events, explain the conduct of themselves and others, and sustain a meaningful life, it is important to examine the properties of everyday life and the properties of the commonly shared social knowledge which permeates everyday life. This provides a framework for understanding the natural flow of social interaction.

Most social interaction consists in the interlocking of action plans which are devised with some intention in mind. Thus, when I receive a letter from a 'long lost' friend who is in distress and decide to reply to him, my intention involves projecting myself into an accomplished end state, and enables me to design an action plan, namely the steps that are necessary in order to achieve this particular goal. In this particular instance I consider the single steps of finding some writing paper and a pen, going to the desk, writing the necessary consoling words, finding an envelope and some stamps, mailing the letter and relying implicitly on other specific properties of social life as these pertain to the postal services, such as 'a duly addressed and posted letter will get to its destination within a period of time through the intervention of an institution, the precise workings of which I don't know, called the postal service' (to use Schutz's, 1953, example). Should I lack any of the necessary paraphernalia, such as pen, ink or paper then I would go and buy these, relying on other resources available to me from my wealth of social knowledge, combining a variety of alternative action plans, such as locating shops, making a purchase, exchanging courtesies, etc. Thus, I devise a step by step plan in which I represent and order the various future acts conceptually, with the end in perspective, shaping the ongoing process of my present.

There is a particular quality to the elements of the action plan described above which is also to be found in any other action plan, or act. To illustrate this point let us present another example of an action plan. Say I have a friend who is going on a long journey to the country, who is known to be quite forgetful, and who is expected to write quite a few letters during the course of this journey. I intend to give him a farewell present. Having designed an action plan, I go and buy some envelopes, writing paper, pen, stamps and wrapping paper. I package the envelopes, writing paper, pen and stamps in the wrapping paper, and add a note of goodwill to present the completed action plan. If one compares this episode with the previous one, it is obvious that there are a number of similar or identical elements. Let us take the element of buying stamps. I go to the post office to buy stamps, in order to send the letter to the long lost friend in one case, in order to complete the present in the other. Depending on the specific action plan within which this particular 'routine' of buying stamps is conceptualized and executed, it acquires different meanings. It is clear that the context within which an element is located provides that element with a distinctive meaning. The action plans differ with respect to the end states to which they are subservient, as do the meanings of the particular elements within each action plan. The observable behaviour, however, is superficially identical in both cases.

Before considering the implications of the contextual changes in meaning that the element undergoes, let us proceed a little further. The simple act will be modified depending on the situational constraints that exist. This can be illustrated as follows. The clerk in the post office where I go to buy the stamps may be a grumpy old man, or a beautiful young woman, or a student I know who has a part-time job at the post office. Each of these specified instances provides the 'buying stamps routine' with distinct situated identities, and thereby modifies further the nature of each act. The simple conclusion is that each act is unique and personalized, just as each performance of a play, as any actor will assure you, is unique, despite the fact that the script is identical.

The question, then, is how does one manage the wealth of hypothetically constructed and/or actually realized specifications of activities in order to construct action plans? Obviously, if one were required to attend to all concrete and hypothetical instances and commit these to memory, this would overload the cognitive processing system and result in breakdown. The elements which enable the construction of my action plans must therefore be idealized abstractions. In projecting or planning specific hypothetical acts none of the concrete instances enters my design. I have an idealized representation of the specific element devoid of the concrete realizations of the idealization that I have experienced. In other words, I dissociate the irrelevant detail from the relevant schema which is crucial for devising my plan. The argument is that: "The social world is a mutually held and sustained matrix of abstraction from the concretely given actualities of experience" (Natanson, 1970, p. 14). Thus, no matter how the meaning of the specific routine of 'buying stamps' is modified through the context of the action plan, and further modified in its executive expression through situational parameters, what remains is an idealized and abstracted representation of specific acts, or events, or persons, which is detached from the variety of their concrete realizations.

The notion of idealized abstractions is developed within Schutz's (e.g.1972, 1973; Schutz & Luckmann, 1974) work through the concept of *typification* and has recently acquired considerable interest in the psychological research on social cognition with the reintroduction of Bartlett's (1932) schema concept. The psychological interest in this field is concerned mainly with the properties of abstract knowledge structures (cf. Bower, Black & Turner, 1979; Cantor & Mischel, 1979; Markus, 1977; Neisser, 1976; Rummelhart & Ortony, 1977; Schank & Abelson, 1977; Taylor & Crocker, 1980; *inter alia*).

Thus, in the conduct of social behaviour, i.e. in devising action plans, or in interpreting acts, the elements of representation one resorts to are endowed with a particular quality. They are highly idealized, consensual, understood and interpreted intersubjectively by all, or at least most members belonging to the same culture. This knowledge is implicitly available to the agent and his or her potential counterpart as 'everybody's knowledge'. Further, this knowledge is objectivated and anonymous, i.e. detached from the agent's and his or her potential counterpart's personal circumstances. This knowledge is part of our common sense knowledge of the world and is of a socialized nature, and therefore supersedes the unique or private knowledge of an agent which is determined through his or her *personal history*. In this sense this knowledge is functionally independent of the individual. We shall now consider the intuitive character of this schematized reality, namely the world of the natural attitude (cf. Douglas, 1971; Gurwitsch, 1962), or the *lebenswelt* (cf. Husserl, 1962).

The taken-for-grantedness of everyday life

The primary characteristic of our experience of this paramount reality is our attitude towards it. It is a taken-for-granted-world. Its reality and existence are never doubted or questioned; whatever activity we engage in or pursue in our everyday lives requires as an essential precondition a tacit acceptance of this reality (cf. Berger & Luckmann, 1966; Gurwitsch, 1962; Pollner, 1974; Schutz, 1972; *inter alia*). "As common-sense men living in the mundane world, we tacitly assume that, of course, there *is* this world all of us share as the public domain within which we communicate, work, and live our lives. Moreover, we naively assume that the world has a history, a past, that it has a future, and that the rough present in which we find ourselves is epistemically given to all normal men in much the same way... [T]hroughout all of the routine elements and forms of existence, we simply assume, presuppose, take it for granted that the daily world in which all of these activities go on is *there*; it is only on special occasions, if at all, that a serious doubt arises as to the veridical character or philosophical signification of our everyday world" (Natanson, 1973, p. xxvi, emphasis in original). Of course, these presuppositions are open to finer analysis, as demonstrated by Evans-Pritchard's (1937) work on the Azande, and Pollner's (1974) exemplary work on 'mundane reasoning'. Even in the case of doubting and questioning in everyday life, the belief in a natural world still holds (cf. Gurwitsch, 1962). Indeed, such instances are examined in detail below and, as will be seen, involve social practices, the effect of which is to buttress further the taken-for-granted life-world and its under-lying unquestioned and unchallenged presuppositions. It is precisely such 'incorrigible propositions' (Gasking, 1965, p. 431) which demon-strate the power of the taken-for-granted attitude towards the reality of everyday life and the type and amount of cognitive work which goes into sustaining the fabric of this reality.

In order to examine the reality of everyday life and the nature of social knowledge and its intersubjective character one needs to adopt a *theoretical stance* (cf. Douglas, 1971, p. 15) towards the social practices that govern our own everyday existence. This stance requires standing back from, reflecting upon and reviewing the experience that is taken-for-granted in everyday life, and involves what Husserl (1962) called the 'phenomenological suspension' or *epoche* (cf. Natanson, 1962; Schutz, 1972). It is precisely this stance which allows us to examine the properties of everyday life, such as its practices, social knowledge and intersubjectivity.

Intersubjectivity and the sociality circle

This 'taken-for-grantedness' of everyday life enables us to develop the basic propositions about how intersubjectivity is obtained in our daily dealings, where we assume others to have the same attitude towards everyday reality. We take it for granted that they also take the life-world for granted. The world is regarded as an intersubjective one.

This aspect of social interaction requires elucidation. Our concern here is with the the minimal requirements for the *maintenance of social reality*. In the illustrations we have employed so far the individuals engaged in interaction had access to the routines of everyday life. This enabled them to design acts and to interpret them. However, it is important to understand the presuppositions which underlie the employment and deployment of such resources and thereby enable flawless interaction to occur. Such resources are the prerequisites to *sociality*. The first and most important condition for social interaction is that the design and execution of action plans must be guided by *intersubjective relevance* considerations. This can be illustrated by reference to cases where there is a lack of intersubjective relevance: it would be difficult to purchase stamps if I went to the local bakery; equally, it would be difficult to buy stamps if I went to the post office and started chatting about the troubles afflicting my long lost friend. In other words, it is important that my personal motives (genuine motives) are translated into routines appropriate to the relevances of the interlocutors who are to be my partners. So, I must first of all know or have access to the social rules in order to be able to employ them. Further, I must also know that the relevance of a particular rule or rules is warranted by the context within which the interaction is to take place. The first moment of reciprocity is thus established by the ascertaining and matching of *intersubjective relevances*. The second moment of reciprocity is *within rule intersubjectivity*, and is integrated into the social rules themselves, since the rules are socially created symbols that enable intersubjectivity. As such they acquire life forms in their continued and collective reproduction in everyday life. These two moments are interdependent and constitute what we shall refer to as the *sociality circle*. This circle is completed when I know that the rules which I regard as relevant to the present context are also regarded by you to be relevant to this context. The sociality circle is crucial to the maintenance of social reality. As long as the circle is unquestioned, as is the case in flawless social interaction, I take the interaction for granted and pursue my interests. However, any interruptions in the circle arising from a mismatch of relevances, or from the employment of rules which are highly idiosyncratic, will result in the breakdown of meaningful conduct. Such interruptions will constitute threats to the taken-for-granted interpretative validity of either moment and the situation will become problematic; new interpretative schemata have then to be initiated and reconstructive activity results (cf. Semin & Manstead, 1979). Finally, it is important to note in this connection that any breakdown in the sociality circle will give rise to conscious reflection. In the uninterrupted execution of my action plans I monitor my conduct reflexively and do so routinely and subjectively. The common sense knowledge that I take for granted is confirmed by its uninterrupted mutual redefinition in the interaction. Only when my action plan is interrupted do I have a different stance towards the immediate reality that confronts me. The reality has become problematic, and through retrospective reflexion I have to review what has gone wrong. Now I regard myself and my acts as objects of my attention. I am caught in thought, trying to grasp, interpret and understand the problem and to reconstruct the reality.

A surprising feature of such problematic situations is that there exists a rich variety of routinely available resources to cope with them. These too are part and parcel of our commonly shared social knowledge. Take examples such as socially embarrassing situations (cf. Manstead & Semin, 1981; Semin and Manstead, 1981; 1982), or traffic accidents, or winning a huge sum of money in a lottery, or solving extremely difficult problems unexpectedly. In our everyday lives we have specific routines which we can use to cope with such instances of 'rule breaking'. Although these instances have low degree of probability of occurrence, they have a high degree of familiarity, for they are part and parcel of our commonly shared social knowledge. We even have routines for the most outlandish events such as extraterrestial beings visiting our planet: The science fiction literature has provided us with a variety of rules for such an eventuality. In fact there is very little that would be *entirely* novel to the experience of the Western mind, if one assumes a normal degree of enculturation.

1.4. Accountability of conduct

We now return to the main theme of the book, namely the recognition, interpretation, and normalization of social situations in which breaches of norms or rules occur. Earlier in this chapter it was observed that an essential and integral part of social interaction is that it is monitored reflexively by each participant. Gehlen (1958) argues that reflexivity is a distinctive characteristic of the human species and is bound up with the social character of language. It is in this context that the concept of accountability acquires importance, for it has been shown to be a distinctive feature of reflexivity (cf. Giddens, 1976, 1979). The concept of accountability has been employed in numerous ways in the literature (cf. Giddens, 1979; Harre, 1979; Marsh et al., 1978; Scott & Lyman, 1968; *inter alia*).

According to Garfinkel (1967), "...the activities whereby members produce and manage settings of organized everyday affairs are identical with members' procedures for making these meanings accountable" (p. 1). In the course of their everyday lives members produce activities, engage in social practices, design action plans, etc., for which they have reasons. These reasons can be articulated and proffered if and when necessary. However, it is not often necessary for actors to provide others with reasons for action, because their behaviours are those of competent actors, and are therefore both warrantable and intelligible. Garfinkel (1967) refers to this aspect of accountability as "the 'uninteresting' essential reflexivity of accounts" (p. 7). By this he means that this type of accounting is 'taken-for-granted', unquestioned and routine. Accounting is thus part and parcel of everyday life. It is only 'uninteresting' insofar as the provision of accounts is not an activity which presents interpretative problems. As Garfinkel (1967) elaborates, "...members take for granted that a member must at the outset 'know' the settings in which he is to operate if his practices are to serve as measures to bring particular located features of these settings to recognizable account. They treat as the most passing matter of fact that members' accounts, of every sort, in all their logical modes, with all their uses, and for every method of their assembly are constituent features of the settings they make observable. Members know, require, count on and make use of this reflexivity to produce, accomplish, recognize, or demonstrate rational-adequacy-for-all-practical-purposes of their procedures and findings" (p. 8). For Garfinkel, therefore, the accountability of actions is a pervaisive matter, and actions are accounted for routinely. Actions are *organised* in such a way that they can be accounted for to others. Garfinkel's particular use of the concept 'reflexivity' follows from these considerations. For him reflexivity provides a methodological principle for looking at the way in which accounts are organisationally embedded in the actions.

Our use of the concepts of accountability and reflexivity differs from Garfinkel's. Generally, the conduct of members is regarded as routine and unproblematic, and is as such 'competent' practice. Even when problematic situations arise members deal with these in a 'routine' manner, resorting to interpretative schemata that are already available to them in their common stock of knowledge. In the course of unproblematic social interaction there is no need to provide accounts for action since these actions are both warrantable and intelligible (Harré, 1979). In the case of 'fractured social interaction', however, explicit accounting is required, and is either initiated spontaneously by the actor who creates the 'fracture', or by bystanders or participants in the form of a direct inquiry of or challenge to the actor. By offering or calling for explicit accounts, the participants recognize that social interaction has been fractured. Before examining in detail the conditions for such activity to occur, we shall consider the type of analysis that we shall employ and the rationale for this analysis.

The role of language in the reflexive monitoring of action is central since it is the means by which the possibility of a commonly shared world is obtained, the medium of practical activity, and the repository of the interpretative schemata through which social interaction is constituted (cf. Berger, 1966; Berger & Luckmann, 1966; Blumer, 1966; Giddens, 1976, 1979). Interpretative schemata are central elements of the commonly shared stock of knowledge and are the means by which the attainment of an accountable social existence is made possible. They provide the 'sense' and 'meaning' through which we apprehend social reality and enable us to understand self and others. As Giddens (1974) puts it, "...understanding is not merely a method for making sense of what others do, nor does it require an empathic grasp of their consciousness in some mysterious or obscure fashion: *it is the very ontological condition of human life in society as such*...Self understanding is connected integrally to the understanding of others. Intentionality, in the phenomenological sense, is not thus to be treated as an expression of an ineffable inner world of private mental experiences, but as *necessarily* drawing upon communicative categories of language, which in turn presuppose definite forms of life. Understanding what one does is only made possible by understanding, i.e., being able to describe what others do, and vice versa. It is a semantic matter, rather than a matter of empathy; and reflexivity, as the distinctive property of the human species, is intimately and integrally dependent on the social character of language"(pp. 19-20, emphasis his). Ordinary language constitutes the medium through which skilled interaction is accomplished. Talk, in this sense, provides the means for both the description of acts and their communication,

and thus constitutes the object of analysis for the examination of
accounting practices in 'fractured social interaction' and its normalization. It is in terms of talk and language that accounting is
organized and can be analysed (cf. Blum & McHugh, 1971; Mills,
1940). In cases of 'fractured social interaction' where some disruption
of the natural flow of social interaction has occurred, actors employ
culturally provided resources for interpreting, explaining and nor-
malizing the problematic situation. The medium through which this is
achieved contains organized practices which are not incidental to the
ongoing social interaction, and common sense accounts of how and
why the incident came about. Before considering the social psychological relevance of this type of analysis, it is necessary to consider
more specifically what has thus far been loosely referred to as the
recognition, interpretation and normalization of 'fractured social
interaction'.

What we have called 'fractured social interaction', 'disruptions',
'breaches', 'social predicaments', and so on, represent instances of
everyday social conduct in which the action is not immediately
'accountable' in terms of the routine monitoring of social interaction.
Some act occurs, which is neither 'intelligible' nor 'warrantable', i.e.,
the actor displays 'incompetence', either in terms of some routine
expectation guiding the situation or with reference to some moral
norms and standards that conventionally guide 'proper' conduct. A
breach of either routine conventions or rules, or a violation of some
moral standards has occurred. These are the outline features which
trigger the onset of those social practices which we shall consider
under the general heading of 'accountability'. The characteristic
feature of such situations is that actors become acutely aware of
themselves as objects, both to themselves, and to others, and assess
their actions in the light of the potential and actual meaning of these
actions to onlookers. Indeed, because the taken-for-granted routines of
everyday life are such that action is implicitly accountable, when a
problematic act occurs against the background of such accomplished
acts it poses the burden of having to be made 'accountable'. The
account may therefore be offered by the actor without requests or
challenges from observers, but if not forthcoming it may be demanded
by those who witnessed the questionable act. These are the
circumstances in which what was referred to earlier as 'attributional
effort' arises. Some act is not immediately interpretable, either in
terms of the expectations and conventions guiding the situation, or in

terms of the moral standards applicable to it. At such points ongoing social interaction is suspended and a retrospective evaluation of the questionable behaviour is made.

However, several conditions have to be met before an actor suspends ongoing social interaction and adopts a retrospective 'theoretical' stance in relation to his or her 'questionable conduct' (cf. Semin & Manstead, 1981). In order for a breach to be recognized as such: (1) The rule(s) and conventions in question must belong to the repertoire available to the actor; (2) the rule(s) and convention(s) must be taken seriously, i.e., be 'authenticated' (cf. Cheal, 1980), otherwise the rules would not derive the force they do as guidelines for action; (3) the actor must be aware of having broken the rule(s) or convention(s) in question; (4) the rule(s) must be recognized by the actor as being applicable to him- or herself; and, finally, (5) the actor must have some awareness that the breach in question has been witnessed by others. It is in the context of the above conditions that 'motives', 'reasons', and 'intentions' form discrete accounts, whether initiated by others, or as elements of the process of self-examination by the actor. Thus, following some breach of social rules or conventions or moral standards the actor's conduct is held up for assessment (cf. Peters, 1958), either by the actor him- or herself, or by the observers of the incident. The ensuing accounting takes place through talk as a practical social activity. Talk is therefore the most appropriate level at which to analyse accountability.

The social psychological significance of analysing language in this context is evident in the plan laid down by Heider (1958), in that the social psychological reality of everyday life is founded upon the common-sense psychology of interpersonal relations. "Since common-sense psychology guides our behaviour toward other people, it is the essential part of the phenomena in which we are interested" (Heider, 1958, p. 5). In such repair activities as are contained in what Mills (1940) refers to as 'motive talk', common-sense psychological explanations and procedures are manifest in explicit form, and represent a psychological reality which is an integral aspect of our practical activities in everyday life. This psychological reality is inseparable from the production of meaningful action and interaction and provides the basis for the possibility of society. Furthermore, 'accounts of conduct' acquire an additional social psychological relevance because they rely on an explicitly grounded 'theoretical aspect' of the reflexive monitoring of conduct, which actors expect each other to sustain.

When actors are required to formulate reasons for their conduct, they are expected to proffer a reasoned explanation of their acts; if this is not forthcoming their reputations may be called into question, by the making of negative dispositional inferences. This particular form of analysis of social psychological practices and psychological reality as manifested in everyday talk provides an alternative perspective to the one that is provided by conventional experimental social psychology. In an analysis of the psychological realities manifested in language (especially in accounting practices), motives, dispositions, intentions, reasons, and so on, are not construed *as private states* of the individual. Instead, these vocabularies of everyday talk (cf.Blum & McHugh, 1971; Mills, 1940) are regarded as relevant to the extent that they are means by which actions are made meaningful and interpreted, and to the extent that they serve a "...social function of coordinating diverse actions" (Mills, 1940, p. 909). Unlike attribution theory, no reference is made to "internal rules" which govern the process of causal inference and associated attribution.

One final point must be clarified before going on to consider the properties of the 'theoretical stance' that follows a breach of conduct, and the characteristics of motive talk. This concerns the correspondence between accounting practices stemming from 'fractured social interaction' and the background circumstances in which the fracture or breach has occurred. A number of authors (e.g., Harré and Secord, 1972) assume that both the production of skilled and competent action and the ability to provide accounts for conduct are grounded in a culturally provided stock of knowledge. However valid this may be, it does not necessarily mean (as Harré seems to assume) that there must be a direct correspondence between the production of action and its accounting. For example, it may be that particular types of action are so routinized that they cease to be consciously attended to (cf. Black, 1962, 1968); there may be differences between the discursive abilities of an agent who accounts for his or her actions and the resources that are employed in the production of the action (Cheal, 1980; Giddens, 1979); the resources for the production of action may rely on tacit knowledge (cf. Polanyi, 1966); the agent may decide to employ a particular accounting practice which has little to do with the particular circumstances and reasons for the act in question; the meaning of the action may be modified as a consequence of new events that are realized, resulting in an account which, because of its temporal disjunction from the original act, is distinctly but not necessarily consciously modified; and so on. These problems concerning the relationship between account and action are not directly relevant to the present analysis, since our concern centres on the types of procedures that are employed in accounting as such. The primary objective is to provide a detailed analysis of the accounting practices that are available and the *public* nature of their acceptance or non-acceptance as resolved in motive talk, the ascription of dispositions and responsibilities, and the application of norms and sanctions.

Let us now return to the processes that occur when a breach of conduct is recognized. We have already noted that ongoing social interaction is suspended in such circumstances. Given that a breach has occurred and is recognized as such by both actor and observers (or is assumed by the actor to be recognized by observers), the actor adopts a 'theoretical stance'. This involves seeing him/herself as an 'object' within the context of the setting in which the untoward act has taken place; the routine monitoring of social interaction is suspended. A retrospective evaluation of the incompetent performance is entailed in this stance, involving both the situated image that the actor has projected as a consequence of the act, and the biographical self-image he or she has conveyed to observers over a period of time. Tedeschi and Riess (1981) refer to this process as "impression management". Thus, in viewing him/herself through the eyes of others, the actor engages in an interpretative process, extrapolating the possible imputations of motive that can be made to him or her on the basis of the 'incident'. This assessment of self is critical in influencing the types of restitutive practices that the actor embarks upon, since the impression created by the breach is likely to be one which spoils the impression the actor believes him/herself to have created thus far; it is, in any case, discrepant with the image that a competent agent is assumed to convey under 'normal' circumstances. In various studies concerned with the examination of interpretative processes that take place following breaches, Semin and Manstead (1981, 1982; Manstead & Semin, 1981; Semin 1981b,c,1982) have demonstrated that actors assume that they have projected a negative image of themselves, even if the breach in question is an unintentional one, such as upsetting a display of goods in a supermarket. The threat of potential negative imputations to the self, in the shape of anticipated negative dispositional inferences that an observer may make, increases with the degree of blame and responsibility that can be inferred from the act (cf. Manstead & Semin, 1981; Semin, 1981b). The reputation of the self is assumed to be called into question, and the potential explanations that observers may advance (i.e., the motives and dispositions that are available to make the action a meaningful one) all have direct negative implications for the actor's reputation. Thus, the suspension of social interaction and the adoption of a theoretical stance involve primarily an assessment of the potential interpretative schemata that may be invoked by observers to explain the incident. Since the incident is one which is not characteristic of a competent member of society, these interpretations all contain potentially negative implications for the actor's reputation. The accounting process in itself provides a socially available means of stemming the flow of possible negative imputations; exactly which accounting practices are employed depends, among other things, upon the type of breach in question. The various types of public accounting strategies available are closely related to the moral evaluations that actors and observers make of each other's conduct, and are therefore related to the moral norms and sanctions to which agents who contravene them can be subjected. Competence in such everyday contexts is defined in terms of what members are commonly expected to know about in everyday life and are thus expected to follow in their routine monitoring of action.

Recognition of the problematic situation, the potential interpretations of the projected self, and the possible imputations that others may make give rise to the practices that are involved in attempts to normalize the situation. Mills (1940) has termed this type of social practice 'motive talk': "Motives are imputed or avowed as answers to questions interrupting acts or programs. Motives are words...They do not denote any elements in individuals. They stand for anticipated situational consequences of questioned conduct. Intention or purpose...is awareness of anticipated consequences; motives are names for consequential situations, and surrogates for actions leading to them. Behind questions are possible alternative actions with their terminal consequences" (Mills, 1940, p. 905). This is very much akin to Dewey's (1922) conception of motives, i.e., that a motive does not precede an act, functioning as an 'innate releaser', but rather is "...an act plus a judgement upon some element of it, the judgement being made in light of the consequences of it" (1922, p.120). Thus motive talk, which can be self-generated, or instigated by the direct question of an observer, not only allows the interpretation of a situation, but is also part and parcel of the process of negotiation through which the normalization of public conduct takes place (cf. Peters, 1958). The actor has to repair the situation and justify or excuse his or her conduct, if possible. "A motive is not necessarily a discreditable reason for acting, but it is a reason asked for in a context where there is a suggestion that it *might* be discreditable. The demand is for justification, not simply explanation" (Peters, 1958, p. 31). Thus, motives act as reasons for action, but they are distinctive from reasons in a general sense (i.e. for ongoing action plans) since in the cases under examination what is at stake is a justification as well as an explanation. Motives are reasons which imply "... a directed disposition in the individual whose conduct is being assessed"(Peters, 1958, p. 35), i.e. a goal assignment is given for action.

Finally, it should be noted that the analytically distinguished phases of (i) the occurrence of untoward behaviour, (ii) the recognition of such an incident, and (iii) motive talk, may in actuality be temporally disjointed or continuous. For example, if I fail to turn up for an important appointment at 10 o'clock in the morning, and later that day happen to meet the person I was supposed to meet, motive talk is likely to ensue (assuming that I become aware of my failure to keep the appointment), even though several hours have elapsed since the transgression.

1.5. Summary

In this chapter we have considered attribution theory as a potential theoretical approach to examining the accountability of conduct. This theory, while by no means possessing the formal properties of a cohesive theory, is nevertheless a moderately unified and well established theoretical perspective in present-day social psychology. In examining critically the shortcomings of this approach we have been led to suggest the framework of an alternative approach , which we have called interpretative social psychology. This is, in fact, a synthesis of several lines of theoretical endeavour, such as symbolic interactionism, cognitive sociology and ethnomethodology, none of which stems from the psychological branch of social psychology.

In spite of the unquestioned ability of attribution models to generate research (cf. Harvey, Ickes & Kidd, 1976, 1978, 1981), our examination of attribution theory identified certain shortcomings which, in our view, limit seriously its applicability for the accountability of conduct. Chief among these shortcomings is the absence of any

awareness of the role played by language and culture in the interpretation of social actions. Instead of regarding social interaction as
progressing within particular cultural and temporal frames which
themselves render actions warrantable and intelligible, attribution
models assume implicitly that extraordinary amounts of cognitive
work need to be invested in the process of understanding any and every
social event. The very fact that the need or call to provide an account
for some action arises in particular kinds of circumstance calls into
question any theoretical approach that fails to specify clearly when
persons begin to question the motives, reasons, intentions, and so on,
of a fellow actor.

By contrast the theoretical approach embodied in interpretative
social psychology recognizes the importance of the role played by
culture in providing a language which incorporates explanatory
concepts in its descriptive terms; in providing rules and conventions
against which the appropriateness of observed behaviours can be
assessed; and in providing social actors with a stock of knowledge
which contains interpretative schemata shared by members of a
common culture, and which enables the more or less flawless
interaction of everyday life. Within this theoretical framework, actions
which correspond to social expectations are not called into question.
Actions which are not immediately warrantable and intelligible,
however, provoke reflexive questioning. Such a perspective on social
interaction provides a fuller and more satisfactory vehicle for
analysing the accountability of conduct than that provided by
attribution theory.

In the final section of this chapter the properties of "problematic"
social episodes were considered, with a view to analysing the way in
which these predicaments are recognized, interpreted, and normalized. It was argued that the unproblematic nature of most social
interaction provides a backdrop against which any hiatus stands out,
provoking the spontaneous provision of an account or the call from
observers to provide such an account. Because the problematic action
is one which falls outside the boundaries of legal or customary
behaviour, the actor is likely to assume that others who witnessed the
action will be inclined to make negative dispositional inferences on the
basis of their observation. The account provided by the actor may be
seen as an attempt to mitigate or nullify these negative inferences, by
excusing or justifying the action. The questioning and ascription of
motives that occur under such circumstances involve judgment and
evaluation.

2

Facework

2.1. Introduction

A fundamental assumption of much of the work discussed in this book is that social interaction is a finely balanced process. As long as the identities projected either explicitly or implicitly by those who interact remain unchallenged, the equilibrium of interaction is sustained. As Lyman and Scott (1972) have put it, "In everyday life people frequently make claims (or are thought to be making claims) of being certain kinds of persons. In a typical case, the individual succeeds in carrying the burden of proof to substantiate his claims" (p.161).

It follows from such an assumption that when the identity claims of one individual are threatened by a slip or flaw in self-presentation, the equilibrium of social interaction is also threatened. Interactants will typically be keen to instigate coping processes which attempt to defend or restore the social equilibrium, since the discrediting of one actor's identity causes implications for other parties to the interaction: they too have committed their identities to the encounter, and short of abandoning the encounter altogether, they will have to try to restore the social equilibrium before further damage is done.

The coping processes which are instigated by the occurrence or threat of some behaviour which disconfirms the identity of an actor are given the generic term 'facework' by Goffman (1955). The present chapter will review and discuss the theoretical and empirical literature on facework, seeking consistently to relate these theoretical and

emprical developments to Goffman's (1955) typology of facework
practices.

2.2. Goffman's typology of facework

In Goffman's (1959) view, the smooth flow of interaction, the
maintenance of the 'expressive order' as he puts it, is upheld by
overlapping definitions of the situation. This perspective admits the
possibility that social interaction may contain events which in some
way threaten any one individual's projected definition of the situation,
thereby creating the potential for 'embarrassment' not only on the
part of the individual but also on the part of the audience

Definitional disruptions of this kind have, Goffman argues, two sets
of implications for social interaction. First, *preventive practices* are
continuously deployed in an attempt to preempt such disruptions.
Secondly, *corrective practices* are utilised when disruptions have
occurred. Thus a dichotomy is drawn between 'avoidance' behaviour,
which is employed to prevent threats to face, and 'escape' behaviour,
which is intended to re-establish social equilibrium. Both types of
behaviour fall under Goffman's rubric 'facework', in that they are
actions taken by the individual to render behaviour consistent with
face; in other words, they are attempts to make events occurring in the
situation correspond with projected definitions of the situation. The
distinction between avoidance and escape manoeuvres does not reside
simply in the occurrence of some threatening event; rather, Goffman
treats all facework activity as preventive facework up to the point
where one or more of the participants in an encounter explicitly — in
most cases, verbally — acknowledge the threatening event and deals
with it by means of a 'corrective interchange' (Goffman, 1955).

The present chapter will introduce Goffman's typology of facework
in some detail and then review studies of facework within the
framework of Goffman's typology. The main focus of attention in this
chapter will be on preventive facework practices, for it is in studies of
such practices that Goffman's influence is most apparent. Chapter 3
will address corrective facework and there Goffman's analysis of the
corrective interchange will be compared with other treatments of
accounts and accounting.

2.2.1. PREVENTIVE PRACTICES

Goffman (1959) sub-divides the general category of preventive practices into two classes: *defensive* practices, i.e. those steps taken by the actor to prevent threat to face and *protective* practices, i.e. those steps taken by the audience to prevent threat to the actor's face.

Defensive practices

Goffman suggests that successful performance by an actor or a team of actors is characterised by three attributes, each of which carries the flavour of Goffman's dramaturgical approach to the study of social interaction. These attributes are dramaturgical loyalty, dramaturgical discipline and dramaturgical circumspection. Each attribute entails the operation of various defensive practices, as indicated below.

Dramaturgical loyalty. This attribute applies particularly to those performances which involve a team rather than a single individual. Loyalty here refers to the requirement for all members to maintain the team line. Thus team-mates should abstain from any action which suggest an internal rift or disagreement between members of the team. Goffman suggests that one of the key problems in maintaining loyalty to the team line is to prevent team members from developing affective ties with the audience, which, if they are sufficiently strong, might involve a transfer of loyalty from team to audience and thereby threaten the team's collective line. High in-group solidarity and systematic changes of audience are identified as key means by which this threat of dramaturgical disloyalty is averted.

Dramaturgical discipline. Goffman refers here to the necessity for actors to remain 'affectively dissociated' from their performance, while nevertheless appearing to be fully involved in it. The threat which is posed by such affective involvement is that the actor who is thus involved will not be "free to cope with dramaturgical contingencies as they arise". The key to dramaturgical discipline resides in the ability to suppress actual emotional response (where it does not accord with appropriate emotional response) and to substitute it with the appropriate responses. Goffman (1959) suggests that teasing is used as an informal initiation device, testing the capacity of new team members to 'take a joke'.

Dramaturgical circumspection. By this Goffman means preparation for all likely contingencies coupled with sufficient awareness of each situation as to allow an actor to adjust the performance to suit prevailing conditions. Goffman cites careful preselection of team-mates and audiences as means by which an actor can reduce the likelihood of disruptive contingencies arising. With respect to prac-tices which allow more exaggerated claims to be made without likelihood of detection, he identifies several key variables: the complexity and length of the performance; the information conditions under which it is staged; the importance to the performer of the consequences which will occur as a result of the performance; the physical distance of a team from its audience; and the degree to which a performance is pre-programmed or scripted. Any practice which leads to these variables operating in such a way as to reduce the likelihood of detection by the audience is therefore a defensive practice (e.g. the use of an agenda at a meeting which diminishes the possibility of uncertainty amongst the performers at that meeting and commensurately reduces the chance of an audience gaining unfavourable impressions about the performers).

The three attributes discussed above would seem to apply only to those situations where an actor is fully involved with the performance at hand. Indeed, the threat to face posed by a lack of these attributes arises from too great an affective involvement with performance on the part of the actor. In a subsequent essay, Goffman (1961) describes another practice, namely *role distance*, which is not allied to any of the above attributes but can, nevertheless, be construed as defensive facework.

Role distance is a practice employed by those who seek to ward off the personal implications of the role they are seen to be performing. The term 'role distance' is used by Goffman "to refer to actions which effectively convey some disdainful detachment of the performer from a role he is performing" (1961, p. 98). In being seen not to be taking their roles seriously, performers "...give themselves some elbow room in which to manoeuvre...should they make a bad showing, they are in a position to dodge the reflection it could cast on them... By exposing themselves in a guise to which they have no serious claim, they leave themselves in full control of shortcomings they take seriously" (Goffman, 1961, p. 99). A rather more formal definition of role distance has been supplied by Stebbins (1969): "[R]ole distance can be defined as an attitude of dislike toward all or part of a set of role expectations which, when enacted, bring the threat of a loss of respect and at least momentary lack of support for one's self-conception from certain reference others present in the situation...[A]ctual performance expressing this predisposition we shall call *role distance behaviour*." (p. 407, original italics). It is apparent that role distance behaviour, as described by Goffman and defined by Stebbins, is a practice by which actors seek to *manage* the impression which they project to others, and that it is therefore an instance of defensive facework.

It is clear, then, that defensive facework practices include not only those techniques employed to sustain dramaturgical loyalty, discipline and circumspection — techniques, that is, which prevent the performer from becoming too immersed in the performance — but also those signs of 'mockery' or 'disdain' for a role which indicate that the performer is anything *but* immersed in the performance.

Protective practices

The practices outlined in the previous section are labelled by Goffman 'defensive', since they are, as he puts it, "techniques through which a set of performers can save their own show" (1959, p. 222). These actor-practices, Goffman suggests, have their counterparts in practices 'employed' by audiences or potential audiences (i.e. bystanders, outsiders) which are *protective*, in that they are aimed at helping the performers to 'save their own show'. These protective practices would fall under the colloquial rubric 'tact'. Goffman notes that two kinds of practices are employed prior to the admission of the audience to a performance. First, outsiders who are in a position to take the role of audience are conventionally supposed to avoid doing so, by means of adopting a pose of tactful inattention. Secondly, outsiders are not supposed to enter regions of interaction to which they have not been invited, and will commonly give some warning if such an entrance has to be accomplished (e.g. knocking on doors before entering).

However, as Goffman points out, the requirement for tact on the part of the audience does not cease once they have been admitted to the performance. They are expected to pay a certain amount of attention, to withold from interruptions, and to avoid creating an 'incident'. Further, when blemishes in performance occur, the audience may 'overlook' such occurrences and may even actively help the performers to cope with crises which threaten the performance. Goffman also notes that the audience is typically more prepared to exercise these kinds of tact when the performer is known to be a novice.

2.2.2. CORRECTIVE PRACTICES

The several practices outlined in the previous section are neither an exhaustive listing of techniques for avoiding threats to the smooth flow of interaction, nor a set of 'moral codes' which are invariably followed. If the latter were the case, then the need for the various techniques reviewed in the present section would be greatly diminished since disruptions would rarely occur. The use of preventive practices does not, in any case, guarantee the avoidance of an embarrassing incident: accidents will happen.

Such incidents typically call for the institution of corrective practices whereby the actor's damaged face can be restored. This is because the incident in question usually reflects not only on the actor whose face has been damaged, but also on the audience, since the interaction to which both actor and audience are parties is founded on mutual claims to acceptability, and a threat to these claims is a threat to the encounter itself. As Goffman puts it, "the encounter finds itself lodged in assumptions which no longer hold" (1956, p. 268). Thus there may be several motives for engaging in facework: the actor will for personal reasons be keen to restore face, and thereby to some extent counteract the negative impressions which others may have formed; the actor may feel some responsibility towards the interaction, and therefore want to engage in facework for social as well as personal reasons; the audience may want to save the actor's face because it identifies with the actor and sympathises with his or her plight; or the audience may want to repair the damage which accrues to the encounter itself, since members of the audience will find their own faces threatened if the encounter breaks down irretrievably. These several complementary motives will naturally operate more powerfully when the embarrassing incident has actually occurred, since the threat is now a reality rather than a possibility or probability.

Thus the incident consists of a threat to face or faces which is acknowledged by the participants who then engage in what Goffman terms a corrective or remedial interchange (Goffman, 1955, 1971). Goffman proposes that the interchange comprises four basic moves apart from the incident itself:

1. *The challenge* "by which participants take on the responsibility of

calling attention to the misconduct; by implication they suggest that the threatened claims are to stand firm and that the threatening event itself will have to be brought back into line" (Goffman, 1955, p. 220). Thus notice is served by one or more parties to the interaction (normally the 'offended parties') that the incident is too serious to be ignored. The typical nature of such a challenge is that the offender is called to account.

2. *The offering* "whereby a participant, typically the offender, is given the chance to correct for the offence and re-establish the expressive order" (Goffman, 1955, p. 220). The ways in which this move can be made constitute the main element of the category 'corrective practices'. Thus the offender can attempt to show that the challenge was unjustified, for one or more of a number of reasons: the 'offence' was really quite a meaningless act; or it was unintentional; or it was a joke; or it was an inevitable product of situational factors outside his or her control. A second approach might be for the offender to acknowledge implicitly or explicitly the offended party's definition of the behaviour in question, in which case the offender may attempt to deny personal responsibility for bringing about the threat or injury (e.g. "Don't blame me, I'm simply doing my job"). A third type of corrective practice is for the offender to acknowledge both the offensive nature of the act and personal causation, but to attempt to show that they can still be trusted as participants. This can be achieved in one or both of the following ways: the offender can offer compensation to the injured parties; or can engage in some kind of self-castigation. Either way, the offender shows awareness that some price has to be paid for the misdemeanour. In his later work, Goffman (1971) has delineated three categories of corrective practice which would fall under the rubric 'offering': *accounts, apologies, and requests.* This threefold distinction will be discussed in detail in Chapter 3.

3. *The acceptance* is the move by which the recipients of the offering intimate that they accept the offering as "as satisfactory means of re-establishing the expressive order and the faces supported by that order" (Goffman, 1955, p. 220).

4. *The thanks* is the final phase of the interchange, in which the person whose offering has been accepted expresses gratitude to those who accepted the offering.

2.2.3.SUMMARY

Goffman's typology of facework practices is summarised in Table 2.1. The fundamental distinction is that between preventive practices

TABLE 2.1. Goffman's typology of facework practices

	Pre-Incident Practices PREVENTIVE	Post-Incident Practices CORRECTIVE
ACTOR PRACTICES	*Defensive* e.g.: dramaturgical loyalty dramaturgical discipline dramaturgical circumspection role distance	*Offering* e.g.: account apology
AUDIENCE PRACTICES	*Protective* e.g.: tactful inattention warning of entrance	*Challenge* e.g.: call for account

which are deployed *before* social interaction is disrupted, and corrective practices, which are employed *after* the disruptive incident is explicitly acknowledged, as in the issue of a challenge or the making of an offering. A further main distinction is that between practices deployed by the *actor* and those deployed by the *audience*. It should be noted, however, that this latter distinction is rather less clear-cut than that between preventive and corrective practices. In everyday social interaction persons oscillate quite rapidly between being actors who perform and being part of an audience to the performances of others. The question of who is the 'actor' and who is the 'audience' is one of some importance in determining which facework practices persons are likely to adopt.

In the case of corrective facework this question is relatively easily settled, for the actor is the person who, at the very least, *believes* himself or herself to be responsible for an incident which has threatened the social equilibrium. It may also be the case that other participants — the audience, for present purposes — see this person as responsible for such an incident.

In the case of preventive facework the question of who is actor and who is audience can be more complex. In some cases the actor is defined by his or her lack of knowledge of the situational requirements. Thus the initiate, the foreigner, the short stay hospital patient, among others, are likely to regard themselves as actors, and to be so regarded by others present — the audience — who are more familiar with the situation. In other cases there is an explicit or implicit sense in which one of the participants is performing for the others, as when a recital is being given, a speech is being made, a story is being told, and so on. However, there are still other cases such as interchanges between close friends or between customer and shop assistant, for example, where the issue is less clear-cut, where no individual stands out from the other participants by virtue of novice status or whatever. Such encounters, which are after all by no means unusual in everyday social life, pose something of a problem for Goffman's typology, for if it is not clear who is actor and who is audience, then it is difficult to predict which kinds of facework practices will be deployed, or indeed to appreciate the need for preventive facework. It is this last point which helps to resolve the problem: if there is no sense in which one participant can be regarded as performing before the others, then the encounter must by definition be either so automated or so familar to the participants that the need for preventive facework practices does not arise. In such encounters facework practices will only be employed if some incident threatens to disrupt the otherwise smooth expressive fabric.

Having outlined Goffman's typology of facework practices, attention will now be focused on empirical studies of facework. These will be reviewed in two sections, the first dealing with sociological studies of a non-experimental nature, and the second with experimental studies from the social psychological literature.

2.3. Empirical studies of facework

Before reviewing these studies in detail, some general observations are in order concerning the appropriateness of different kinds of methodology and evidence for the validation of Goffman's conceptual scheme.

Goffman's own preferences in this regard are quite explicit. In the preface to *the presentation of self in everyday life* he justifies his own exclusively observational and conceptual approach by arguing that "...the illustrations together fit into a coherent framework that ties together bits of experience the sender has already had and provides the student with a guide worth testing in case studies of institutional social life" (p. xii). Elsewhere he refers to his own methodology as "unsystematic, naturalistic observation" (1971, p. xv). While admitting that such an approach has serious limitations, he rejects traditional research designs on the grounds that "the variables which emerge tend to be creatures of research design that have no existence outside the room in which the apparatus and subject are located" (1971, p. xvi). In particular, Goffman is critical of traditional research designs because the resulting research is conceptually weak: "Understanding of ordinary behaviour has not accumulated, distance has" (1971, p. xvi).

It is clear that Goffman has little faith in the use of experimental methods in the study of everyday social behaviour, and that among systematic methodologies his preference is for the case study. Goffman's reservations notwithstanding, experimental studies of facework are reviewed below, not with a view to validating or invalidating Goffman's typology of facework practices, but simply to advance as broad a range of empirical evidence on facework as possible. It could be argued that Goffman's objection to experimentation on the grounds of conceptual poverty is inapplicable where the experiments explicitly seek to address ideas derived from Goffman's own conceptual analyses. His other main objection to experimental methods, namely the inability to generalise from experimental findings, is less easily answered. However, to the extent that the findings of different experiments point to the same conclusions, it could be argued that such findings transcend the limitations of the laboratory.

This review of the evidence on facework begins with the less inherently problematic category of non-experimental studies conducted by sociologists, and will then proceed to a review of the experimental work in this area, before concluding with an integrating summary.

2.3.1. SOCIOLOGICAL STUDIES OF FACEWORK

Gross and Stone (1964) content analysed 1000 recollections of embarrassing episodes and classified these into three broad categories. They suggest that the categories provide insight into the role requirements for normal social interaction, and they label these requirements *identity, poise*, and the *maintenance of confidence*. A brief resumé of the meanings they attach to these requirements indicates that they contain both implicit and explicit notions of defensive practices.

In Gross and Stone's terms, the *identity* of an individual

> ...is established when others *place* him as a social object by assigning him the same words of identity that he appropriates for himself or announces. It is in the coincidence of placements and announcements that identity becomes a meaning of the self (Stone, 1962, p.93).

The establishment of this 'coincidence of placements and announcements' is critical, and Gross and Stone identify three defensive practices in which the performer engages in order to achieve this coincidence. First, actors should attend to the coherence between personal appearance, which is one aspect of announcement, and the setting in which they appear. Further, they should be careful to ensure that 'reserve' and/or 'abandoned' identities are not incongruent with the performance of the 'dominant role' in any given interaction. Finally, and rather obviously, actors should devote their attention to dominant role performance.

By *poise*, Gross and Stone mean the performer's control over various elements of self and setting. They identify five such elements: spaces, props, equipment, clothing, and body. In brief, they argue that the performer's self, and those aspects of the situation which are under the performer's control, need to be maintained in a constant state of readiness, and therefore in good repair. This kind of maintenance of self and situation is clearly a defensive practice. Gross and Stone point to the private rehearsal of "spontaneous" public speech as an instance of such maintenance.

While they regard identity and poise as central role requirements for initiating normal social interaction, Gross and Stone contend that *maintenance of confidence* is needed if this interaction is to continue. As the interaction stabilises, so the participants begin to build up expectations of one another. Gross and Stone point out that violations of such expectations constituted the greatest single source of embarrassment among their subjects' recollections of embarrassing incidents. In order that others might have confidence in the expectations they develop towards them, actors should maintain themselves in role, or at least avoid abrupt changes in identity. This can also be seen as a defensive practice, in that loss of confidence in a performer might reasonably be expected to foreshadow a less positive appraisal of that person.

Gross and Stone do not overlook the protective practices engaged in by the audience. They note that the standards of role performance nearly always allow for flexibility and tolerance, and that the operation of such norms allows all participants to assume that they will not be held strictly to account for minor aberrations in performance. Gross and Stone also claim that a norm of 'giving the other party the benefit of the doubt' operates, and suggests that this is particularly the case at the outset of interaction, when due scope is given to the performer to play a desired role.

Gross and Stone's conclusions regarding role requirements and performance norms relate to Goffman's analysis of preventive facework practices in several respects. Most fundamentally, their concept of identity is very similar to Goffman's concept of face, and their point that the performer should attend to the coherence between announced identity and other features of the social setting echoes Goffman's point that the line taken by the performer should be both internally consistent and consistent with other evidence introduced during the interaction.

Gross and Stone's concept of poise overlaps considerably with the attributes of dramaturgical discipline and dramaturgical circumspection, held by Goffman to characterise successful performance. Clearly, the performer who lacks discipline in becoming affectively immersed in the performance, or lacks circumspection in failing to appreciate the prevailing conditions, is not one who is poised. It is not surprising, therefore, to find that the practice of privately rehearsing what will later be presented as a 'spontaneous' public speech, cited by Gross and Stone as an example of poised behaviour, is akin to the defensive practices discussed by Goffman in connection with dramatrugical circumspection (e.g. the 'scripting' of public performances). Furthermore, the requirement that performers maintain themselves in role, which is the principal meaning of Gross and Stone's concept of maintenance of confidence, is similar in many respect to the practice of sustaining the line which has already been adopted, the key feature of Goffman's notion of dramaturgical loyalty. Finally, the performance norms referred to by Gross and Stone are a perfect illustration of Goffman's point that audiences are prepared to exercise tactful inattention when minor blemishes in performance occur.

There is clearly a high degree of consistency between the attributes regarded by Goffman as necessary for successful interaction and the role requirements outlined by Gross and Stone, and consequently a similar consistency between the kinds of practice described as sustaining the attributes and role requirements. To the extent that Gross and Stone's categories and concepts were derived from their analysis of recollections of embarrassing incidents, their paper can be regarded as providing empirical support for Goffman's conceptualisation of facework.

A rather different type of approach to the non-experimental study of facework is represented by Emerson's (1970) case study of behaviour during gynaecological examinations. Whereas Gross and Stone relied for their case material on their subject's recollection of embarrassing incidents, Emerson selected for analysis a situation in which the 'official' definition of reality is inherently precarious. The gynaecological examination, Emerson points out, is precarious for two reasons: "First, it is an excellent example of multiple contradictory definitions of reality... Second...there is a substantial threat from participants' incapacity to perform" (1970, p.76). In other words, the gynaecological examination is a situation in which (a) 'reserve' or 'abandoned' identities incongruent with the dominant role performance are difficult to discard fully; and (b) considerable demands are made on the poise of each participant, and the need to maintain confidence is at a premium.

Of course, the gynaecological examination is a situation in which the roles of 'actor' and 'audience' are relatively easy to allocate. As Emerson points out, "...the staff assume the responsibility for a credible performance. The staff take part in gynaecological examinations many times a day, while the patient is a fleeting visitor" (p.77). In identifying the use of preventive facework practices, one would therefore look to the patient's actions for evidence of defensive practices, and to the actions of the staff for evidence of protective practices. For the patient's part, the defensive practices apparent from Emerson's analysis are primarily examples of dramaturgical discipline. The main requirement of the patient is that she be nonchalant about what is happening: she should be attentive to the situation, but her voice should be controlled and self-confident, her facial expression should be neutral, her gaze should not be directed at the physician unless he is talking to her. As Emerson puts it, "Her role calls for passivity and self-effacement... The self must be eclipsed in order to sustain the definition that the doctor is working on a technical object and not a person" (p.83).

The preventive practices engaged in by the medical staff — the audience, for present purposes — are more numerous. Among the various actions described by Emerson, the following are unambiguously protective practices, designed to help the patient to maintain face. First, there are features of the setting in which the examination takes place. Emerson cites such features as divisions of space, decor, and equipment, arguing that these "are constant reminders that it is indeed 'medical space'" (p.81). Furthermore, the staff wear medical uniforms, they exclude from the setting any lay persons who might serve to mitigate the medical quality of the setting, and a female nurse is typically present to counteract any non-medical connotations of a male doctor and female patient being alone in such circumstances. Verbal exchanges with the patient are facilitated by the use of scientific terminology, or by the use of euphemisms. One way or another, instructions to the patient avoid sexual imagery. Finally, the gynaecological examination is highly routinised. Emerson observes that "Routine technical procedures organise the event from beginning to end, indicating what action each person should take at each moment... There is little margin for ad-libbing during a gynaecological examination" (p.82-83). All these aspects of staff behaviour prior to and during the examination seem to represent protective counterparts to the dramaturgical circumspection which Goffman describes as one category of the defensive practices deployed by actors. The audience in this case comprises a team which attempts to ensure that the actor is able to behave in accordance with the medical definition of the situation, and thereby maintain face.

Over and above such dramaturgical circumspection, the staff themselves must display poise during the examination. In particular, the physician has to strike the appropriate balance between the need to be formal and technical, so as to resist any hints of intimacy, and the need to be friendly and soothing, so as to relax the patient and avoid insulting her by failing to treat her as a person. According to Emerson, the doctor achieves the requisite qualities of friendliness and soothingness "by radiating concern in his general manner, offering extra assistance, and occasionally by sacrificing the task requirements to 'gentleness'" (p.85). It is clear that the doctor has to exercise a form of what Goffman calls dramaturgical discipline in this respect, appearing at once both disinterested in and concerned for the patient's feelings and personality. The ultimate goal of this discipline, however, is not to manage his own public image, but rather to enable the patient to manage hers. As Emerson observes, "Reality in gynaecological examinations is challenged mainly by patients" (p.85), the exceptions to this being cases where novice medical students are participating in the examination.

Emerson describes various types of events which threaten the medical definition of reality during a gynaecological examination. Patients may cry, express pain, or withdraw attention from the scene to the extent that they do not immediately respond to instruction. Patients may be inappropriately modest or inappropriately immodest with regard to nudity. Patients may express inappropriate concern about unappealing aspects of their bodies. Emerson notes that "The foremost technique in neutralising threatening events is to sustain a nonchalant demeanour even if the patient is blushing with embarrassment, blanching from fear, or moaning in pain" (p.88). In other words, the staff tactfully fail to acknowledge those features of the patient's conduct which are dissonant with the official reality. When these features are too salient to be ignored, staff can *redefine* them. Thus signs of embarrassment or sexual arousal may be redefined as 'fear', 'ticklishness', or whatever. Humour may also be used in order to communicate with patients about the events at hand with a degree of detachment. Thus the doctor can respond to a patient's protests by lightly ridiculing them without actually ignoring them. All these actions on the part of the staff are clear examples of Goffman's category of protective practices, in that the audience is either 'overlooking' blemishes in the actor's performance or actively helping the actor to cope with events which threaten her performance.

Emerson's final example of the means by which threatening events are neutralised concerns the teamwork of the nurse and physician. Emerson argues that one of the main purposes served by the presence of the nurse is to provide a team mate for the doctor: "Team members can create a more convincing reality than one person alone. Doctor and nurse may collude against an uncooperative patient, as by giving each other significant looks" (p.90). This strategy would seem to fall beyond the bounds of protective facework, in that the concern of the audience team is no longer to help the patient to carry off her performance. Indeed, one could argue that when the patient becomes so uncooperative as to evoke this unsympathetic collusion, the facework practices deployed by the audience are directed primarily towards maintaining their own faces in awkward circumstances. By behaving uncooperatively, the patient loses the protection extended by the originally sympathetic audience.

These two sociological studies of facework provide us with findings and observations that are broadly consistent with Goffman's (1955) typology. Through their analysis of recollected embarrassing incidents, Gross and Stone (1964) demonstrate that dissonance between face and setting, lack of poise, and inconsistency of face within an encounter all provoke embarrassment. The means by which these threats to social equilibrium may be averted are clearly instances of preventive facework practices. Actors should make their self-presentation appropriate to the setting (dramaturgical circumspection), avoid undue affective involvement in their performance (dramaturgical discipline), and maintain a consistent line (dramaturgical loyalty).

Emerson's (1970) observations on behaviour during gynaecological examinations show how participants manage a precarious situation. It might be thought that this situation is so extreme as to be anomalous, but Emerson contends that the difference between this encounter and routine interaction is one of degree, not kind: "[T]he gynaecological examination merely exaggerates the internally contradictory nature of definitions of reality found in most situations" (p.91). The particular value of Emerson's analysis from the present point of view is that it highlights the use of protective practices by an audience. Because of the essentially passive role played by the patient during the examination, there is little she can do but attempt to retain poise. The medical team, on the other hand, has to ensure that features of the setting are consistent with the medical 'line' that needs to be projected (dramaturgical circumspection), and to retain a delicate poise between instrumental and affective interaction (dramaturgical discipline). Over and above these audience counterparts to the defensive practices described by Goffman, Emerson's analysis demonstrates the key role played by three techniques by which the medical team neutralise threats arising from the patient's behaviour: tactful inattention, redefinition, and humour. Each of these techniques is a means by which some inappropriate aspect of the patient's behaviour can be incorporated into a medical definition of the encounter.

2.3.2. EXPERIMENTAL STUDIES OF FACEWORK

Let us now turn to experimental investigations of facework to see what light they cast on the causes and consequences of the use of facework practices. A series of experiments concerned with face maintenance have been conducted by Brown and Garland (Brown, 1968, 1970; Brown & Garland, 1971; Garland & Brown, 1972).

Brown (1968) started from an interpersonal bargaining perspective. He notes at the outset of the paper that the unfair reduction of one bargainer's outcome by an opponent typically results in retaliation and mutual loss. Drawing on Goffman's analysis of facework, Brown reasoned that the explanation for such findings is that the bargainer has a powerful concern to avoid losing face before an audience. The need to maintain face is split by Brown into *face-saving* and *face-restoration*, which parallels the distinction between preventive practices and corrective practices. His (1968) study was concerned with retaliation following exploitation, which Brown regards as the central means by which face-restoration is accomplished. This emphasis on retaliation as a corrective practice appears to be a consequence of Brown's interpersonal bargaining perspective. It is interesting to note that Goffman treats retaliation as a peripheral means by which face can be restored, and that he specifically identifies games as encounters in which the "aggressive use of face-work" takes place (Goffman, 1955, p. 221). The point is that in the normal course of social interaction the aggressive use of facework is limited by the fact that such aggression constitutes a further threat to the expressive order of the encounter. Retaliation, then, may be regarded as a corrective practice, but one which is highly person-oriented rather than situation-oriented and which requires a rather special game-like encounter. Bearing these limitations in mind, we can return to Brown's experiment.

Subjects were observed by an 'audience' (supposedly classmates) while they took part in a modified version of Deutsch and Krauss' (1960) two-person bargaining game. For the first ten trials of this game the naive subject was systematically exploited by his opponent. Then the subject received 'audience feedback' to the effect that he had looked "foolish and weak", or "good" despite the exploitation because he had "played fair". There followed a further ten trials, in which the subject could choose between gradually more potent retaliation, at increasing costs, and outcome maximisation. The final manipulations concerned whether or not the subject was told that his opponent knew the costs of retaliation on the second set of trials.

The results of this experiment unequivocally supported Brown's hypotheses: negative feedback produced significantly greater retaliation than positive feedback, despite the fact that retaliation involved the sacrifice of the retaliator's own outcomes. Furthermore, this retaliatory behaviour was employed to a significantly greater extent when the exploited bargainer supposed that his opponent was unaware of the costs of his retaliation. It is interesting to note that subjects who received negative feedback reported a significantly greater concern with "appearing strong" to their opponents during the second ten trials than did subjects in any other condition.

In his second paper, Brown (1970) discarded the interpersonal bargaining paradigm in favour of investigating face-saving in the context of embarrassment. The aim of the two experiments reported in this paper was "to determine whether the earlier research on face-saving in interpersonal bargaining...could be extended to explain behaviour following experimentally induced embarrassment" (Brown, 1970, pp. 257-258). However, the parallel between these studies and the 1968 experiment is confounded to some extent by the fact that the second paper shifts its concern from corrective practices to preventive practices. The 1970 paper reports two closely related experiments which used as a dependent variable the extent to which subjects were prepared to forego monetary profits in order to avoid being embarrassed in front of an audience. In the first of these studies, Brown predicted that monetary sacrifice would be highest when the task was embarrassing *and* the subject believed the audience to be ignorant of potential rewards; in other words, an interaction was predicted between 'task embarrassment' and 'audience knowledge'.

The results of this experiment provided general support for this prediction. Subjects who performed the more embarrassing task *and* believed that the audience was ignorant of their potential rewards sacrificed significantly more on average than subjects in other conditions. No differences in sacrifice of payoff were found between the other three conditions, although the scores fell in the predicted order. Self-report data indicated that fear of looking foolish or feeling embarrassed was a significantly more potent reason for not maximising payoff for subjects in the high task embarrassment condition than for those in the low task embarrassment condition.

The second experiment sought to examine the effects on face-saving of manipulating audience characteristics. Brown noted that previous studies had investigated the effect of audience role and identity on such dependent measures as task performance (e.g. Henchy & Glass, 1968) and positivity of self-presentation (e.g. Jones, Gergen & Davis, 1962). Experiment 2 of the 1970 paper was designed to determine the relationship between audience role and identity on the one hand, and face-saving on the other. The results indicated that a significantly greater amount of reward was sacrificed by subjects in an 'evaluative audience' condition than those in a 'non-evaluative audience' condition. No support was found for the prediction that greater face-saving would occur before a female audience than before a male audience (subjects were male).

The conclusions to be drawn from the studies reported in Brown's (1970) paper are clear enough: there is a tendency for people to engage in costly preventive practices in order to avoid being embarrassed before an audience. Across the two experiments, rather more than half the subjects chose not to maximise their payoff by engaging in the most 'public' form of performance; the data suggest that these subjects found that the cost in terms of face incurred by such a public performance were greater than the economic costs of engaging in the preventive practice of facework, and therefore chose a less financially rewarding but more private form of performance. Furthermore, this preventive practice was adopted to a significantly greater extent when the experimental task was reported by subjects as being more embarrassing and of the 41 subjects in the two experiments who performed the more embarrassing task and declined the larger payoff, 29 (i.e. 71%) gave fear of embarrassment or fear of looking foolish as their reason for not maximising their payoff. It is important to note, however, that the facework induced by Brown's experimental procedure would appear to have a purely self-preservative function. The reasons given by subjects for not maximising their payoff appear to have been purely concerned with the preservation of their own image in the eyes of the audience: there was no evidence of concern on the part of these subjects to avoid threatening the expressive order of the encounter. This might have been a consequence of the somewhat rarified nature of the laboratory encounter. The typical experimental encounter is one in which the maintenance of expressive order is unlikely to be a salient factor.

Brown and Garland (1971) continued to examine facework primarily as a defensive practice, once again using as their dependent measure subjects' willingness to sacrifice monetary rewards in order to avoid performance of an embarrassing task, namely singing in public. Two experiments were reported, the first of which explored the effects on face-saving of self-evaluation, degree of acquaintanceship with the audience, and anticipated revelation of the audience's evaluation. It was expected that face-saving would be greater when task-specific self-evaluation was low, when the audience was said to consist of acquaintances rather than strangers, and when subjects anticipated receiving evaluative feedback from the audience. Analysis of the length of singing time revealed a significant difference between the high and low self-evaluation conditions: as predicted, the average singing time was significantly shorter in the low self-evaluation condition. No other significant effects were found.

The absence of empirical support for the other two hypotheses prompted the second experiment. In this study the acquaintanceship variable was extended to run from 'close relationship' through 'acquaintanceship' to 'complete strangers'. In a fourth condition, subjects were told that the audience was composed of strangers, but that they would meet the audience after singing. Analysis of length of singing time revealed a significant effect due to audience identity. Further analysis indicated that subjects sang for a significantly shorter time before close friends than before acquaintances or strangers, contrary to expectation; and that subjects sang for a substantially shorter duration when they did expect to meet strangers afterwards than when they did not expect such a meeting. The significant reversal of the predicted relationship between acquaintanceship and face-saving warrants some discussion and is particularly interesting in the light of Goffman's model of facework which, as we have seen, emphasises the fact that participants will take precautions to prevent the disruption of each other's projected definitions of self as well as their own.

Throughout his work Goffman shows us examples of the kinds of social limitations that impinge on the line that an actor takes in a given encounter. Naturally, one of the most important of these limitations is the degree to which a given audience is likely to be encountered in the future. Before an audience which is unlikely to be encountered again, an actor can take an extravagant line, without regard to the possibility that future encounters might reveal facts which do not accord with his current presentation. The reverse of this coin is that the actor will be free to have his current presentation discredited, with little fear of the embarrassment which might ensue during future encounters with the present audience. Goffman's analysis therefore provides a neat explanation of Brown and Garland's findings that embarrassment and face-saving were more likely to occur before an audience of close friends rather than acquaintances, and before an audience of strangers whom one is expecting to meet rather than an audience of strangers whom one does not expect to meet.

With the inclusion of the 'close friends' and 'future interaction' conditions, Brown and Garland clearly constructed an experimental encounter more characteristic of everyday life encounters. Although the facework with which they were concerned was still essentially a defensive practice, the fact that this defensive practice was found to be adopted more extensively in contexts having an explicit or implicit 'after-life' is indicative of the greater care taken by actors in an encounter which is likely to be repeated. This is consistent with the notion that the concern of those engaging in facework is directed in part towards the preservation of a basis for future interaction, as well as a more selfish concern with their public image.

Garland and Brown (1972) reported two further experiments which are closely related to those just discussed; indeed the experimental task and the dependent measure of face-saving were identical. The main concern of the first experiment was to investigate sex differences in face-saving behaviour. No hypotheses about sex differences in face-saving were made, but Garland and Brown noted that the bulk of previous (non-experimental) literature on the question of sex differences in embarrassment and blushing suggests that females are more easily embarrassed than males (e.g. Darwin, 1872; Buytendijk, 1950; Sattler, 1966). The results indicated that female subjects engaged in significantly more face-saving than males when singing before a female audience. This finding led Garland and Brown to analyse their data carefully, particularly since it represented a significant reversal of their expectation that face-saving would be greatest before male audiences. Of particular interest was the tendency (non-significant) for female subjects to report themselves as feeling less similar to the female audience than to the male audience. Garland and Brown interpreted this feeling of dissimilarity as arising from the subjects' differential attributions of singing ability to male and female audiences, citing the fact that when potential subjects were being screened for participation in this experiment, females had rated their voices much more positively than males.

Following up this interpretation, Garland and Brown conducted a second experiment, investigating the effect on face-saving of manipulating the supposed 'singing ability' of the audience. Half the subjects were told that the female audience consisted of 'poor' singers, while the other half were told that the female audience consisted of 'excellent' singers. The prediction was that face-saving would be greater before the 'excellent' singer audience than before the 'poor' singer audience, and the results provided strong support for this hypothesis. Thus feelings of similarity or equal status to the audience with respect to the task in hand might function to reduce face-saving on the part of the actor.

Garland and Brown noted (p. 287) that Woolbert (1916) has suggested that an expert audience might be seen as less inclined to act in an understanding fashion toward an actor who has performed poorly than an amateur or lay audience. This relates closely to the earlier discussion concerned with differences between encounters staged for the purposes of laboratory experiments and everyday life encounters. It seems quite likely that unless (as with Garland & Brown's second experiment) subjects are instructed that the audience is non-expert, they will make the assumption that they are being evaluated from a vantage point conferred by superior skill. It is suggested that actors' perceptions of the degree of similarity between their skill at the task and that of the audience might be a crucial factor in determining how self-centred their employment of facework will be. Where an audience is seen by actors as being *more* skilful than themselves, they are likely to engage in defensive practices; however, if actors regard the audience as being *less* skilful than themselves, they are likely to engage in protective practices. In other words, one's perception of one's skill relative to other parties to the interaction may be an important determinant of one's feeling of responsibility for maintaining the expressive order of the encounter: a greater sense of responsibility should reflect itself in a greater willingness and concern to protect the self-presentations of other participants — and thereby protect the encounter itself.

Further experimental evidence on the use of facework practices comes from studies conducted by Modigliani (1971) and Archibald and Cohen (1971). Modigliani (1971) used a facework index, consisting of eight categories, six of which were aimed at capturing what Modigliani felt to be "some major forms of facework" (Modigliani, 1971, p. 20). Facework behaviour was coded into these categories by trained observers, who watched and heard each subject as he answered questions during a 'staff interview'. This interview was part of the experimental procedure for all subjects in four 'public' conditions (i.e., public failure, mitigated public failure, public success and mitigated public success), and it followed manipulations of success and failure which had been surreptitious manipulations of task difficulty and appropriate feedback. Presumably through lack of sufficient resources, Modigliani only obtained facework codings for the two public failure conditions (i.e. public failure and mitigated public failure). The six categories representing facework responses to the staffman's questions are as follows (the examples given in parentheses are those supplied by Modigliani, 1971, p.20):

1. Defensively changing the subject (e.g. "I don't know, but how much longer is this thing going to go on?").

2. Introducing information excusing the performance (e.g. "Flourescent lights really affected my concentration").

3. Introducing redeeming or self-enhancing information (e.g. "I'm usually much better at mathematical type tasks.").

4. Minimising failure by derogating the task (e.g. "For my money, solving anagrams is pretty meaningless and boring.").

5. Denying failure (e.g. "I doubt anyone could solve those in ten minutes.").

6. Fishing for reassurance (e.g. "I really messed you guys up pretty bad, didn't I? I'm really sorry.").

This index includes one preventive practice (category 1) and five corrective practices (categories 2 through 6). The corrective practices are all offerings made by the offender to his audience and consist of excuses (categories 2 and 3), justifications (categories 4 and 5) and apology (category 6).

Since facework data were only available for two of the original six treatments, Modigliani only reported correlation coefficients between facework and other dependent measures. For the public failure and mitigated public failure conditions combined, a significant positive correlation was found between facework and reported embarrassment, and a significant negative correlation was found between facework and a measure of the subject's impression of how he was evaluated by the audience. These correlations are hardly surprising: one might argue that they tell us more about the validity of Modigliani's facework coding system than they do about facework itself. Thus Modigliani demonstrated that facework can be observed and coded in a reliable and reasonably valid fashion.

Archibald and Cohen's (1971) paper investigated facework in the context of their broader concern with the relative ability of 'approval' and 'consistency' explanations of the links between self-evaluation, self-presentation and reactions to feedback from others. They reasoned that an approval interpretation predicts that low self-evaluation subjects would simply engage in more facework than high self-evaluation subjects; and that a consistency interpretation predicts that low self-evaluation subjects would engage in more facework where evaluative feedback was positive whereas high self-evaluation subjects would engage in more facework where evaluative feedback was negative. Four basic facework strategies were measured by means of a post-experimental questionnaire: *role distance, denial of responsibility for outcomes, discrediting* of those who had given the feedback, and general *derogation* of feedback source. While use of role distance is clearly a preventive practice, denial of responsibility and discrediting and derogating the source of feedback are corrective practices. Analysis of the role distance data revealed that subjects with low self-evaluation reported themselves to be less involved in the interaction than high self-evaluation subjects, and particularly so when they anticipated continuing the interaction. Role distance was the only facework strategy which varied as a function of factors other than evaluative feedback from others: subjects who received negative feedback were significantly more likely to feel unlucky, to discredit the feedback source and to derogate the feedback source. The only other significant finding was an interaction showing that significantly more discrediting of feedback source occurred when low self-evaluation subjects anticipating future interaction received negative feedback. All these findings tend to support an approval interpretation, for the independent variable which exerted most influence on facework ratings was negative feedback, i.e. disapproval.

Further data of interest were reported by Archibald and Cohen in the shape of correlations between their measures of facework and embarrassment. These revealed that their 'specific' measure of embarrassment (based on scales 'embarrassed — not embarrassed' and 'ashamed — unashamed') correlated significantly and positively with *derogation* and significantly but negatively with *role distance*. Their 'general' measure of embarrassment (based on scales 'confident — shaken', 'tense — relaxed', 'at ease - self conscious', and 'awkward — poised') correlated significantly with all measures of facework, negatively with role distance and positively with the other three. The negative correlation between role distance and both measures of embarrassment is particularly interesting. Archibald and Cohen's explanation of this finding is as follows:

> Although we have no way of checking on the time sequence in which the various facework strategies were used, since actual feedback did not affect role distance, it seems reasonable to assume that the subjects who failed, and particularly those who expected to have to face others...defensively detached themselves from the embarrassing effects of anticipated disapproval. That this strategy worked is suggested by the large negative correlations between role distance and embarrassment; that is, the more role distance that the subjects established, the less embarrassed they were by disapproval when they actually received it (Archibald & Cohen, 1971, p. 296).

Extending Archibald and Cohen's line of thinking a little further, it could be argued that a significant *positive* correlation between embarrassment and facework measure would be indicative of the relative poverty of that facework strategy. Derogation was the only one of Archibald and Cohen's measures of facework which did correlate significantly and positively with their 'specific' measure of embarrassment. This would seem to be consistent with the above reasoning, in that derogation of the source of negative feedback can be construed as a 'last ditch' attempt on the part of the actor to stave off embarrassment. If this rather speculative interpretation is allowed, then one might infer from Archibald and Cohen's data that role distance is the most effective facework strategy of those which they chose to measure, followed by discrediting the source of feedback, denial of responsibility and derogating the feedback source, in that order.

Another kind of approach to studying the effects of the experience of embarrassment upon subsequent face-saving behaviour is represented by Apsler's (1975) experiment. Apsler noted that Goffman's analysis of embarrassment suggests that an embarrassing incident:

> has a relatively specific influence on embarrassed individuals' behaviour. Embarrassed individuals are concerned about the effect an

embarrassing incident has on the image that they are attempting to project to the others in the situation. Consequently, their behaviour is directed at the other persons involved in the embarrassing situation...in order to correct their damaged image, the image formed of them by others in the situation (Apsler, 1975, p. 146).

Apsler's study was designed to test a prediction based on this reasoning. It was hypothesised that an embarrassing incident would influence the embarrassed individual's behaviour towards others who were involved in the incident, but would have relatively little impact on the individual's behaviour towards others who were unaware of the incident. This hypothesis was tested by manipulating embarrassment and then presenting subjects with a request for help, either from somebody who had witnessed the embarrassing incident or from someone who was unaware of it. While the results provided strong support for the prediction that embarrassed subjects would comply with the request more than unembarrassed subjects, there was no support for the 'Goffman hypothesis' that compliance would be maximal when the request came from someone who had witnessed the incident.

Apsler argued that these findings suggest that embarrassed individuals experience negative affect, in the form of embarrassment, and seek to relieve this negative affect through some positive experience; complying with a request for help is just such an experience. However, it is not clear that the hypothesis derived from Goffman was adequately tested. While the experiment was carefully designed to convey to the subjects in the non-observer request condition that the person making the request had not witnessed the subject engaging in a number of embarrassing tasks, observation of an individual performing these tasks from the other side of a one-way mirror does not fully capture the interdependent nature of the social encounters with which Goffman is concerned. Apsler's subjects cannot reasonably be said to have been participating in an analogue of everyday social interaction. From the embarrassed subjects' perspective, the pressures to restore face in the eyes of those who had witnessed the embarrassing incident would not have been especially great, since these witnesses were total strangers with whom they would be unlikely to interact in the future. Furthermore, it is not clear whether compliance with a request for help is an instance of corrective

facework, regardless of who made the request. Goffman's discussion of
corrective practices focuses on the explanations provided by the
performer responsible for the incident on the premise that the
interaction would flounder unless the offender makes an offering
which is accepted by the audience. The request for help made by
Apsler's confederates represents a subsequent phase of the 'interaction', removed from the embarrassing incident. Compliance with the
request would not have explained the subject's embarrassing
behaviour. It is therefore unclear whether or not Apsler's findings
have any serious implications for Goffman's analysis of facework. On
balance it seems that his study has more to do with the expiation of
negative affect (cf. Regan, Williams and Sparling, 1972) than with the
prevention or correction of negative appraisals.

This discussion of Apsler's study concludes the review of experimental studies of facework. To summarise, experimental procedures
have been devised which lead the individual subject to feel that he
looks foolish in the eyes of an audience. Brown and Garland's studies
showed that individuals subjected to such procedures will try to
defend their public image, even if this defense is economically costly.
Modigliani's study demonstrated that the use of facework practices
(all but one of which was corrective) varies directly with experimen-
tally-induced embarrassment, and inversely with the individual's
impression of how he or she is evaluated by others. There is firm
experimental support, therefore, for Goffman's most fundamental
assumption, that embarrassing incidents and threats to face lead
performers to engage in facework.

Archibald and Cohen's findings were more complex: of particular
interest is the fact that role distance, the only preventive practice
which they measured, was *negatively* related to embarrassment, while
the corrective practice of derogating the source of feedback followed
the pattern of positive correlation between facework and embarrassment found by Modigliani. This pattern of correlations is, of course,
highly consistent with Goffman's distinction between preventive and
corrective facework practices. Although a negative correlation
between use of a facework practice and the experience of embarrassment cannot be regarded as a *necessary* condition for that practice to
be classed as preventive, it should be a *sufficient* condition for this
purpose since corrective practices must, by definition, be preceded by
an interactional offence and should therefore be positively correlated
with measures of affect associated with such incidents.

Finally, Apsler's study is the only one of those reviewed which specifically sought to test an hypothesis derived from Goffman's analysis of facework, and was the only one which failed to provide support for this analysis. He found that embarrassed persons were more likely than controls to comply with requests for help — whether or not these requests were made by witnesses to the embarrassing incident. However, it was argued that Apsler's study probably failed to establish the conditions necessary for a test of Goffman's approach, and that the implications of his findings therefore remain ambiguous.

2.4. Conclusions

The evidence reviewed in this chapter is consistent with Goffman's typology of facework. Strain is created when the self-presentation of one party to an encounter is discredited, whether it be through the individual's own behaviour, through some aspect of the setting, or through another person's actions. Actors take various kinds of measures to forestall the strain created by these discordant incidents and, in may cases, particularly where the audience is well-disposed towards the actor, actors can expect the audience to cooperate with them in preventing this strain.

Insofar as the evidence reviewed is consistent with Goffman's analysis of facework, it can be argued that Goffman's implicit model of man is validated. The nature of Goffman's model of man is summarised by Kreilkamp (1976) as follows: "Goffman's view is that without a presentation of self, a self is not possible. The self does not really exist until presented; and the presentation of self immediately connects the self to the social matrix, since every presentation implicitly considers how others will react to the self presented. Further, one modifies that presentation to fit one's sense of what others will tolerate or welcome" (p. 137).

Whether this model of the person as fragmented self is either intuitively attractive or an appropriate means of understanding behaviour in close personal relationships is not at issue here. The point is that this model of the person undoubtedly helps us to analyse and comprehend human behaviour in many kinds of social interaction. We are deeply concerned with the way in which others evaluate the face we present — we therefore strive to present this face in a way which is likely to result in positive evaluations. When we imagine that some facet of our behaviour blatantly discredits this presentation, or when others suggest through their actions that our behaviour reflects poorly on us, we take steps to recast that behaviour in a more positive light. The next chapter examines more closely the means by which this recasting is achieved.

3

Motive Talk

3.1. Introduction

In this chapter we shall be concerned with what Mills (1940) has called "vocabularies of motive", and what subsequent theorists call "motive talk". As we have seen in Chapter 1, Mills argued that motive talk arises when "acts are in some way frustrated. It is then that awareness of self and of motive occur. The 'question' is a lingual index of such conditions" (1940, p.905). So motive becomes an issue when a line of action is punctuated by a question. The question may be posed implicitly, either by the actor him/herself, or by the nonverbal behaviour of one or more bystanders. The question may be posed more explicitly in the form of a direct enquiry or challenge made by one or more bystanders. Either way, the posing of a question indicates to the actor that his or her behaviour could be regarded as questionable, and that alternative behaviours of a more desirable or appropriate nature could have been enacted. As Mills put it: "Behind questions are possible alternative actions with their terminal consequences" (1940, p. 905). Individuals respond to such implicit or explicit questions by engaging in motive talk, that is by announcing a motive or imputing a motive or by calling on another or others to avow a motive. "The goal of motive talk", notes Hewitt (1976), "is to lay bare the consequences of a particular line of conduct — that is, to make explicit the object toward which it is proceeding" (p. 130).

It is clear from the above that the actor whose behaviour either is or could be regarded as inappropriate, untoward or outrightly offensive is one who is likely to engage in motive talk, either as a result of the question(s) posed by witnesses, or because the actor anticipates or imagines that his or her behaviour could be questioned. Such an actor faces a social predicament, if we follow Schlenker's (1980) definition of a predicament as "any event that casts aspersions on the lineage, character, conduct, skills, or motives of an actor" (p.125). Because questions of motive arise when some real or imaginary interactional offence has been committed, it should be possible to analyse motive talk within the conceptual framework provided by Goffman's (1955) notion of "corrective cycle".

In his 1955 analysis of the corrective cycle, Goffman identified four distinct phases: challenge, offering, acceptance, and thanks. Goffman's (1971) extension of this analysis refers to the corrective process that follows on interactional offence as the "remedial interchange". The idea underlying the concept of remedial interchange is that any given act can be given a variety of readings by the actor and by those who witness the act, and that the remedial work which follows can best be understood by assuming that the actor is working on the basis of a 'worst case analysis', i.e. a reading which maximises the offensiveness of the act and/or its negative implications for the actor's moral status. Thus remedial work can be construed as being directed towards curtailing this maximally negative interpretation of the act. Goffman suggests that the transformation of the potentially offensive into the currently acceptable is accomplished by using one or more of three 'devices': apologies, requests, and accounts.

Both apologies and accounts clearly fall into the 'offering' phase of Goffman's (1955) corrective cycle, in that they follow from an explicit challenge, or the actor's perception that such a challenge could be made if the worst possible interpretation were placed on the act. As will be seen, the status of requests in terms of Goffman's (1955) typology is rather more equivocal. Below we shall examine the three categories of motive talk identified by Goffman, along with a fourth category, 'disclaimers', identified by Hewitt and Stokes (1975).

3.2. Varieties of motive talk

3.2.1. APOLOGIES

Apologies are easily distinguished from some other varieties of motive talk in that they are neither attempts on the part of the actor to deny or mitigate responsibility for an untoward or inappropriate act, nor attempts to deny or mitigate the negativity of the act's consequences. In short, apologies accept responsibility and acknowledge blameworthiness. By apologising, the actor admits that the act in question was indeed offensive, and that he or she was responsible for the act. How, then, do apologies help to mitigate negative evaluation of the actor? Through an apology, the actor acknowledges the social 'fact' that some offence has been committed, thereby affirming his or her adherence to the norm or rule that has been violated, and thus implying that the transgression will not recur. As Schlenker (1980) puts it, "*Apologies are designed to convince the audience that the undesirable event should not be considered a fair representation of what the actor is 'really like' as a person...* In order to accomplish this goal in situations where the undesirable event appears to have been caused by one's own actions, blame must be attached to a 'self' that no longer exists or has changed sufficiently that audiences do not need to be concerned about a repeat of the offense. Thus, a current 'good' self is split off from the past 'bad' self that was responsible for the undesirable event. Such self-splitting is contained in *all* apologies" (p.154, orginal emphasis).

This notion of 'splitting' of the self in apology originates with Goffman, who argues that "apologies represent a splitting of the self into a blameworthy part and a part that stands back and sympathizes with the blame giving, and, by implication, is worthy of being brought back into the fold" (p. 144). This provides us with an idea of how apologies perform the function of mitigating negative evaluation of the actor, but tells us little about the components of an apology. According to Goffman (1971), a full apology has several characteristic features: expression of embarrassment and regret; indication that the actor knows what he or she should have done; sympathy with the use of a negative sanction; rejection of the offensive behaviour; self-vilification; espousal of the 'correct' behaviour; avowal that in the future this correct behaviour will be enacted; performance of penance; and volunteering of restitution.

Tedeschi and Riess (1981) contend that of these several characteristic features of apologies that Goffman identifies, the first — which they interpret as the expression of guilt, remorse, or embarrassment — is the most important and is the one which is usually explicit. In their view, "To express guilt is to admit a kind of moral indebtedness which (the actor) acknowledges should be paid... The expression of guilt reveals that the offender believes in the cultural or societal rules that were broken by his behaviour. It is therefore clear that as compared to someone who accepts no blame for such an action, the guilty person requires less punishment for purposes of deterring similar future behaviour" (p. 297). By comparison, "... remorse is more concerned with the harm done to the victim. Remorse suggests that the problematic behaviour was not typical of the actor, whose values would normally preclude performing such behaviour. Thus, remorse ... tends to mitigate the degree of negative reaction of others to the offender" (p. 298). Tedeschi and Riess continue by arguing that embarrassment occurs when an actor behaves publicly in a fashion discrepant with the identity he or she wishes to project: "Thus, embarrassment communicates to others that the identity disrupted by the predicament is an authentic one, since if the actor did not sincerely believe her own presentations she might not be so concerned about the discrepant behaviour. Embarrassment itself as an emotional reaction thus plays a role in restoring the identity in question" (p. 299).

These three facets of the apology — guilt, remorse and embarrassment — differ in their focus, as Tedeschi and Riess point out. The main focus of guilt is upon the violation of rules. Remorse focuses on the harm that befalls the victim of the actor's behaviour. Embarrassment focuses on the actor's public image, or rather what the actor perceives that image to be. Thus each of these three reactions makes salient a different aspect of the offensive act — the fact that it violates shared rules, its offensiveness to others, or its implications for the actor's identity. Clearly, the three reactions are not mutually exclusive; it seems likely that whichever aspect of the interactional offence is most salient in the eyes of the participants (especially the actor) will help to determine which reaction is most prominent in any ensuing apology. Whichever aspect of the apology is most salient, it seems clear that the effectiveness of the apology as a means of minimizing negative evaluation of the actor resides in the acknowledgement that some offence has been committed, which affirms adherence to the norm or rule involved and implies that the transgression will not recur. The element of self-castigation which is inherent in apology is significant, because by overplaying it the actor can shift the onus from self to the audience, who might well feel obliged to reject the actor's more extreme self-accusations.

3.2.2. REQUESTS

While apologies typically *follow* the act in question, and are therefore quite clearly 'corrective' strategies in Goffman's (1955) terminology, requests typically *precede* the potentially offensive act. Goffman (1971) defines the request as the "asking license of a potentially offended person to engage in what could be considered a violation of his rights" (pp. 144-145). In fact the object of making a request is similar to that of apologizing, for the person who makes a request admits the potential offensiveness of the forthcoming action, and thereby affirms awareness of the norm or rule which he or she might be seen as violating. The actor begs leave of the potential challengers and claimants, so as to be allowed to act in a manner which the latter might otherwise regard as offensive. The hope of the actor who makes a request is that the person(s) who might be offended by the proposed act will respond by making what Goffman (1971) calls an "offer". As Goffman puts it, "the value to the potential offender of doing this is based, of course, upon the character of the offers... The assumption is that when a violation is invited by (the person) who ordinarily would be its victim, it ceases to be a violation and becomes instead a gesture of regard performed by this person" (1971, p. 145).

The power of the request as a means of transforming the potentially offensive into the currently acceptable can be illustrated by comparing the likely evaluative reactions to an actor who simply helps him/herself to a cigarette from somebody else's pack, with the reactions to an actor who makes a request ("Can you spare a cigarette?") and receives an offer ("Go ahead, help yourself") before taking one. By making a successful request, the potential offender transforms what would be seen as irritating and presumptious behaviour on his or her part into a small act of generosity on the part of the potentially offended party. An interesting point here is that it is difficult for the latter to turn down the request without appearing miserly and discourteous. It is for this reason that requests are not often rejected; indeed, the main restraint on requests may arise from within the individual who makes them rather than from those to whom they are made, as noted by Milgram (1977, pp. 4-6). One way in which the individual to whom the request is made can resist the unknown implications of agreeing to an open-ended request (e.g. "Will you do me a favour?") without appearing to be too unsympathetic is by stalling (e.g. "That depends on what it is"), which can itself be construed as a preventive facework strategy.

3.2.3. DISCLAIMERS

Disclaimers also precede the potentially offensive act. Hewitt and Stokes (1975) define the disclaimer as "a verbal device employed to ward off and defeat in advance doubts and negative typifications which may result from intended conduct. Disclaimers seek to define forthcoming conduct as not relevant to the kind of identity – challenge or re-typification for which it might ordinarily serve as the basis" (p.3). The disclaimer precedes some act or statement that conflicts with the assumption underlying the disclaimer. Thus the individual who begins "I haven't thought this through at all, but.." and then goes on to give you the benefit of his or her thoughts on a particular issue is taking care to disclaim the negative implications that might arise from his or her thoughts being illogical or ill-informed. Similarly, the individual who begins "I am no good at playing tennis, but..." and then goes on to agree to play is being careful to disclaim the negative implications that might arise from his or her performance being substandard.

Hewitt and Stokes (1975) have identified five types of disclaimer, which they call hedging, credentialing, sin licensing, the cognitive disclaimer, and the appeal for suspension of judgement. A typical instance of *hedging* is the prefacing of an act or statement with the phrase "I'm no expert, but...". As Hewitt and Stokes observe, "The phrase signals to hearers that they should treat factually faulty statements or deeds that have the wrong effects as the normal prerogative of people who are not and do not claim to be expert in what they are doing" (p.4). The hedging disclaimer signals that the forthcoming act is tentative; the actor is not committed to the act, in the sense that he or she is willing to have his or her mind changed by someone who does claim expertise, and is uncertain about how the act will be received.

The classic example of *credentialing* is the phrase "I'm not prejudiced — some of my best friends are...". Here the individual seeks to avoid the loss of esteem that he or she knows is likely to accompany an attribution of racism, by claiming special credentials, ostensibly through friendship, that qualify him or her to make a prejudicial statement without being regarded as prejudiced. This differs from hedging in that here the speaker is more committed to the forthcoming act and also knows that the act is likely to result in an undesired typification (e.g. racist). It is interesting to consider whether any credentials do in fact derive from claimed friendships with members of a racial or social group. Instead, it may be the speaker's knowledge that the forthcoming act is likely to produce a negative dispositional attribution that is instrumental in establishing the speaker's credentials. Hewitt and Stokes observe that "Knowledge is a credential because it establishes the actor as one who may have *purpose* in what he is doing, so that others cannot easily regard him as an unknowing representative of a particular negative type" (1975, p.5, emphasis theirs).

The *sin licence*, according to Hewitt and Stokes, is the type of disclaimer employed by an actor who is committed to an act and certain that it will be evaluated negatively, but does not expect to be denigrated in a particular way (e.g., as a sexist). Typical of sin licences is the prefacing statement, "This may be against the rules, but...". Hewitt and Stokes comment that this type of disclaimer "is an effort to invoke in a specific situation the more general and commonly recognized principle that there are occasions on which rules may legitimately be violated..." (1975, p.5).

Cognitive disclaimers are defined by Hewitt and Stokes as those which are used when an actor thinks that others are likely to regard him or her as out of touch with the empirical facts of the situation at hand, as a result of what he or she says or does. An example of such a disclaimer would be "This may sound crazy, but...". By anticipating that others may doubt his or her rationality, the actor attempts to reassure others that there is no loss of cognitive capacity on his or her part. The ability to appreciate that what is about to be said or done may strike others as bizarre suggests that the actor's grasp of the situation is still congruent with the way in which others see it.

The *appeal for the suspension of judgment* is characterised by Hewitt and Stokes as an attempt by the actor to persuade others to withold their negative evaluation of an act until it is complete or can be placed in 'proper' context. Examples of such disclaimers would be "Don't jump to any conclusions, but..." or "Let me finish what I am saying before you react".

We are now in a position to consider the features of disclaimers which make them effective as preventive facework, and also to compare disclaimers with requests. Hewitt and Stokes (1975) state that "Disclaimers seek to define forthcoming conduct as not relevant to the kind of identity – challenge or re-typification for which it might ordinarily serve as the basis" (p.3). Implicit here is the notion that the disclaimer tries to establish an explanatory context in which the forthcoming act appears excusable or justifiable. In other words, it seems that disclaimers, to the extent that they are effective, work in the main by transforming the meaning of the act in a way that removes or reduces its evaluative implications for the actor. Hedging, for example, operates by excusing the actor for negative outcomes on the ground that he or she lacks the information or skill required to produce a positive outcome. Credentialing operates principally by attempting to deny others the right to reproach the actor on the grounds that his or her (self-proclaimed) credentials make it unlikely that the act is in fact offensive. Sin licensing operates by claiming that no violation will occur (e.g. "What I'm going to do may not be within the letter of the law but it is within its spirit") or by arguing that such violation as will occur is legitimized because, for example, the benefits outweigh the costs. Cognitive disclaimers attempt to ensure that the forthcoming act is perceived by others as purposeful and under cognitive control, rather than random and irrational, and thereby to maximize the likelihood that others will assume that the act has some justification. Finally, appeals for the suspension of judgement operate by seeking a deferral of the evaluative process until further events reveal the acts in question to be justified or excusable.

Disclaimers share with requests the quality of being prospective acts, which are undertaken by the actor in the expectation that his or her conduct will be questioned. However, requests differ from disclaimers in that they make no attempt (in themselves) to present the forthcoming act as anything other than a norm or rule violation. The effectiveness of the request as a facework strategy lies in the actor's admission that the act is potentially offensive. This admission makes it clear to others that the actor is aware of the norm or rule which might be violated, and also has sufficient respect for that norm or rule to be concerned about the possibility of violating it. Disclaimers, as we have seen, often go beyond the simple admission of potential offensiveness: they seek to excuse or justify the forthcoming act in advance, or to deny others the right of reproach for the act, or at least to delay the moment when reproach might be made. Of course, where a disclaimer does admit that the forthcoming act might be offensive to others, it serves to indicate awareness of and respect for the norm or rule in question, and some of its effectiveness as facework probably stems from this demonstration. This seems especially true of most forms of hedging; of those forms of credentialing (e.g. "This may sound sexist, but...")

where no credentials as such are supplied beyond the knowledge of the possibility of negative typification; and of those forms of sin licensing (e.g. "I know this isn't good form, but...") where the disclaimer does not go beyond an acknowledgement that rules or norms are likely to be violated. On the whole, however, disclaimers do more than pay lipservice to ideal cultural standards, and in this respect they differ from requests.

There are, naturally, other differences between requests and disclaimers. The most salient among these is the fact that a request seeks the permission of the potentially offended party before the questionable act is performed, whereas the disclaimer is typically just a preface to a statement or action which is performed without waiting for a response from those to whom the disclaimer is addressed. The actor who makes a request is therefore in a better position to know prior to the act itself whether it is likely to cause offence to others. However, the range of potential violations which can be handled by prefacing them with a request is rather tightly circumscribed. On the whole, the rule violations which are negotiated via requests are of a rather trivial kind, such as queue jumping, smoking in the company of non-smokers, helping oneself to the last remaining portion of food, and so on. Each of these violations *could* be handled by a sin licence disclaimer, but the actor would almost invariably be regarded more favourably if the violation were preceded by a request and the granting of permission. Only when the nature of the violation is such as to make the request-offering cycle too cumbersome is a sin licence likely to be no less acceptable than a request. For example, if someone wishes to gain entry to a conversation or debate in which he or she has no formal part to play, that person may preface an opening remark with "I know I'm speaking out of turn, but...". Correspondingly, the violations that are prefaced with disclaimers are generally of a more serious kind, in that they may cause graver offence. Making a potentially racist or sexist remark is not the sort of act for which the individual can normally seek permission; if he or she wants to make the remark in question without being typified as a racist or sexist, then prefacing it with a credentialing disclaimer is the only viable preventive facework strategy. Instead of asking others permission to make a racist or sexist remark, the individual fends off the possible attribution of racism or sexism by claiming credentials that protect him or her from such typification. On the whole, therefore, disclaimers will tend to be employed where the potential violation is of a more serious character.

It is interesting to note that where requests are used in connection with acts that *are* potentially highly offensive (e.g. "Would you like me to be frank about my reactions to your paper?"), they are unlikely to be any more effective than a disclaimer, since the permission granted in response to such a request may be less than heartfelt.

3.2.4. ACCOUNTS

The first unified treatment of accounts was that of Scott and Lyman (1968). They began their analysis by defining the term 'account': "An account is a linguistic device employed whenever an action is subjected to valuative inquiry... By an account...we mean a statement made by a social actor to explain unanticipated or untoward behaviour..." (1968, p. 46).

From this definitional basis, Scott and Lyman proceed to develop a typology of accounts. Following Austin (1961), they draw a fundamental distinction between what are termed "excuses" and "justifications". According to Austin, in a situation in which someone has done or is said to have done something unwelcome, or wrong or untoward, that person may attempt to defend his or her conduct in one of two ways: "One way of going about this is to admit flatly that he, X, did do that very thing A, but to argue that it was a good thing, or the right and feasible thing, or a permissable thing to do, either in general or at least in the special circumstances of the occassion. To take this line is to *justify* the action... A different way of going about it is to admit that it wasn't a good thing to have done, but to argue that it is not quite fair or correct to say *baldly* 'X did A'... perhaps he was under somebody's influence, or was nudged... it may have been partly accidental or an unintentional slip... In the one defence, briefly, we accept responsibility but deny that it was bad: in the other, we admit that it was bad but don't accept full, or even any responsibility" (1961, p. 2). It can be seen then, that these two types of account address different elements in the attribution of responsibility for an offensive act. Excuses deny some or any measure of responsibility for what is admittedly an offensive act. Justifications deny some or any measure of offensiveness in an act for which the individual admits responsibility.

Scott and Lyman go on to provide an instructive listing of the kinds of account that fall into these two classes. Among various types of excuse, they distinguish *appeals to accident, appeals to defeasibility,* appeals to biological drives, and *scapegoating*. Typical examples of each of these subcategories would be, respectively: excusing one's lateness by claiming that one's car has broken down; excusing one's upsetting behaviour towards another person by claiming lack of intent or lack of knowledge of the outcome; excusing one's amorous advances towards another person by claiming that one has uncontrollable sexual drives; and excusing one's offensive behaviour by claiming that it is simply a function of another person's pathology or deficiency.

In distinguishing between various types of justification Scott and Lyman draw on Sykes and Matza's (1957) earlier typology of 'techniques of neutralization'. This includes *denial of injury, denial of victim, condemnation of condemners, and appeal to loyalties*. Scott and Lyman add two further types of justification, which they call *sad tales* and *self-fulfilment*. In denying injury, the individual justifies the questionable act by asserting that it harmed nobody. In denying the victim, the act is justified by claiming that the victim deserved injury. In condemning the condemners, the individual justifies the act by asserting that others do similar or worse things and go unpunished or uncondemned. In appealing to loyalties the act is justified by claiming that it served another to whom the actor is deeply committed. In telling a 'sad tale' the actor presents autobiographical evidence designed to justify the act. Finally, by invoking self-fulfilment the act is justified on the grounds that it leads to some enlightenment.

Schönbach (1980) has suggested an extension and modification of the Scott and Lyman taxonomy. The extension consists of the addition of two further categories, namely 'concessions' and 'refusals', to Scott and Lyman's categories of excuses and justifications. The concessions category is not really an accounts category, consisting as it does of offerings which acknowledge the offensiveness of the questionable act and the actor's responsibility for the act. Table 3.1 shows the divisions and subdivisions within the concessions category that are specified by Schönbach. These differ from each other only in the degree to which guilt or regret are expressed, or the extent of restitution offered. Overall it seems reasonable to regard these different concessions as apologies rather than accounts, since their facework potential resides exclusively in the actor's recognition that a norm or rule has been violated.

TABLE 3.1. Schönbach's concessions typology

C	Concessions
C1	Explicit acknowledgement of own responsibility or guilt.
C1.1	Full confession of guilt, without reservations.
C1.2	Partial confession of guilt, with reservations.
C2	Explicit abstention from excuse or justification. Concession of inappropriateness of excuses or justifications in the present case.
C3	Expression of regret concerning the failure event (comission or omission).
C3.1	Expression of regret concerning own responsibility for the failure event.
C3.2	Expression of regret concerning the consequences of the failure event.
C4	Restitution or compensation.
C4.1	Appeal to restitutions or compensations already performed.
C4.2	Offer of restitutions or compensations.

Schönbach's refusals category does not consist of accounts, either, for as he himself points out, the important element common to the facework strategies within this category is the refusal to provide an account. These attempts to avoid excusing or justifying one's behaviour are called "meta-accounts" by Scott and Lyman (1968). Among Scott and Lyman's meta-accounts are mystification, referral, and identity switching. To these Tedeschi and Riess (1981) have added another three: deferral, restatement of intentions, and empty explanations. In *mystification* the actor states that there are reasons for the action in question but that these cannot be revealed because they are confidential or too complicated to explain. *Referral* simply involves the actor telling the questioner to ask somebody else (e.g. someone in authority) for an account. *Identity switching* denotes an actor's refusal to provide an account on the grounds that his or her identity or status relative to the questioner do not oblige him or her to do so. *Deferral* is very similar to Hewitt and Stokes' "appeal for the suspension of judgement" disclaimer, in that the actor asks others to defer evaluative judgements of the questionable acts. Whether this appeal for deferral is classified as a disclaimer or a meta-account would seem to depend only on whether it precedes or follows the questionable act. In *restating intentions*, the actor simply states his or her intentions in performing the act, rather than excusing or justifying the act. *Empty explanations* are simply statements to the effect that the act was performed because the actor wanted to perform it, without explaining why he or she wanted to do so.

The contents of Schönbach's refusals category are shown in Table 3.2. It is apparent that three of the six principal sub-categories are very similar to three of Scott and Lyman's meta-accounts. Specifically, refusal R4, (Denial of right of reproach), is similar to Scott and Lyman's identity switching; refusal R5 (Referral to other sources of information) is similar to Scott and Lyman's referral; and refusal R6 (Evasions or mystifications) is similar to Scott and Lyman's mystifications. Schönbach's remaining three refusals sub-categories seem reasonably straightforward.

TABLE 3.2. Schönbach's refusals typology

R	Refusals
R1	Claiming the failure event has (thus) not occurred.
R2	Explicit refusal of a confession of guilt.
R3	Unrestricted attribution of guilt to other persons.
R3.1	Unrestricted attribution of guilt to the *accuser*
R4	Denial of the right of reproach.
R4.1	Denial of the right of reproach on the basis of own identity or role in relation to the accuser.
R4.2	Denial of the right of reproach in view of the negative qualities or deeds of the accuser. (See also E4.1, J7.1)
R5	Referral to other sources of information.
R6	Evasions or mystifications.

Schönbach's modification of Scott and Lyman's (1968) typology resides in certain detailed changes to the specifications of excuses and justifications. Schönbach's expanded version of the excuse category is shown in Table 3.3. Excuse E1 (Appeal to own human shortcomings) is the account counterpart to Hewitt and Stokes' (1975) "hedging" disclaimer: in both cases the focus is on the actor's own limitations, implying that his or her conduct should not be judged too harshly in view of these shortcomings. Whether a given appeal is a disclaimer or an excuse turns solely on whether it is made before or after the act in question. Excuse E2 (Reasons for the appeal to own shortcomings) consists of a number of factors which temporarily debilitate the actor. Among these, three are worthy of comment. Excuse E2.3 (Appeal to one's own negative past) is in effect an excuse variant of Scott and Lyman's "sad tales" justification: Schönbach contends that the appeal to one's own negative past, for example a deprived childhood, can serve as an excuse. Whether a specific appeal is to be construed as an excuse or as a justification must depend on whether it is being employed to exculpate the actor or to justify his or her actions. Schönbach's excuse E2.6 (Appeal to loyalties) is also an excuse variant of one of Scott and Lyman's justifications: Schönbach observes that the repentant Nazi who admits the horrors of the Third Reich but claims former ignorance and belief in the Führer is *excusing* his or her conduct, while the staunch Nazi who still claims his allegiance to his or her oath to the Führer and still believes in Hitler's mission is *justifying* his or her conduct. Schönbach's excuse E2.7 (Appeal to the specific external circumstances of the situation) is one that embraces Scott and Lyman's "appeals to accident" excuse as a particular instance of the more general case. There is some overlap between Schönbach's excuse E3 (Appeal to own effort and care before and during the failure event) and Scott and Lyman's excuse type "appeals to defeasibility".

TABLE 3.3. Schönbach's excuses typology

E	Excuses
E1	Appeal to own human shortcomings.
E1.1	Appeal to insufficient knowledge or skill.
E1.2	Appeal to will impairment.
E2	Reasons for the appeal to own shortcomings.
E2.1	Appeal to biological factors, e.g. arousal.
E2.2	Appeal to illness, addiction, drunkenness.
E2.3	Appeal to one's own negative past. (See also J 4.1)
E2.4	Appeal to provocations by other persons.
E2.5	Appeal to duress by powerful agents.
E2.6	Appeal to loyalties. (See also J5)
E2.7	Appeal to the specific external circumstances of the situation. (See also J2.1)
E3	Appeal to own effort and care before and during the failure event.
E4	Appeal to shortcomings or misdeeds of *other persons* as frame of reference for the evaluation of the failure event: A mild judgment is appropriate.
E4.1	Appeal to shortcomings or misdeeds of the *accuser* as a frame of reference for the evaluation of the failure event: A mild judgment is appropriate. (See also J7.1, R4.2)
E5	Appeal to the participation of *other persons* in the failure event.
E5.1	Appeal to the participation of the *accuser* in the failure event.

The former stresses the effort and care of the actor, while the latter claims lack of intent or knowledge of the outcome of the act; what these two appeals share is the claim that the actor did not act with malice or intention to upset. However, it seems likely that these claims would be made under rather different circumstances, with Schönbach's E3 being more likely to be offered in contexts where accusations of carelessness and/or lack of motivation arise, and Scott and Lyman's being more likely to be offered where there is scope for doubt about the actor's intention to produce negative consequences. These two types of excuse would seem to be sufficiently different from each other to maintain the distinction between them. Schönbach's E4 excuse (Appeal to shortcomings or misdeeds of other persons as frame of reference for the evaluation of the failure event) is again an excuse analogue of one of Scott and Lyman's justification types, namely condemnation of condemners. Schönbach notes that an appeal to the negative attributes of others can serve as an excuse (argument: others are no better, so don't blame me), as well as a justification (argument: others do similar things that nobody complains about, so don't take offence at my actions). Schönbach's final excuse subdivision, E5 (Appeal to the participation of other persons in the failure event), would appear to be a more general version of Scott and Lyman's scapegoating excuse. In scapegoating the questionable act is claimed to be a function of another's pathology or deficiency; in Schönbach's E5 excuse others have helped to produce the questionable act, but not necessarily by virtue of any deficiency. So scapegoating seems to be a particular case of the more general E5 excuse type.

Schönbach's expanded version of the justifications category of accounts is shown in Table 3.4. Most of the major subdivisions within

TABLE 3.4. Schönbach's justification typology

J	Justifications
J1	Denial of damage.
J2	Minimization of the damage
J2.1	Minimization of the damage in view of the circumstances which demanded the failure event. (See also E2.7)
J2.2	Appeal to the positive consequences of the failure event.
J3	Appeal to the role of the victim.
J3.1	Justification of the damage with qualities of the victim.
J3.2	Justification of the damage with acts of the victim.
J4	Appeal to the right of self-fulfilment.
J4.1	Appeal to the right of self-fulfilment in view of one's own negative past. (See also E2.3)
J5	Appeal to loyalties.(See also E2.6)
J6	Appeal to positive intentions.
J7	Appeal to shortcomings or misdeeds of *other persons* as frame of reference for the evaluation of the failure event: Ego's moderation should be acknowledged. (See also E4)
J7.1	Appeal to the shortcomings or misdeeds of the *accuser* as a frame of reference for the evaluation of the failure event: Ego's moderation should be acknowledged. (See also E4.1, R4.2)

this category are identical or equivalent to justification types noted by Scott and Lyman. The exceptions to this are J2 (Minimization of damage) and J6 (Appeal to positive intentions). Minimizing damage is clearly related to denying damage; however, there is a key difference between the two appeals, in that the former does acknowledge an element (however small) of offensiveness in the questionable act, while the latter makes no such concession. To the extent that these two appeals are likely to be employed in different contexts and met with different reactions it is worth distinguishing between them.

Tedeschi and Riess (1981) have also modified and expanded Scott and Lyman's (1968) typology of accounts. Within the general category of excuses, they identify three sub-categories, denial of intention,

TABLE 3.5. Tedeschi and Riess' excuses typology

LACK OF INTENTION OR ASSERTION THAT EFFECTS WERE
NOT PLANNED
    Accident
    Failure to Foresee Consequences (Plea of Ignorance)
        Effects unforeseeable
        Lack of information
        Poor judgment
        Distraction by other events
        Misrepresentation of events by others
        Mistake
        Lack of time for deliberation (e.g., crisis)
        Inadvertancy
    Mistook Identity of Target Person
    Lack of Capacity (e.g., infancy, mental retardation etc.)
LACK OF VOLITION OR ASSERTION OF LACK OF BODILY CONTROL
    Physical Causes
        Drugs
        Alcohol
        Physical illness (e.g., fainting spell, temporary paralysis, etc.)
        Exhaustion
    Psychological Causes
        Insanity or mental illness
        Overpowering or uncontrollable emotions (e.g., fear, anger, jealousy)
        Coercion by others
        Hypnotised
        Brainwashed
        Somnambulism
    Lack of Authority
DENIAL OF AGENCY
    Mistaken Identity (I didn't do it)
    Amnesia and/or Fugue State

---

denial of volition, and denial of agency, as shown in Table 3.5. Within the denial of intention sub-category, it can be seen that they distinguish four types of excuse, namely accident, plea of ignorance, mistaken identity, and lack of capacity. Where an act was accidental, or its effects were not or could not be foreseen, or where it was performed in the mistaken belief that the target was someone else, or where it was performed by someone believed to be incapable of intending the action in question, the act should be regarded as unintentional.

Within the denial of volition sub-category, Tedeschi and Riess distinguish three types of excuse, namely those involving physical causes, those involving psychological causes, and those claiming lack of authority. What these excuses have in common is that while they accept that the actor physically caused certain negative effects, they assert that the actor did not have full control over his or her body at the time of acting. This lack of control may be due to physical factors, such as drugs, illness or exhaustion; or to psychological factors, such as insanity, brainwashing or coercion; or to the fact that the actor lacked authority to perform an action that would have prevented the negative effect.

Within the denial of agency sub-category, Tedeschi and Riess distinguish two types of excuse, mistaken identity and amnesia/fugue state. In the first case the actor accepts that the act in question has negative effects but denies that he or she was the actor ("it must have been someone else you saw"). In the second case the actor effectively denies agency by claiming that he or she has no recollection of the actions in question: if the actor is apparently unaware of having performed an act, how can he or she be held responsible for it?

Tedeschi and Riess' typology of excuses is a more systematic treatment than the typologies proposed by Scott and Lyman (1968) and Schönbach (1980). The types of excuse identified by Scott and Lyman can be accommodated comfortably within Tedeschi and Riess' typology, with the exception of "scapegoating". It is not apparent how this type of excuse, in which an actor claims that the act in question was a response to others' questionable attitudes or behaviours, can be regarded as an instance of denying intent, volition, or agency, for no direct attempt is made to deny any of these elements. Rather, the actor who employs the scapegoating excuse seeks to set his or her action in the context of the deficient attributes or actions of other persons, and thereby mitigate his or her own blameworthiness. This suggests that

Tedeschi and Riess' typology of excuses may need to be expanded in order to accommodate excuses which appeal to mitigating circumstances. The only excuse types identified by Schönbach that do not fit neatly into Tedeschi and Riess' typology are those involving the role played by persons other than the actor (i.e. E4 and E5). In the case of the E5 excuse (Appeal to the participation of other persons in the failure event), this seems to be an instance of excusing one's conduct by denying exclusive agency (e.g. "It wasn't just me that did it, others were also involved"). In the case of the E4 excuse (Appeal to the shortcomings or misdeeds of other persons as a frame of reference for the evaluation of the failure event), it is difficult to see how this can be construed as denying intent, volition, or agency. This raises the question of whether such an appeal can properly be regarded as an excuse. When an individual claims that "Others are no better than me", he or she is not so much denying responsibility for the act in question as arguing that the context provided by others' behaviour mitigates the offensiveness of the act. It therefore seems more appropriate to exclude this account type from the general category of excuses, and to regard it simply as a justification.

With regard to justifications, Tedeschi and Riess argue that these may be classified into ten major categories. These, along with their sub-divisions, are shown in Table 3.6. Tedeschi and Riess observe that "Most of the categories relate the action in question to some norm or rule of society or the particular social group. The norm or rule prescribes or allows the behaviour or defines it as morally neutral (or good). Thus, through the justification the actor offers a socially acceptable description of an action that might have been perceived as strange, unsuccessful, meaningless, bad, immoral, unethical or unexpected by others" (p.287). Several of Tedeschi and Riess' types of justification are similar or identical to justification types mentioned by Scott and Lyman (1968) and by Schönbach (1980). Thus Scott and Lyman's "appeal to loyalties" and "self-fulfilment" justifications have direct counterparts in Tedeschi and Riess' typology, and there is considerable overlap between Scott and Lyman's "denial of injury", "denial of victim", and "condemnation of condemners", and Tedeschi and Riess' "effect misrepresented", "appeal to norms of justice", and "social comparisons", respectively. Likewise, Schönbach's J1, J2, J3, J4, J5 and J7 justification types all have their counterparts in Tedeschi and Riess' scheme.

TABLE 3.6. Tedeschi and Riess' justifications typology

Appeal to Higher Authority
      God, Satan, or spirits commanded
      Government official commanded
      High status or high prestige person commanded
      Organizational rules stipulated
Appeal to Ideology
      Nationalism or patriotism
      For the revolution
      To protect society or mankind
      To promote the religion or sect
      Against oppression
Appeal to Norms of Self-Defence
      Self-defence
      Reciprocity
      Revenge on associate of provoker
            Clan and gang wars
            Guilt by association
Reputation Building
      Protection from coercion
      Credibility maintenance
      Machismo
Appeal to Loyalties
      Friend
      Long-standing understanding or relationship
      Gang or group
      Peer group, sex, race, etc.
Appeal to Norms of Justice
      Derogation of victim
      Equity, equality, and social welfare norms
      Law and order
Effects Misrepresented
      No harm done (no victim)
      Benefits outweigh harm
Social Comparisons
      Condemn the condemners
      Scapegoating
Appeal to Humanistic Values
      Love
      Peace
      Truth
      Beauty
Self-Fulfilment
      Psychological health
      Catharsis of pent-up emotions
      Personal growth
      Exerting individuality
      Mind expansion and self-actualisation
      Conscience or ego-ideal

Let us now consider those types of justification identified by Tedeschi and Riess but not appearing in the typologies of Sykes and Matza (1957) or Schönbach (1980). "Appeals to higher authority" seek to shift responsibility for the act in question to a person or group of persons whose authority is recognized, and thereby to have the act perceived as being legitimate. As Tedeschi and Riess put it, "A person may assert that God, Satan, corporation or organizational rules, persons in power, or 'voices' commanded him to do as he did" (p.287). "Appeals to ideology" invoke a system of ideas or symbols and attempt to present the act in question as one that promotes these ideologies. Acts of violence against other humans are often justified as 'necessary' to protect or to further religious, patriotic, or revolutionary aims. "Appeals to norms of self-defence" try to present the act in question as a response to an unprovoked attack on the actor by others, in other words a 'justifiable' act of self-defence. In some cases the appeal to the self-defence norm may be coupled to an appeal to the norm of reciprocity (e.g. "An eye for an eye, a tooth for a tooth"). In some cultures and sub-cultures the self-defence norm may take the form of permitting or even prescribing revenge on friends and relatives of the attacker, as well as the person who made the attack. "Reputation building" justifications are those which seek to justify an act by presenting it as necessary to maintain a positive public image or reputation. Acts of aggression may be 'justified' in this way by arguing that unless one resists another's coercive actions, that other's use of coercion will continue or expand; or by claiming that they are necessary to establish the credibility of one's threats; or by arguing that they demonstrate machismo. Finally, "appeals to humanistic values" such as love, peace, truth, beauty, and so on, seek to present the act in question as one that promotes these values. Tedeschi and Riess cite the 'justification' by Nazi medical researchers that their experimentation on concentration camp prisoners furthered human knowledge as an example of such an appeal.

It is also necessary to consider those types of justifications noted by Scott and Lyman (1968) or Schönbach (1980), but *not* included in Tedeschi and Riess' typology of justifications. The "sad tales" justification identified by Scott and Lyman has no direct counterpart in Tedeschi and Riess' scheme, but careful consideration of what is achieved by telling a sad tale suggests that it does *not* justify an action for which the actor freely admits responsibility. Rather, the actor's presentation of information about his or her dismal past seeks to influence others' perceptions of the actor's responsibility for the act in question. In effect, the telling of a sad tale amounts to the description of mitigating circumstances. As such, the sad tale account type is more reasonably construed as an excuse than as a justification, and should perhaps be classified along with the scapegoating excuse, as an appeal to mitigating circumstances. Turning now to Schönbach's typology, his J6 (Appeal to positive intentions) justification has no direct counterpart in Tedeschi and Riess' scheme. However, the J6 justification would seem to be an extraordinarily broad type of justification, which could embrace any of the justifications noted by Tedeschi and Riess which appeal to norms or values (e.g. appeal to ideology, appeal to humanistic values, appeal to norms of justice, and so on). Overall, therefore, Tedeschi and Riess' typology of justifications is more complete than the other typologies, in that it includes all justification types which are present in other typologies, and goes on to identify further types of justification which are either absent from or only implicit in these other typologies.

3.3. A synthetic typology of accounts

We are now in a position to synthesize previous account typologies into a single and comprehensive scheme. Tedeschi and Riess' typologies of excuses and justifications form the basis of this synthesis, but are revised or modified to accommodate points arising from other typologies. The resulting typology is shown in Table 3.7.

TABLE 3.7. A synthetic typology of accounts

A. EXCUSES

A1 Denial of intent ("I did not intend to produce these results")

   Accident

   Unforeseen consequences, due to:
       lack of knowledge
       lack of skill or ability
       lack of effort or motivation
       environmental conditions

   Identity of target person mistaken

A2 Denial of volition ("I did not want to perform this act")
   Physical causes

temporary (e.g., fatigue, drugs, illness, arousal)
semi-permanent (e.g., paralysis, blindness, deafness)

Psychological causes originating in:
self (e.g., insanity, overpowering emotion)
others (e.g., coercion, hypnotism, brainwashing)

Lack of authority ("I would like to help you, but I do not have the authority to
do so")

A3   Denial of agency
Mistaken identity ("It wasn't me, honest")
Amnesia ("I can't remember anything about it")
Joint production ("It wasn't only me who did it")

A4   Appeal to mitigating circumstances ("I am not entirely to blame")

Scapegoating - behaviour in question was a response to the behaviour or
attitudes of another or others
Sad tales - selected arrangement of facts highlighting dismal past

B.   JUSTIFICATIONS
B1   Claim that effect has been misrepresented
Denial of injury (no harm done)
Minimization of injury (consequence only trivially harmful)

B2   Appeal to principle of retribution
Reciprocity (victim deserving of injury because of his/her actions)
Derogation (victim deserving of injury because of his/her qualities)

B3   Social comparison
(Others do same or worse but go unnoticed, unpunished or even praised)

B4   Appeal to higher authority
Powerful person(s) commanded
Higher status person(s) commanded
Institutional rules stipulated

B5   Self-fulfilment
Self-maintenance (catharsis, psychological or phsyical health)
Self-development (personal growth, mind expansion)
Conscience (acted in accordance with)

B6   Appeal to principle of utilitarianism
Law and order
Self-defence
Benefits outweigh harm

B7   Appeal to values
Political (e.g., democracy, socialism, nationalism)
Moral (e.g., loyalty, freedom, justice, equality)
Religious (e.g., charity, love, faith in deity)

B8   Appeal to Need for Facework
Face maintenance ("If I hadn't acted like that I would have lost credibility")
Reputation building ("I did that because I wanted to look tough")

With regard to excuses, Tedeschi and Riess' three main categories of excuse, namely denial of intent, denial of volition and denial of agency, are retained virtually unchanged. However, a fourth category is added, called appeal to mitigating circumstances, and this includes scapegoating and sad tales. Appeals to mitigating circumstances are defined as attempts to shrug off responsibility for the questionable act by attributing some of the responsibility either to the characteristics or behaviours of other persons (i.e., scapegoating), or to the environment (i.e. sad tales).

With regard to justifications, Tedeschi and Riess' typology has been revised to a greater extent, although some categories are unchanged. Beginning with category B1 (Claim that effect has been misrepresented), this is essentially the same as Tedeschi and Riess' "effect misrepresented" justification except that the "benefits outweigh harm" sub-type has been transferred elsewhere, and a new sub-type has been added in order to accommodate accounts which attempt to minimize the degree of harm perpetrated by the act in question.

Category B2 (Appeal to principle of retribution) is a new cateogry based on Tedeschi and Riess' "appeal to norms of self-defence". It is argued that the latter category confounds justifications based on two quite distinct principles, those of *retribution* and *utilitarianism*. Appeals to the principle of retribution focus on recompense for evil, that is the notion that the victim deserves injury because of some act he or she has committed (reciprocity) or because his or her qualities (race, sex, caste, religion, nationality, etc.) make him or her intrinsically deserving of injury (derogation of victim). Such appeals, it is contended, are quite distinct from those which seek to justify an act in terms of the utility of its consequences. Self-defence clearly is not a justification based on the retributive principle; rather, an act of violence committed in self-defence is justified in terms of the consequences of action or inaction, i.e. the preservation or loss of the actor's life.

Category B3 (Social comparison) is equivalent to Tedeschi and Riess' category of the same name. However, the sub-types identified by those authors are dropped because their use of the term scapegoating in this context (which, confusingly, is different from what Scott and Lyman mean by the same term) really does not differ from the meaning of condemning the condemners. In both cases, an act is justified by pointing out that others do similar or worse things but are not criticized for such behaviour.

Category B4 (Appeal to higher authority) is again very similar to Tedeschi and Riess' category of the same name. However, the sub-types are reorganized so that they simply distinguish between commands from powerful persons (i.e. those who are feared by the actor), commands from high status persons (i.e. those who are respected by the actor), and the stipulations arising from institutionalized rule systems.

Category B5 (Self-fulfilment) is another closely based on Tedeschi and Riess' category of the same name. Here too the sub-types are reorganized in order simply to distinguish between acts which supposedly maintain the self's equilibrium, acts which develop or expand the self, and acts which accord to the dictates of one's conscience.

Category B6 (Appeal to principle of utilitarianism) derives in part from Tedeschi and Riess' category "appeal to norms of justice". The "law and order" sub-type is retained, because acts that are justified on the grounds that they help to preserve law and order are appeals to the social utility of the acts in question. As mentioned above, the self-defence justification is also seen as belonging to this category, since the focus of the appeal is on the consequences of the act rather than on the goodness or evil of the action itself. It is also clear that Tedeschi and Riess' "benefits outweigh harm" justification, which they located in their "Effect misrepresented" category, is an appeal to the principle of utilitarianism. On the other hand, the "derogation of victim" justification clearly does not belong in this category and has already been dealt with as an instance of an appeal to the principle of retribution. Finally, the "equity, equality, and social welfare" sub-type identified by Tedeschi and Riess cannot be regarded as appeals to social utility; rather, they are seen as appeals to the *values* of equity, equality and social welfare.

Category B7 (Appeal to values) incorporates not only the appeals to equity, equality and social welfare, just mentioned, but also three separate categories of justification in Tedeschi and Riess' typology, namely "appeal to ideology", "appeal to loyalties", and "appeal to humanistic values". It is argued that these categories of justification are all cases of appealing to values, i.e. abstract principles which are by implication positively evaluated by the actor. Values, in turn, may be classified into three groups: political, moral and religious.

Finally, category B8 (Appeal to need for facework) reflects the content of Tedeschi and Riess' "reputation building" category.

Justifications which appeal to the need for facework are interesting because they themselves are of course instances of facework. Such appeals seek to mitigate the perceived offensiveness of the questionable act by explaining that it was done in order to maintain face or to enhance one's public image.

3.4. The relationships between different forms of motive talk

Having considered each of the main forms of motive talk, we are now in a position to examine systematically the relationships between them. One obvious distinction that can be drawn between requests and disclaimers, on the one hand, and apologies and accounts, on the other, is that the first two are prospective while the latter two are retrospective in relation to the act in question. So one fairly simple basis for distinguishing between different forms of motive talk is the moment in time at which they appear, where the reference point is provided by the questionable act.

A second means of distinguishing between the different forms of motive talk arises from a consideration of the means by which they counteract any negative impressions arising from the potentially offensive act. As we have seen, apologies and requests do this by simple acknowledgement that a norm or rule has been or will be violated, together with the implicit message that this violation is atypical of the actor. Excuses counteract negative impressions by denying full, or in some cases any, responsibility for the questionable act. Justifications accept responsibility for the act but deny that it was at all offensive, or at least claim that it was not as offensive as it may have appeared to others to be. So here we have three types of attempt to counteract negative impressions: simple acknowledgement of potential rule or norm violation; denial of responsibility; and denial of offensiveness.

Disclaimers, however, do not fit especially neatly into this threefold distinction. As was noted above, disclaimers usually seek to change the way in which the forthcoming and potentially offensive act is perceived by others, either by disavowing in advance any claim to expertise and thereby excusing one's performance by denying intent to produce aversive consequences, or by defining the act in advance as one that is inoffensive, despite appearances to the contrary. In other words these types of disclaimer would seem to operate by attempting to deny responsibility or deny offensiveness, in which case they could be regarded as "prospective excuses" and "prospective justifications", respectively. Other kinds of disclaimer, however, do not appear to make any attempt to excuse or justify conduct in advance; instead, such disclaimers merely acknowledge the possibility that the forthcoming act might give offence to others. So disclaimers fall into each of the three categories noted above, i.e. acknowledgement of potential rule or norm violation, denial of responsibility, and denial of offensiveness.

Indeed, this is not the full extent of the problem of locating disclaimers within this threefold category system, because some disclaimers (e.g. credentialing, sin licences) may, if we follow Hewitt and Stokes' (1975) definitions and examples, in some cases fall into one of these three categories and in other cases fall into another. This can be illustrated by reference to two of Hewitt and Stokes' examples of sin licences: one goes "I know this is against the rules, but..." (Hewitt and Stokes, 1975, p.5), and is no more than an acknowlegement of rule violation; another goes "What I'm going to do is contrary to the letter of the law but not its spirit..." (Hewitt and Stokes, 1975, p.5), and seeks to justify the action in advance by denying that any injury will be done. A similar kind of distinction can be drawn between two of Hewitt and Stokes' examples of credentialing: one goes "I know what I'm going to say seems anthropomorphic, but..." (Hewitt and Stokes, 1975, p.4), and does no more than acknowledge the possibility of a norm violation and consequential typification; another goes "I'm not prejudiced — some of my best friends are Jews, but..." (Hewitt and Stokes, 1975, p.4), and seeks to justify the action in advance, again by denial of injury. This analysis of the fit between disclaimers and the threefold category system developed in relation to the means by which apologies, requests and accounts try to counteract negative impressions of the actor leads us to conclude that some of Hewitt and Stokes' categories of disclaimers are too broad. The disclaimers they describe as falling within a given category do not necessarily share the same means of counteracting negative impressions of the actor. Instead of persisting with Hewitt and Stokes' disclaimer categories, it might be more fruitful to distinguish between *acknowledging disclaimers*, i.e. disclaimers that acknowledge the possible infraction of norm or rule by the forthcoming act; *excusing disclaimers*, i.e. disclaimers that attempt to deny some or all of the actor's responsibility for the forthcoming and potentially offensive act;

and *justifying disclaimers*, i.e. disclaimers that attempt to deny that the forthcoming act is at all offensive, or as offensive as it might appear. This way of distinguishing between disclaimers does no violence to the concept of disclaimer, as elaborated by Hewitt and Stokes (1975), and has the great advantage of permitting the integration of disclaimers into the categories of motive talk developed above. The results of such an integration are shown in Table 3.8, which shows how the different forms of motive talk considered in this chapter break down into the six cell matrix formed by crossing the 'time' factor (prospective and retrospective) with the 'means of face maintenance/restoration factor' (acknowledgement, excuse, and justification).

TABLE 3.8.: The relationships between different forms of motive talk

Time	Means by which face is maintained or restored		
	Acknowledgement of possible rule or norm violation	Attempt to define act as excusable	Attempt to define act as justifiable
Prospective	Requests; acknowledging disclaimers	Excusing disclaimer	Justifying disclaimers
Retrospective	Apologies	Excusing accounts	Justifying accounts

This classification of different forms of motive talk highlights the points of similarity and points of difference between them. One important point of difference is *not* shown in Table 3.7, however, which is that requests differ from all other forms of motive talk in that they are posed as *questions* to others, whereas the other forms of motive talk are essentially *responses* to the real, imagined, or anticipated questions posed by others to the actor. As noted earlier, the fact that requests seek the permission of others to engage in a potentially offensive act probably sets fairly tight limits on the nature of the act (in particular its offensiveness) in connection with which a request can be employed successfully. This raises the more general question of the relationship between an act and its context on the one hand, and the likelihood that a particular form of motive talk will be employed and how it is received, on the other. This question is considered below, first by examining theoretical analyses of the conditions under which particular forms of motive talk are likely to be offered and accepted, and then by examining the published research that tackles this issue.

3.4.1. FACTORS INFLUENCING THE USE OF AND REACTIONS TO FORMS OF MOTIVE TALK

Identity negotiation

The main thrust of a justifying disclaimer or account is its attack on the legitimacy of an actual or potential challenge from another. Thus a successful justification often indicates an illegitimate challenge. This is not particularly important if the justification is offered in anticipation of a challenge (i.e. as a disclaimer), or in response to an unvoiced challenge. However, it does mean that an overt challenge of an act which is then easily justified poses a threat to the challenger's face. Attributions of irrationality, insensitivity, or even paranoia might be made to an individual whose challenge is effortlessly revealed to be quite illegitimate. This shows the crucial nature of the remedial interchange, in that it carries implications for the identities of challenger as well as challenged. As Scott and Lyman put it in relation to accounts: "Every account is a manifestation of the underlying negotiation of identities" (1968, p.59).

Scott and Lyman's treatment of accounts and identity negotiation tends to focus on the implications of an account for the identity of the person who offers it. Of course, this is a key point of interest, for it is by definition the one who proffers an account whose identity is most under threat. However, the identity of the challenger is also negotiable, and there are certain junctures in the remedial interchange at which his or her identity is especially open to negotiation. For example, the manner in which a given account or apology is received by the challenger will to some degree situate the latter's identity for the remainder of the encounter. Also, the relationship between the challenge and the presumed offense will help to situate the challenger's identity. Either issuing a challenge that is patently illegitimate, or failing to issue a challenge that is equally patently legitimate will tend to threaten the challenger's identity. He or she therefore has to be sensitive to the minimal conditions under which a challenge can be issued, that is the conditions under which a supposedly offensive act can reasonably be called into question.

Relative power and status

A key factor determining these minimal conditions for the successful issuing of a challenge, as well as the likelihood that the offering made in response to such a challenge is successful, is the relative power and/or status of challenger and challenged. As Scott and Lyman observe, "Where hierarchies of authority govern the social situation, the institutionalized office may eliminate the necessity of an account, or even prevent the question from arising. Military officers are thus shielded from accountability to their subordinates" (1968, p.57). In similar vein, Goffman notes that "Folklore imputes a great deal of poise to the upper classes. If there is any truth in this belief it may lie in the fact that the upper-class person tends to find himself in encounters in which he outranks the other participants in ways additional to social class. The ranking participant is often somewhat independent of the good opinion of others and finds it possible to be arrogant, sticking to a face regardless of whether the encounter supports it" (1955, p. 222n).

It seems reasonably clear that where the relative power and/or status of challenger and challenged are discrepant, this will have implications for the remedial interchange. Where the challenger enjoys greater power or higher status than the challenged, there will probably be less concern from both parties with the legitimacy of the challenge, with correspondingly fewer justifications being offered. The challenged party is also likely to attempt to tailor his or her offering so as to make it accord with the perceived expectations of the challenger. Finally, any offering is likely to be less successful where the challenger has higher relative power and/or status than where the power/status relations are equal. Where the challenged individual enjoys greater power or higher status than the challenger, the reverse of these expectations should obtain.

Background expectations, offensiveness and offerings

The effectiveness of an offering made by an actor whose behaviour has been called into question is reflected in the extent to which it restores the *status quo ante*. In the context of accounts, Scott and Lyman observe that "Accounts may be honoured or not honoured. If an account is honoured, we may say that it was efficacious and equilibrium is thereby restored in a relationship" (1968, p. 52).

The main variable identified by Scott and Lyman as governing the honouring of an account is the extent to which it accords with the "background expectancies" of the other interactants. These background expectancies will vary to some degree from one social milieu to another. Actors who do not share the background expectancies of the milieu in which an account is introduced are less likely to have that account honoured. Scott and Lyman suggest that "In interacting with others, the socialized person learns a repertoire of background expectations that are appropriate for a variety of others. Hence the 'normal' individual will change his account for different role others... The incapacity to invoke situationally appropriate accounts, i.e., accounts that are anchored to the background expectations of the situation, will often be taken as a sign of mental illness" (1968, p. 58). For accounts to be successful, therefore, they must fit with the background expectations of the other participants. It might be felt that this point is almost tautologous, for it seems to argue that accounts which are acceptable, in the sense of being congruent with background expectations, are more likely to be accepted. However, an acceptable account is not necessarily an account that will be honoured (as will be seen below). When an account is introduced into a social context in which its vocabulary of motives is unacceptable, it is likely, according to Scott and Lyman, to be regarded as *illegitimate.* Thus an account which might be honoured by friends may be treated as illegitimate in a court of law. When an account states grounds for action which cannot be normalized in terms of much more general, 'taken-for-granted' background expectancies, Scott and Lyman suggest that it will be regarded as *unreasonable.* Thus accounts which appeal to the higher authority of 'voices' that commanded the individual to perform the questionable act are likely to be construed as unreasonable, and Scott and Lyman note that "...unreasonable accounts are one of the sure indices by which the mentally ill are apprehended" (1968, p. 54).

A second variable governing the honouring of accounts is the offensiveness of the questionable act. Quite simply, as the offensiveness of the act increases, so the power of the account to minimize that offensiveness or to mitigate the individual's responsibility for the act must diminish. Scott and Lyman suggest that "An account is treated as *illegitimate* when the gravity of the event exceeds that of the account" (1968, p. 54). More specifically, it could be argued that as the offensiveness of the act increases, so certain types of motive talk are likely to be more successful than others at restoring the social equilibrium. It seems likely that the first casualty of increasing offensiveness is the justification, since the aim of justification is to deny or minimize the offensiveness of the questionable act. Excuses may still be effective in conjunction with acts that are too offensive for justifications to be successful. However, excuses are also likely to be regarded as illegitimate when the questionable act is highly offensive. Scott and Lyman note that "accidentally allowing a pet turtle to drown may be forgiven, but accidentally allowing the baby to drown with the same degree of oversight may not so easily be excused" (1968, p. 54). Where the act in question is highly offensive, it is likely that the only form of offering that will be effective is abject apology.

To summarize, Scott and Lyman's prescriptions for an account to be successful are that it should be: (a) acceptable (i.e. employ a vocabulary of motives shared by the recipients); (b) reasonable (i.e. state grounds for action which can be integrated into common-sense knowledge of causality); and (c) adequate (i.e. appropriate to the offensiveness of the act in question). These are the qualities of an account which in Scott and Lyman's view determine its honourability, i.e. its worthiness of being honoured. It may seem odd that the *credibility* of an account is not regarded by them as central to its honourability but, as Goffman (1971) has noted, "The goodness or badness of an account must, of course, be distinguished from its trueness or falseness. True accounts are often good, but false accounts are sometimes better" (pp. 142-143).

3.5. Empirical studies of motive talk

3.5.1. APOLOGIES

Two studies on apologies have been reported by Schlenker and Darby (1981; Darby and Schlenker, 1982). The Schlenker and Darby (1981) study examined when apologies are used and the forms that apologies take by asking their subjects to imagine themselves as the central character in each of two scenarios in which they inadvertantly bump into another person in a public place. The vignettes describing this incident were manipulated so as to vary the offender's responsibility for the act (high or low) and the consequences of the act (high, medium, or low). Having read each of the two scenarios, subjects answered some questions, and were advised that their answers should reflect how they would act if they were the central character in the situation described.

The questions assessed how likely subjects were to use each of six elements of apologetic behaviour, two types of nonapologetic response, and two types of account for the incident. The apology elements were as follows: (1) "say 'Pardon me' to the other person and walk away without doing or saying anything else"; (2) "say 'I'm sorry'"; (3) "express feelings of remorse about the situation (e.g. you might say, 'I'm "very sad about this' or 'I feel so badly about this')"; (4) "offer to help the person in some way"; (5) "do or say something to get the other person to forgive you"; and (6) "say something to castigate yourself (put yourself down) about the situation (e.g., you might say 'How stupid of me' or 'How clumsy of me' or 'I feel foolish')". The two nonapologetic responses were: (1) "say or do nothing with regard to the other person"; and (2) "acknowledge the other person's presence through some nonverbal behaviour (e.g., making eye contact, smiling, or making some other facial expression), but not say anything to the other person". The two account types were: (1) "do or say something that might decrease your responsibility for the situation (e.g. you might say, 'I didn't notice you standing there' or 'I tripped' or 'someone bumped into me and I fell into you')"; and (2) "do or say something that might try to minimize the amount of harm that was done (e.g., you might say, 'No harm done' or 'I'm glad to see that you're all right' or 'It doesn't look as if you're hurt too badly' or something similar)".

Responses to these questions indicated that subjects were unlikely simply to walk away from the incident without doing anything. Acknowledging the other's presence by nonverbal behaviour was considered more likely, but only in the low consequences condition. Excuses (i.e. account type 1) were more likely to be used when responsibility was low rather than high. There was no significant variation across conditions in the use of justifications (i.e. account type 2). Both excuses and justifications had only intermediate likelihoods of use.

With respect to the apology elements, it was found that the most likely one to be used was saying "I'm sorry", which was especially likely to be used when the consequences were described as medium or high, as opposed to low. The more perfunctory apology ("Pardon me") was more likely to be used when the consequences were low rather than medium or high, and was especially likely to be used when consequences were low and responsibility was high. Expressions of remorse and offers of help were judged to be more likely where the consequences were medium or high, rather than low. Requesting forgiveness and engaging in self-castigation were most likely to occur when both responsibility and consequences were high; in both cases the consequences manipulation had no impact on likelihood of use within the low responsibility condition.

In summary, the results of Schlenker and Darby's (1981) study show that apologies were the most favoured means of handling the predicament, and that the kind of apology likely to be offered became more elaborate and self-blaming as the actor's responsibility for the incident and the consequences of the transgression increased.

Darby and Schlenker's (1982) paper reports two experiments which examined the reactions of children of different ages to the use of apology following a transgression. The transgressions used in these experiments were described in the form of vignettes which were read to the children. In the first experiment the vignette depicted a child who was walking down a corridor at school and inadvertently bumped into another child who was carrying a stack of dishes. Both responsibility for and consequences of this transgression were described as high or low, yielding four possible versions of the vignette. Each child heard only one of these four versions. The offender was described as reacting to the transgression in one of four ways: (1) walking away without making any apology; (2) making a perfunctory apology ("Excuse me"); (3) making a "standard apology" ("I'm sorry, I feel badly about this"); and (4) making a "compensation apology" ("I'm sorry, I feel badly about this. Please let me help you"). Each child heard all of these reactions, and after each reaction had been described was asked a number of questions. These were designed to assess perceptions of the offender's blameworthiness, entitlement to forgiveness, punishability, degree of penitence, "goodness" or "badness" as a person, and likability. Main effects due to the apology manipulation showed that as apologies became more elaborate, so the offender was blamed less, forgiven more, judged to be a better person, and liked more. On each of these measures, the no apology condition differed reliably from the perfunctory apology condition, which in turn differed reliably from both of the more elaborate apology conditions. However, only the forgiveness ratings differed reliably between the standard and compensation apology conditions.

Apologies only influenced perceptions of punishability when the

offender's responsibility for the incident was high. Here the compensation apology produced the lowest ratings, differing significantly from
the two intermediate apology conditions, which in turn differed
significantly from the no apology condition. Only the penitence ratings
were affected by the interaction between apology type and children's
age. The youngest age group (average age 6.1) thought the offender
was very sorry *regardless* of the offender's reaction to the indicent. The
two older groups (average ages 9.3 and 12.3) rated the offender as more
sorry when some apology was made than when no apology was made,
and thought that the offender was increasingly sorry as the apology
became more elaborate.

In the second experiment reported by Darby and Schlenker the
vignette read to the children described a child who, while playing on a
see-saw with another child, jumped off (high intentionality) or fell off
(low intentionality) and thereby caused the other child to be knocked
to the ground. The offender's motive for this action was varied
orthogonally to the intentionality manipulation. In the "good motive"
condition, the offender had noticed that the see-saw was breaking and
was trying to slow it down to save the other child from injury. In the
"bad motive" condition, the offender was trying to scare the other
child by going fast. As in the first experiment, each child-subject heard
one of the four possible versions of the vignette and all four versions of
the offender's post-incident behaviour, again ranging from no apology,
through perfunctory, standard, and compensation apologies. Subjects'
perceptions of the offender were assessed by questions similar to those
used in the first study.

The apology manipulation influenced some perceptions indepen-
dently of age. As apologies became more elaborate, so the offender was
seen as less blameworthy and was evaluated more favourably. Other
measures were signifantly influenced by the interaction between age
and apology type. These measures included ratings of the offender's
likeability, penitence, punishability, and entitlement to forgiveness. In
each case older children (particularly the 12 year olds) were more
responsive in their ratings to the type of apology made by the offender.
The oldest group were singificantly more negative than the youngest
group in their ratings of the offender who made no apology at all. The
impact of the apology variable on some measures was also qualified by
interactions with the intentionality and motive manipulations. Thus
the effectiveness of apologies in reducing punishability ratings was
confined to the low intentionality condition. The influence of apology

type on evaluations of the offender was more pronounced in the good motive than in the bad motive condition, with the result that although motive type made no difference to evaluation when *no* apology was made, evaluations of the offender were more positive in the good motive than in the bad motive condition as long as *some* apology was made. Finally, forgiveness ratings were higher when the offender had a good motive rather than a bad motive, except when intentionality was high and no apology forthcoming.

These two experiments show that apologies are effective in reducing negative repercussions for an individual who commits a transgression. The mitigating effects of apologies were more pronounced for older children than for younger children, although this was more apparent in the second study than in the first. Darby and Schlenker interpret these findings as evidence that younger children are less able than older children to integrate and weight information when forming social judgments. Specifically, the investigators suggest that the younger children may form judgments immediately after hearing the story (or, in real life, witnessing the incident), and do not adequately incorporate post-incident events into their initial reactions.

3.5.2. REQUESTS

There is a remarkable dearth of empirical work on the power of requests to transform potentially offensive actions into acceptable actions. There is, however, some evidence which shows that individuals are not particularly attentive to the specific content of a request where compliance with the request involves relatively little effort or cost. Langer, Blank and Chanowitz (1978) examined compliance with requests addressed to individuals who were just about to use a photocopier. The request made by the experimenter was to be allowed to use the machine first, to copy either 5 or 20 pages. If the number of pages the experimenter wanted to photocopy was smaller than the number being copied by the subject, the request was defined as asking a "small favour"; if the subject had fewer pages to copy than the experimenter, the request was defined as asking a "large favour". One of three types of request was made: (i) *request only*, i.e. "Excuse me, I have 5 (20) pages. May I use the xerox machine?"; (ii) a request involving '*placebic information*', i.e. "Excuse me, I have 5 (20) pages. May I use the xerox machine, because I have to make copies?"; or (iii) a request involving '*real information*', i.e., "Excuse me, I have 5

(20) pages. May I use the xerox machine, because I'm in a rush?". The dependent measure was simply whether or not the subject complied with the request.

Langer et al. predicted that where the request was for a small favour, placebic information requests would be as effective as real information requests, with both these requests being more effective than the simple request only. The rationale for this prediction was that requests for small favours would be processed 'mindlessly', such that a request for a small favour coupled with any reason would evoke a compliance 'script' (cf. Abelson, 1976). Where the request was for a large favour, however, it was expected that subjects would process the semantic content of the request more carefully, with the result that the placebic information request would evoke no more compliance than the request alone, and less compliance than the real information request. The results supported these predictions. If requests for small favours were accompanied by a 'reason', compliance was greater than where no reason was given, even if the reason conveyed no information. However, when the request was for a large favour, compliance was affected by the adequacy of the reason given.

This study suggests that requests for relatively small favours are more likely to succeed in eliciting compliance when they take a certain *form*, regardless of the specific *content* of the request. Requests for larger favours, however, are more likely to succeed if they are accompanied by information which could be construed as a reason for granting leave. There is a clear need for further research on requests, both to establish the replicability and generality of Langer et al.'s (1978) findings, and to assess the effectiveness of requests in diminishing negative evaluations of the actor, as well as the potential of different request types to induce compliance.

3.5.3. ACCOUNTS

Mehrabian (1967) reported a study in which the impact of motive talk variables on the reactions of other participants was examined. His prime concern was to investigate the effectiveness of an 'alternative tactic' to the apology often employed by those who usurp the rights of others. Mehrabian reasoned that when one person (offender) violates the rights of another (target), transient negative attitudes towards the offender will be elicited from the target. These transient negative attitudes are assumed to be maximal in the absence of an apology by the offender. The effectiveness of an apology in diminishing these negative attitudes, however, will be mitigated if the offence is repeated. As Mehrabian puts it, "The diminishing value of apology as a function of repetition of offence is partially due to the admission of guilt associated with apology" (1967, p. 688). The alternative tactic to apology investigated by Mehrabian is the cognitive reconstruction of the offence such that admission of guilt and the attendant negative attitudes on the part of the target are minimized. Thanking somebody for waiting instead of apologising for being late would be an example of such cognitive reconstruction.

Using vignettes depicting hypothetical social situations, Mehrabian investigated the impact of three variables on attitudes toward the offender. These were *ambiguity of offence* (ambiguous, unambiguous), *type of communication* (none, apology, cognitive manipulation), and *sex of target* (male or female). Subjects were instructed to take the role of the target in six vignettes, and to rate degree of dislike and irritation felt towards the offender on a 7-point scale. It was predicted that some communication would be more effective than no communication in countering feelings of dislike and irritation; and that cognitive manipulation would be more effective in ambiguous situations than in unambiguous ones.

Both these predictions were supported by the results. It was also found that in unambiguous situations an absence of communication elicited more negative attitudes than in ambiguous situations, which seems quite straightforward. There was no significant effect involving sex of target. If the power to diminish negative attitudes is taken to be a measure of effectiveness of motive talk, these findings suggest that in unambiguous situations apology is more effective than cognitive restructuring, which in turn is more effective than no communication at all; in ambiguous situations, however, apology or cognitive restructuring are equally effective and superior to no communication at all.

Mehrabian did not discuss his study and its findings in terms of accounting. Nevertheless, his experiment could be construed as a comparison of the effectiveness of apologies and accounts, where the latter were represented by an 'effect misrepresented' type of justification, the effect of which was to deny the existence of an offensive act by thanking the target person for witholding a claim to rights. From the accounting perspective, however, the comparison between these two offerings (apology and account) across levels of ambiguity is effectively a comparison across levels of offensiveness of the act; this is because the ambiguity manipulation was confounded with the manipulation of the offensiveness of the act. In broad terms, therefore, it would seem that the negative attitudes elicited by a less offensive act (i.e. when the target is not sure that it *is* offensive) can be countered just as effectively by an account as by an apology; but that where there is no doubt about the offensiveness of the act, an apology is more effective than an account, which is in turn better than no offering at all. This conclusion, already somewhat strained by equating cognitive manipulations with accounts, is difficult to translate into the theoretical context of the honouring of accounts, since honouring involves factors over and above attitudes towards the offender. Intuitively, however, it seems possible that unambiguously offensive acts would be handled better by apologies than by accounts, if only because they afford the offender less potential for an account than do acts which are ambiguously offensive. This study at least serves to remind us that apologies are means by which social equlibrium can be restored, and that in some cases an apology might be more effective, from the offender's point of view, than an account. Unfortunately, Mehrabian did not manipulate the degree to which apologies had been offered for similarly offensive acts previously; as he himself notes, the repeated use of apology as a tactic for diminishing negative attitudes following an offence is likely to be accompanied by a decline in effectiveness of this tactic.

The most extensive empirical study of accounts published to date is that conducted by Blumstein (1974). His questionnaire experiment was designed to identify factors which predict the honouring of accounts (i.e. the restoration of interactive equilibrium following an account); and to test the notion that honouring an account involves the meaningful integration of several elements. Among such elements Blumstein identified three pertaining to the moral character of the offender. First, he assumed that the *moral worth* of the offender would influence the honouring of accounts, in that an offender who is perceived to be incorrigible is saddled with the attribution that the source of offensive behaviour is the offender and not the environment. Secondly, he argued that mitigation of personal responsibility would be an important factor, with perceived *personal causation* impairing the offender's moral worth and thereby reducing the chances of an account being honoured. Finally, he drew on Goffman's analysis of apology in assuming that *penitence* would help to restore the moral character of the offender and enhance the likelihood of an account being honoured.

Two of the remaining elements identified by Blumstein have already been raised in connection with Scott and Lyman's (1968) analysis, namely the *credibility* and *adequacy* of the account, that is its internal and external consistency, and its appropriateness to the offence and its circumstances. Blumstein supposed that (other things being equal) accounts are honoured to the extent that they are deemed credible and adequate. Account credibility therefore occupies a more central role in Blumstein's model than it does in Scott and Lyman's discussion of account content and honouring.

Blumstein also assumed that the *relative status* of offender and offended would influence the honouring of accounts. He predicted that persons of lower status would be more constrained to honour accounts provided by superiors, but pointed out that relative status should influence only the *overt honouring* of an account, with the subordinate's private assessment of the account's *honourability* remaining unaffected by the fact that it emanates from a superior.

The final element identified by Blumstein was the *offensiveness* of the act in question. It was assumed that the honouring of an account would vary inversely with the offensiveness of the act it sought to justify or excuse.

In short, Blumstein expected that incorrigibility, personal causation and offensiveness would have negative effects on moral worth, and on the credibility, adequacy and honouring of accounts; that penitence would have a positive effect upon these same measures; and that honouring would be a joint function of the credibility and adequacy of an account, with adequacy being partly determined by credibility. He also anticipated that relative status would have a clear impact on honouring, but a diminished effect on account adequacy.

This model was tested by analysing subjects' reactions to social situations, which were presented to them in the form of short vignettes. Three aspects of these vignettes were manipulated: situation type, of which there were six (e.g., machinist failing to wear goggles, student failing to turn up for basket-ball team practice session); account type, of which there were six (e.g., denial of injury, appeal to a higher loyalty); and relative status, of which there were three levels (demander superordinate, demander and accounter equal, demander subordinate). Thirteen dependent measures were derived from subjects' responses to questions about each of the six vignettes they received.

The results showed that significant amounts of variance in the dependent measures were explained by the manipulations of situation type and account type; the relative status manipulation, however, failed to explain significant amounts of variance on any of the dependent measures other than the relative status dependent measure. The manipulation of account type explained larger percentages of variance across most of the dependent measures, including honouring, than did the manipulation of situation type. This fact led Blumstein to conclude that his data lend "systematic support to the assertion that people do not react so much to what we do, but rather to the interpretation we provide for our acts" (1974, p. 558).

The vast majority of the findings discussed by Blumstein concern relationships between dependent measures. Regression analysis revealed that the perceived moral worth of the accounter, the degree to which he was seen as penitent, the offensiveness of his violation, and his status relative to the offended person all had independent and significant effects on honouring. Contrary to expectation, how appropriate or legitimate the demand was seen to be, how likely it was thought that the offence would be repeated, and the extent to which the accounter was seen as personally responsible for his violation did not have a direct bearing on honouring. This latter finding, that personal causation was not an important determinant of honouring behaviour, is especially interesting in view of the fact that it did have an independent and significant effect on account adequacy.

This distinction between the honourability of an account and the extent to which it is in fact honoured is the most interesting implication arising from Blumstein's findings. It is particularly relevant to the previously raised issue of how status and power differentials between participants affect the vulnerability of each to being called to account, and the likelihood of each person's account being accepted by the other. Blumstein's findings provide some support for the notion that a demander of subordinate status is constrained to honour unacceptable accounts from a superordinate accounter. The fact that penitence affected honouring but not honourability is also interesting: this suggests that an 'unacceptable' account might be honoured if it is accompanied by a display of penitence, and would tend to confirm Goffman's assertion — and the implication of Mehrabian's (1967) study — that apology is a potent means of restoring social equilibrium. The fact that Blumstein found offensiveness to affect honouring but not honourability is less easily understood. It seems unlikely that the acceptability of an account is independent of the offensiveness of the act for which the offender is accounting: there must be a point at which the offensiveness of the act is so great that an adequate account becomes impossible. If this is the case, then it has to be concluded that the range of offences employed in Blumstein's study was insufficient to bring out this relationship.

Moral worth was the only measured variable to explain significant amount of variation in all the accounts measures. It would appear that accounters of high moral worth were seen to produce accounts that were more credible, more acceptable, and more likely to be honoured. However, this is only the case if we accept the inferential sequence which is implicit in the causal model postulated by Blumstein. It is also possible that subjects' perceptions of the moral worth of the accounter were influenced by the account produced, rather than the other way round. In fact, this point is acknowledged by Blumstein (p.564), and he notes that the inclusion of the account manipulation in the regression analyses produced a significant reduction in the moral worth regression coefficients, which suggests that the observed relationships between moral worth and account variables were a function of the account. This is hardly surprising in view of the fact that the vignettes used in this study provided minimal information (other than the account itself) on which to base judgments of the moral worth of the offender. However, it clearly might be the case that moral worth influences account variables in remedial interchanges where greater information about the offender's moral worth is available, and one might expect this influence to be particularly marked in the case of account credibility: it seems probable that accounters who are perceived to have low moral worth do not have their accounts believed as readily as those who are perceived to have high moral worth, and this lack of credibility would, in turn, negatively influence adequacy and honouring.

The question of how to interpret the meaning of the significant moral worth regression coefficient highlights a major drawback of this study. Although it is described as an "experiment", the majority of the findings are based on relationships between dependent measures. The correlational nature of these data naturally means that the question of causality in the observed relationships remains open. This point is never explicitly acknowledged by Blumstein who, throughout the paper, refers to non-account measures as "independent measures" and at one point refers to these measures as "causal factors" (p.565). In effect, we are asked to accept on trust the validity of the sequence of causality posited by his model, for this model does not receive unequivocal support from the findings. It nevertheless provides the basis for the distinction drawn between 'dependent measures' and 'independent measures', and for the choice of dependent variables throughout the regression analyses. None of the 'independent measures' (i.e. non-account measures), except for relative status, is a product of systematic variations in the content of the vignettes, and half of them have a purely inferential basis. As with moral worth, the data indicated that a larger proportion of the variance in incorrigibility, personal causation and penitence was explained by the account manipulation than by the situational manipulation. The observed relationships between these measures are therefore especially open to the possibility that the direction of causality is the reverse of that assumed by Blumstein.

One possible explanation for the failure of the relative status manipulation is the fact that status differences were conceptualized in terms of differential experience and knowledge. Thus, in the vignette in which one team-member asks another why he missed the last practice session, the two interactants are fellow players who have been team-members for the same length of time (equal status); or the demander is team captain (high relative status of demander); or the demander is a younger player who has recently joined the team (low relative status of demander). The point is that differences in this kind of relative status are less likely to have effects on the degree to which persons feel constrained in making demands or providing accounts than status differentials based on power to influence the other's instrumental outcomes.

A similar point arises in connection with a field study reported by Ungar (1981), who examined the impact of status of offender and presence/absence of an excuse on the reaction of bystanders to a (staged) minor transgression. The incident took place on a subway platform, and involved a male confederate accidentally kicking over a briefcase which a female confederate had set down on the platform. The female confederate was standing next to a female bystander, who served as the subject, and had earlier engaged this bystander's attention by asking her the time. Status was manipulated by the offender's dress (suit, tie, and expensive coat, vs. overalls, flannel shirt, and construction helmet). The excuse variable was manipulated by (i) having the offender simply walk on after the offence, without saying anything; (ii) having the offender stop briefly after knocking over the briefcase and say "You shouldn't have left it there; someone might've tripped over it"; or (iii) having a third confederate who was also standing near the subject say, as the 'victim' retrieved her briefcase, "She shouldn't have left it there; someone might've tripped over it". In terms of the synthetic typology of accounts developed above, this excuse is best characterized as an 'appeal to mitigating circumstances', in that responsibility for the incident is ascribed to the offended party.

Following the incident, an observer posed questions to the subject which elicited two types of response: a blame measure, reflecting the extent to which the offender was seen as being to blame for the incident; and a derogation score, reflecting whether or not the subject made disparaging or negative remarks about the offender. It was found that status exerted no influence on blame scores, but that the offender was blamed more when no excuse was given than when an excuse was provided — irrespective of whether the excuse was made by the offender or a third party. However, status did influence derogation, with the 'low status' offender being derogated more than his 'high status' counterpart, whereas the excuse variable failed to influence derogation. Ungar interprets this latter finding as evidence that the provision of an excuse failed to transform the transgression into an acceptable act.

While this study may be felt to be preferable to the studies carried out by Mehrabian (1967) and Blumstein (1974), in that reactions to an *in vivo* incident were examined, as opposed to reactions to a written vignette, there are nevertheless several problems associated with Ungar's experiment. First, the nature of the excuse proffered in the excuse present conditions seems to be out of keeping with the sort of account which would normally be provided in relation to such an offense. The provision of a more typical account type (e.g. denial of agency: "I didn't mean to knock over your case)", particularly if prefaced by a sign of penitence (e.g. "I'm sorry ..."), might have been more effective in mitigating the extent to which the offender was derogated. Secondly, the status manipulation did not systematically manipulate the relative status of offender and victim, so it did not result in conditions relevant to Scott and Lyman's (1968) observations about relative status, although it should be added that Ungar was not seeking explicitly to test predictions derived from the Scott and Lyman analysis. A third point is that the manipulation of status by dress did not reflect in any direct fashion the differential power of offender and victim to influence each other's outcomes. Two final points are that Ungar's study only examined a limited set of reactions to the transgression, and that these reactions were those of a bystander rather than those of the victim. These last two limitations arise almost inevitably from the fact that the incident was *in vivo* in a field setting, since there are clear ethical and procedural problems involved in casting members of the general public in the role of victim and then cross-examining them carefully to assess their reactions to the offence.

It might be felt that the findings of these studies of accounting do not amount to much. Mehrabian's (1967) study demonstrates that while accounts and apologies are equally effective means of reducing the incidence of negative attitudes towards an offender when the offensiveness of the act is equivocal, apologies are clearly more effective than accounts where the act is unambiguously offensive. Blumstein's (1974) study produced a multiplicity of results. Taken as a whole, however, the findings show that while it *is* possible to influence reactions to offensive acts by the provision of accounts, the extent of this influence is limited. The most important limiting factors were shown to be the offensiveness of the act in question and the relative status of the two parties. Certainly, common sense strongly suggests that there must be a point on the continuum of offensiveness beyond which accounts cease to be effective; and also that status considerations will substantially modulate the relationship between the perceived adequacy of an account and its actual effectiveness in restoring social equilibrium. Ungar's (1981) study shows that the provision of an excuse for an offence mitigates the extent to which the offender is seen by bystanders to be blameworthy for the incident, irrespective of whether the excuse is made by the offender or another bystander, but does not reduce the degree to which the offender is derogated following the incident. One consistent feature of the findings of these studies is that accounts are limited in their power to stem negative evaluations of the offender. Accounts for highly offensive acts and accounts which make no show of penitence for the offense are unlikely to restore interactive equilibrium.

More might have emerged from these studies had they done greater justice to the richness of the taxonomies of motive talk previously described. However, none of these studies produced findings which address the relative efficacy of different varieties of account. In the case of Mehrabian's (1967) study this is not wholly surprising, both because the study preceded the publication of Scott and Lyman's (1968) taxonomy, and because the study is in any case independent of the sociological tradition in this field of inquiry. Ungar's (1981) study examined the consequences of the presence or absence of one type of excuse, rather than manipulating excuse type. Although Blumstein's (1974) study did manipulate account type, the six account types used were not selected, as far as we can judge, with a view to comparing the effectiveness of different elements of an existing typology of accounts; certainly, no data are presented concerning the relative effectiveness of the different account types. One issue that clearly needs to be investigated, therefore, is how the many different forms of motive talk that have been identified interact with actor attributes and contextual features to determine the credibility, adequacy, acceptability and honouring of a given offering.

Another question in need of an answer is how frequently the elements distinguished in typologies of motive talk are employed in naturally occurring offerings. One difficulty with any typology is that the elements distinguished within the typology appear to have equal status with each other, whereas their actual occurrence or deployment in everyday life is likely to vary considerably across elements. The examination of this issue requires the use of a methodology in which the offerings are provided by respondents, rather than investigators. A questionnaire variant of such a methodology has been employed by Schönbach (1980) in developing his 'typology of account phases'. An observational variant of this methodology was employed by Much and Shweder (1978) in their study of what children say in 'situations of accountability'. During 60 hours of observation, these investigators recorded 630 situations of accountability — defined as "behavioural episodes which carry the potential that someone will be called to account" (p. 24) — in a nursery school class with children aged 3 to 5 years, and a kindergarten class with children aged 5 or 6 years. To determine the extent to which these children were 'culturally competent', Much and Shweder classified the rules associated with these situations of accountability according to a fivefold scheme.

In this scheme they distinguish between five "cultural control mechanisms": regulations, conventions, morals, truths and instructions. *Regulations,* they argue, are historical, have their source in a specifiable authority who can change them and whose power is the validation for these rules. Regulations have no truth value, and the consequence of transgression is penalty. *Conventions* are potentially historical, originate in 'custom' rather than individuals, have no truth value, and are validated by consensus. The consequence of violation is social disapproval. *Morals* are ahistorical (as seen by the people who hold such rules), 'a priori', unalterable, and intrinsically valid. Their truth value is indeterminable and the consequence of breach is moral culpability. *Truths* are also ahistorical and unalterable, and have their source in logic and experience. Truths can usually be validated via empirical data, sometimes in conjunction with logical criteria. They are validated by first-hand experience or by the consensus of 'experts', and have analytic or synthetic truth value. The consequence of breach is error. *Instructions* are similar in many respects to truths, except that they are evaluated in the contexts of means and ends. They are 'recipes' for achieving specified goals. They originate in experience and their validation is synthetic. The consequence of breach is ineffectiveness.

When Much and Shweder examined the distribution of their 630 situations of accountability across these five types of cultural control mechanisms, they found that the majority of the breaches were of regulations, conventions, and morals. Breaches of truths and instructions were less than 8% of all recorded instances, and the proportions of breaches falling in each of the 5 categories were stable across the two classrooms observed. Much and Shweder went on to examine *breach recognitions,* i.e. the challenges or accounts provided in anticipation of a challenge that initiated situations of accountability. They found that adults (i.e. teachers) in both classroom settings made more than the expected number of breach recognitions relating to regulations, while children made more than the expected number of breach recognitions relating to morals. The investigators note that there are at least three ways in which this finding can be interpreted: "One way ... is that teachers are more concerned with maintaining social order in the classroom than are children. A second interpretation is that teachers lack sufficient legislative authority to induce respect for *their* rules. A third interpretation is that conventional rules ('Greet people when they say hello') and moral rules ('Don't damage another person's property') are not as restricted in their range of application as are regulations, which, in our study, tend to be rules designed for a special context, namely school. The breach recognition data may indicate that children are more likely to recognize the legitimacy of rules which they experience in a wide variety of contexts (at home as well as at school, for example)" (p. 35). Much and Shweder also observe that these three interpretations are not mutually exclusive, and that at the very least these data suggest that children are differentially responsive to the infraction of different types of rule.

Also supportive of this conclusion were the results of finer-grained analyses in which the *type of utterance* made in each situation of accountability was related to the type of rule which had been (or was thought to have been) breached. They found that kindergarten accounts associated with breaches of regulations and conventions typically made references to *circumstances, consequences* and *precepts.* References to circumstances cite the conditions which form the context of the questionable act. Consequences refer to the anticipated outcomes of acts, and attempt to show that breaches are desirable because they lead to positive outcomes, or that rule following would lead to undesirable outcomes. Precepts cite some generalization intended to guide behaviour which is said, at least implicitly, to override the rule which has been breached. References to *acts* were found to occur most typically in kindergarten accounts associated with breaches of morals. These utterances include denials that the act in question has occurred; denials that the accused performed the act; and attempts to redefine the act in such a way that it is not seen as blameworthy. Much and Shweder comment that the association between breaches of morals and references to acts suggests that "... the force or validity of moral breaches is not negotiable and that one must instead appeal to the interpretation that no breach occurred" (p. 37). References to *epistemics* were found most typically in kindergarten accounts for breaches of truths and instructions. Utterances which make such references are concerned with the limits and bases of knowledge. These accounts do not question the *applicability* of the rule, but rather the ultimate *validity* of the rule. Finally, references to *intentional states* were found to occur most typically in kindergarten accounts associated with breaches of instructions. Accounts which employ these sorts of utterances assume that the actor's goals, wants and preferences are criteria for evaluating his or her actions.

The fact that children's breach recognitions were more likely to occur in conjunction with some types of rule than others, together with the fact that kindergartners' utterance types tended to vary across different rule types, led Much and Shweder to conclude that "... various cultural control mechanisms ... may well be differentiated and at work in regulating the conduct of five- and six-year-olds" (p. 38). A key advantage of Much and Shweder's research strategy over the vignette methodology employed by other researchers in this field is the ecological validity of their findings. It seems clear from the results of their study that young children are more sensitive to breaches of some types of rule than others, and that the nature of the utterances they provide as accounts varies systematically with the type of rule that has been breached. The combination of naturalistic setting and non-reactive methodology enhances confidence in the validity of these findings. This advantage is partly offset by some disadvantages of their research strategy, however. First such a strategy is highly time-consuming and labour intensive, and secondly, it sheds little light on the evaluative reactions of bystanders and challengers to the accounts provided by actors, unless one is prepared to infer the nature of these reactions from post-incident verbal and nonverbal behaviour. A further limitation of the Much and Shweder study, from the point of view of the theoretical concerns of the present chapter, is that their classification of utterance types does not map neatly onto any of the existing typologies of accounts. Much and Shweder refer to their corpus of accounts as "excuses", yet it would seem that references to acts are clearly justifications rather than excuses, if one follows Austin's (1961) distinction. References to conditions, however, may either be excuses (e.g. "appeal to mitigating circumstances") or justifications (e.g. "appeal to principle of retribution"). It is therefore difficult to draw any conclusions from their findings about the circumstances in which different account types are likely to be used.

The methodology of studying naturally-occurring, rather than experimenter-provided, accounts was also used by Felson and Ribner (1981) in their study of offerings made by male offenders convicted of grossly deviant acts, namely criminal homicide or felonious assault. Felson and Ribner drew their sample of accounts from the entries made on the 'commitment blotter' by 226 males incarcerated in New York State prisons in 1977 who had received their sentences for murder, manslaughter or felonious assault. Felson and Ribner examined the types of account provided by these offenders, the extent to which these account types were related to characteristics of the criminal act, and the extent to which the account types were related to the severity of sentence received. Six 'account types' were distinguished: denial of guilt, admission of guilt, legal excuses (i.e. accidents), other excuses (e.g. drink, drugs, state of mind), legal justifications (i.e., self-defence), and other justifications (e.g. mentions of victim wrong-doing, conflicts with victim, helping another). Characteristics of the criminal act that were distinguished were: outcome of act for victim (death or survival), sex of victim (male or female), and degree of exertion involved in act (three or more blows vs. fewer than three blows).

With regard to the frequency of occurrence of each account type, excuses were found to be relatively infrequent, comprising just under 19% of all cases. The claim that the act was accidental was more frequent than other types of excuse. Justifications were much more frequent than excuses, and accounted for more than half of all cases. The justifications were divided almost equally between self-defence and other types. In just under one-third of all cases, no account was offered; rather, guilt was either denied (c. 17%) or admitted (c. 14%), without further explanation. In explaining the preponderance of justifications over excuses, the investigators suggest that the nature of the offences in question is important: "Homicides and assaults result from interactions that often involve aggressive actions by the victim. The norms of self-defence and (negative) reciprocity readily apply in these circumstances" (p. 141).

Excuses of accident were less likely to be used if the actor had delivered more blows to the victim, but more likely to be employed if the victim died. Clearly, it is difficult to claim that an act was accidental if components of the act were repeated. On the other hand, it may be possible to argue that the *death* of the victim was accidental, without specifying whether some lesser degree of harm had been intended. When the victim was female, self-defence justifications were less likely to be employed, which may simply reflect the belief (or fact) that such an account would not be regarded as credible. Excuses (both accidents and other types) were more likely to be given where the victim was female. Felson and Ribner note that while this may simply reflect the fact that harming females is more difficult to justify, it may also result from the greater likelihood that conflicts between the sexes are emotionally intense. Admissions of guilt were less likely and denials of guilt more likely when the victim survived. This might appear simply to reflect lesser remorse on the part of those whose victims survived and a correspondingly greater inclination to claim innocence. However, Felson and Ribner also point out that those who committed an assault and then admitted their guilt may have had their charges reduced and therefore be underrepresented in the present sample, since state penitentiaries are reserved for those convicted on serious charges.

The impact of account type on severity of sentence was confined to the denial of guilt category. Denial of guilt resulted in heavier sentences for those convicted of murder or first degree assault, but not for those convicted of manslaughter or second degree assault. Felson and Ribner anticipated that denial of guilt would result in heavier sanctions for those convicted of an offence, due to the failure to show any penitence for the offensive act. However, they did not anticipate that this effect of denial would be confined to the more serious charges of murder and first degree assault. Because the major difference between murder and manslaughter, and between first and second degree assault relates to the judged *intent* of the actor, it seems that remorse is especially important where the intention to cause harm is perceived to be high. Whether or not the denial of guilt has a similar effect on others' reactions when the offence is of a different nature but is still seen as high in intent is a matter for further research. Of course, denial of guilt is *not* likely to influence others' reactions negatively if they are unconvinced of the actor's guilt.

Herein lies the main limitation of Felson and Ribner's study. By limiting their investigation to cases in which guilt has already been determined, the researchers (as they themselves acknowledge) set limits on the generalizability of their results. They therefore suggest that "future research should examine the effect of accounts given prior to and during trial on conviction" (p. 141).In the context of the general study of motive talk, as opposed to more specific research in criminal contexts, it should be added that future research should examine the antecedents, distributions, and consequences of motive talk offerings occurring naturally under a wide variety of circumstances. While it would probably be difficult to find non-criminal circumstances in which the accounts for offences are made by actors are readily accessible and the reactions of others are readily quantifiable, Felson and Ribner's study provides a good model for future research on motive talk in natural settings.

3.6. Summary and conclusions

The four principal forms of motive talk — apologies, requests, disclaimers, and accounts — were analysed, both in terms of their respective properties and in relation to each other. One point which emerges very clearly from this analysis is that the vast majority of previous work on motive talk has been concerned with the development of typologies of accounts, and to a lesser extent with empirical studies of accounts, with relatively little attention being paid to apologies, requests and disclaimers.

Tedeschi and Riess (1981) have provided the beginnings of an analysis of the properties of apologies, by distinguishing between apologies expressing guilt, remorse and embarrassment. The studies of Schlenker and Darby (1981; Darby & Schlenker, 1981) implicitly employ a rather different typology, which distinguishes between apologies on the basis of their 'completeness', ranging from perfunctory apologies to those requesting forgiveness. Their findings suggest that as responsibility for and the consequences of a transgression increase, so the type of apology proffered becomes more elaborate or complete, and that older children are more sensitive to the mitigating effects of apology than are younger children. The studies by Mehrabian (1967) and Blumstein (1974) show that simple expressions of penitence are effective means of face restoration, and Mehrabian's study suggests that penitence might be more effective than attempting to account for unambiguously offensive acts. Apart from the tangentially relevant study by Langer et al. (1978) on 'mindlessness' in complying with requests, there is a complete dearth of research examining the use of and reactions to requests or disclaimers. The conditions under which people feel able to make requests for permission to act in a manner that might give offence and the factors influencing others' responses to such requests need to be studied. Hewitt and Stokes' (1975) description of the disclaimer pinpointed a form of motive talk not considered by Goffman (1971). However, their analysis of the different varieties of disclaimer was found to be problematic in certain respects. Again, empirical work is needed in order to establish when people make disclaimers and how others respond to them. It was suggested that one factor influencing the making of disclaimers rather than requests is the potential offensiveness of the forthcoming act. The more offensive the act is thought to be, the more likely it is that a disclaimer, rather than a request, will be made.

Consistencies and inconsistencies between the various typologies of accounts were identified, and an attempt was made to develop a typology of accounts that embraces previous typologies and is internally consistent. This 'synthetic' typology of accounts was then located in a more general conceptual framework that identifies shared and distinctive properties of different forms of motive talk. Two dimensions were identified: first, the time at which the offering is made, in relation to the questionable act; secondly, the means by which the actor's face is maintained or restored by the offering.

Finally, the factors governing the success of forms of motive talk in restoring social equilibrium were considered, with particular attention to the honouring of accounts. The relative status and power of the interactants, the degree to which the offering fits background expectancies, and the offensiveness of the questionable act were all identified as relevant factors. The notion that relative status influences the honouring of accounts was supported in Blumstein's study. Some support for the idea that accounts which accord with others' expectations are more likely to be successful was found in Felson and Ribner's (1981) study, in that offenders who were convicted of criminal acts but who denied their guilt received stiffer sentences — but only when they were charged with acts high in perceived intent. Insofar as Ungar's experimenter-provided excuse failed to accord with bystanders' expectations of the type of offering that should be made under the circumstances of his staged transgression, then his findings are also consistent with the notion that successful accounts are those which fit background expectancies. Finally, the provision that the influence of accounts is limited by the offensiveness of the questionable act was supported by the findings of Mehrabian (1967) and Blumstein (1974). Clearly, more empirical studies of all forms of motive talk, including accounts, are needed, and investigators would do well to follow the example set by Much and Schweder (1978) and Felson and Ribner (1981) in studying how different forms of motive talk are distributed in natural contexts. In particular, future research in this field should seek to examine how different forms of motive talk relate to characteristics of offences, and to the reactions of other participants.

4

Attribution of responsibility

4.1. Introduction

In the present chapter we shall address the question of what responsibility means and how it is employed in everyday life. This issue of responsibility ascription is intimately bound up with the accounting practices that we have discussed so far, and is also related to the general problem of how social order is maintained through the collective social practices of society's members which will be considered in the next chapter. Responsibility ascription is a central issue not only because it involves a class of practical activities through which persons in everyday life exercise mutual control in order to sustain a regulated, orderly, rule-bound and moral existence, but also because these activities have their institutional counterparts in the legal and judicial processes through which society administers justice. It is therefore hardly surprising that the study of ways in which responsibility is assessed has featured prominently in social psychological, philosophical, sociological and legal research.

Social order in any society rests on commonly shared social practices which enable mutual understanding among members of that society. Such practices provide guidelines for the organization and coordination of everyday activities, as well as broad criteria for assessing the acceptability of conduct in given contexts. One cannot conceive of *social* life in the absence of shared social practices. Such social practices, i.e. rules, conventions, codes, provide recipes for dealing not only with the 'usual', but also with the 'extraordinary', the 'unusual'.

Hart (1968), for example, in considering contexts where no centrally organized systems of punishments for contraventions exist suggests that: "...the social pressure may take only the form of a general diffused hostile or critical reaction which may stop short of physical sanctions. It may be limited to verbal manifestations of disapproval or appeals to the individual's respect for the rule violated; it may depend heavily on the operation of feelings of shame, remorse, and guilt"(p. 84). However, like most formal systems of thought, legal systems have arisen from common-sense conceptions of order and control. Therefore the examination of common-sense conceptions of responsibility in legal philosophy (cf. Feinberg, 1965; Hart, 1968, 1948/9; Hart & Honoré, 1959; Ross, 1975) provides a useful insight into the workings of responsibility in everyday life. The concept of *rule* plays an important role in Hart's (1968) considerations on law. Referring to 'primary rules' he emphasizes that: "Rules are conceived and spoken of as imposing obligations when the general demand for conformity is insistent and the social pressure brought to bear upon those who deviate or threaten to deviate is great. Such rules may be wholly customary in origin: there may be no centrally organized system of punishments for breach of the order" (1968, p. 84). Indeed, as he points out on several occasions, the legal system draws considerably on common-sense considerations concerning responsibility. Thus, there exists in legal philosophy a formidable body of material which has a bearing on social psychological considerations of responsibility. This material consists of formalized accounts of the widely shared practices which are used in making judgments about 'faulty' action; it thus provides another perspective on the accountability of conduct, aside from the kinds of social practices that were examined in the two previous chapters. Conceptions of responsibility developed in juris-prudence are based on a formal rendering of 'current' and commonly held moral and normative ideas and practices. They therefore constitute an invaluable source in the examination of the everyday usage of the concept of responsibility. Among the various treatments of responsibility in legal philosophy (cf. Harris, 1979), those of Hart (Hart, 1963, 1968; Hart & Honoré, 1959) are the best known. Hart's analyses of responsibility and its ascription are founded upon a commitment to the philosophy of ordinary language analysis. This analytic premise underlying Hart's approach to responsibility suggests that all discourse is reducible to ordinary language discourse. Equally pertinent to our present considerations are the writings of

Scandinavian legal theorists (e.g. Ross, 1975). These authors equate legal rules with 'rule ideas'. The latter are psychological occurrences represented by an internalized normative system of statements about conduct along with positive or negative imperative stimuli. Although there are differences between these two schools of thought in analytic jurisprudence, the analyses of responsibility concepts that they provide are invaluable in aiding a social psychological understanding of the attribution of responsibility. This is particularly true in view of the fact that social psychological work in this area, despite repeated attempts for conceptual clarity, is replete with examples of intuitive ideas about responsibility and its attribution, and haphazard pursuits of non-replicable research ideas (cf. Fincham & Jaspars, 1980; Fishbein & Ajzen, 1973; Hamilton, 1978; Vidmar & Crinklaw, 1974). It is with a view to exploring the possibility of a conceptual framework for social psychological research in this field that we shall turn to legal-philoso-phical treatments of the concept of responsibility, having first examined Heider's (1958) 'model' of responsibility attribution. However, a disclaimer should be made before we embark on this analysis. In examining legal-philosophical treatments of responsibility in the context of Heider's model, we seek neither to locate equivalences between legal contexts and everyday contexts, nor indeed to gloss over the undeniably substantial differences that exist between legal and everyday attributions. Rather, our concern is to examine the ways in which responsibility is conceptualized from a legal philosophical perspective, with a view to bolstering the conceptual foundations of social psychological work on responsibility attribution.

4.2. Conceptions of responsibility and its attribution: a selective overview

Attribution of responsibility has occupied a relatively central position in social psychology during the last two decades. This is due partly to Heider's (1944, 1958) theoretical considerations on the subject, and partly to what may with hindsight be regarded as an historical accident. The historical accident was the rather counterin-tuitive finding reported by Walster (1966) , in connection with an experimental study concerned with the effect of severity of conse-quences of an accident on attribution of responsibility for that accident. First, we shall discuss Heider's model in some detail. Then we shall present some ideas from the philosophy of law. This will be done with two aims in mind. The first is to prepare the ground for a discussion of Hamilton's (1978) extension of Heider's model which employs some legal concepts in an attempt to establish correspondences between Heider's ideas and those in legal philosophy. The second aim is to prepare the ground for the concluding section of the present chapter, where we shall draw on some ideas from legal-philosophical analyses of the concept of reponsibility in order to examine everyday meanings and uses of the concept of responsibility. Following this, we shall discuss Hamilton's (1978) work. Finally, the research which has been conducted in the wake of Walster's (1966, 1967) studies of the attribution of responsibility for accidents will be discussed briefly in order to illustrate a typical social psychological approach to responsibility attribution.

4.2.1. HEIDER'S MODEL OF ATTRIBUTION OF RESPONSIBILITY

The concept of responsibility is addressed in one of Heider's early papers (Heider, 1944). In his discussion of 'Social Perception and Phenomenal Causality', Heider distinguishes the concept of causality as used in everyday social explanation from its use in science. He accords with Fauconnet's (1928) notion of "...a causality peculiar to man, different from the causality which connects natural phenomena..." (Fauconnet, 1928, p. 277; quoted by Heider, 1944, p. 360). This distinction between personal and impersonal causation has been lost sight of in contemporary attribution theory, as we have already seen in the course of Chapter 1. It is interesting that in developing these considerations the notion of attribution of responsibility occupies a broader meaning for Heider than merely the attribution of responsibility for faulty action in particular. This broader meaning of responsibility attribution is apparent partly from Heider's treatment of the general problem of the explanation of action, where responsibility attribution is one of the arguments employed in making a special case for personal causation, and partly from the connection drawn by Heider between responsibility and social and moral order. In this regard, Heider contends that "...crime violates society and menaces its life. It must be annihilated so that moral order can be rehabilitated. But the crime is a *fait accompli*; it cannot be annulled. Therefore, a substitute has to be found, a symbol of the crime whose destruction replaces the destruction of the crime, and the beings which are considered responsible for the crime" (1944, p.360). He goes on to quote Fauconnet once more: "Is a first and personal cause anything else but a cause conceived in such a way that it can be held responsible, that it can furnish something fixed and constant to which sanction can be applied?"(1928, p. 278, cited in Heider, 1944, p. 361) Thus, in an attempt to develop a concept of 'personal causation' and to promote 'person' as a unit of analysis Heider raises diverse issues. It is in this context that he touches on the concept of responsibility, but even then within the broader context of social order and control, relying here mainly on Fauconnet's work. This theme, which is certainly pertinent to a social psychological understanding of the concept of responsibility, and is also relevant to related issues such as selfhood and personhood, and social order and control, was not addressed again in the social psychological literature until recently (cf. Gauld & Shotter, 1977; Shotter, 1981). We shall return to this theme later in this chapter and in some detail in the next chapter. In fact these general considerations were not central to subsequent social psychological research in this field. Instead, Heider's brief treatment of the attribution of responsibility in his book on *The Psychology of Interpersonal Relations* (Heider, 1958) was to exert a much stronger influence on the development of social psychological research.

Heider's (1958, p.112ff) comments on the attribution of responsibility are made in the context of his general analysis of the naive psychology of everyday life. Partly because of this, they are both brief and ambiguous. In a sense he identifies the problem of responsibility attribution as one which incorporates the analysis of action and the subjective properties involved in action, such as intention. He suggests, for example, "...that the issue of responsibility includes the problem of attribution of action. That is, it is important which of the several conditions of action — the intentions of the person, personal power forces, or environmental factors — is to be given primary weight for the action outcome. Once such attribution has been decided upon, the evaluation of responsibility is possible" (Heider, 1958, p.114). Heider also identifies five 'levels', or conditions under which persons may be held responsible. As Fincham and Jaspars (1980) have noted, Heider's description of these levels clearly implies that the ascription of responsibility extends *beyond* the naive analysis of action. The five levels are as follows:

(1) *Global association*, where the actor is held responsible for acts which are *in any way* associated with him/her, e.g. being held

responsible for deeds committed by members of your nation at a distant point in history.

(2) *Impersonal causation*, where the actor is held responsible if he or she was instrumental in producing the observed effects — even though these consequences could not have been foreseen. Despite the fact that they were not foreseen by the actor, effects are taken to imply a negative reputation if they are bad and a positive one if they are good.

(3) This level, often referred to in the literature as *foreseeability*, is where the actor is held responsible, "...directly or indirectly, for any aftereffect that he might have foreseen even though it was not a part of his own goal and therefore still not a part of the framework of personal causality" (Heider, 1958, p. 113).

(4) The fourth level, *personal causation*, is where the person is held responsible for effects which were intended.

(5) Finally, the fifth level, sometimes referred to as *justifiability*, is where the intentions and motives of the actor are seen as part of a chain in which they are subject to preconditioning by environmental factors. Motives are therefore not ascribed exclusively to the actor. The actor is held responsible only to the extent that his or her intended behaviour was unjustifiable.

There are two features of this fivefold distinction introduced by Heider which seem to have escaped careful attention in the subsequent social psychological literature. The first is that the concept of responsibility was elaborated upon by Heider (1944, 1958) as a conceptual tool to identify and circumscribe personal *versus* impersonal causation, along with the various intermediate modes, as they are employed in 'naive psychology' for the explanation of actions *in general*, rather than the attribution of responsibility for faulty action *in particular*. The second, related feature is that the fivefold distinction was never intended to represent a developmental ladder or sequence. This much has been established by Fincham and Jaspars (1980), following personal communication with Heider.

The subsequent research dvelopments in social psychology have nevertheless employed the *particular* and narrower meaning of responsibility for faulty action, and taken the five levels or types to represent the developmental stages in responsibility attribution. This latter interpretation of the five levels as age-related stages stems from Shaw and Sulzer's (1964) work, which served as an empirical paradigm for later studies. These authors regarded the five 'levels' as representing "different levels of maturation" (p.39) and therefore anticipated that subjects' reactions to vignettes would vary as a function of age. They also suggested that the behavioural context, i.e. the situation in which the actor is witnessed, may vary with respect to the level of responsibility implied (cf. Fishbein & Ajzen, 1973; Shaw & Reitan, 1969; Shaw & Sulzer, 1964). However, the developmental interpretation of Heider's model does not appear to be as appropriate as the initial applications of the 'levels of responsibility' suggested. Indeed, recent work on the developmental stages of Heider's model (cf. Fincham & Jaspars, 1979, 1980; Harris, 1977; Sedlak, 1979; *inter alia*) indicates that the criteria of responsibility contained in the model are already employed by even the youngest children in the samples used in the experimental work.*

4.2.2. RESPONSIBILITY AS RULES: CONSIDERATIONS FROM LEGAL PHILOSOPHY

A possible alternative interpretation and extension of Heider's model is obtained if one regards the five types of responsibility attribution as different *rules* for the attribution of responsibility. Indeed, such an interpretation appears highly plausible if one examines the analyses of responsibility advanced within legal philosophy. We shall now turn, therefore, to an examination of some relevant legal-philosophical expositions of responsibility. Subsequently, an extension of Heider's model advanced by Hamilton (1978) will be examined in some detail, because this refinement of Heider's model contains the promise of a useful theoretical basis on which social psychological research can proceed.

In legal analyses of responsibility a distinction is to be found between the *conditions* or *criteria* of responsibility and the *meaning* of responsibility (cf. Hart, 1968; Ross, 1975). Obviously, the basic condition for someone being held responsible consists in an alleged offence having taken place. This constitutes the basis for

* cf. Fincham & Jaspars's (1980) review for the development work in this field.

somebody being held morally or legally responsible. "The first step in this reaction is to call the person responsible to account, to demand a more detailed explanation from him of what has taken place. If this leads to the assumption that a number of conditions, the conditions of responsibility, are fulfilled, the accused is found guilty and liability established; he receives censure or, in the legal context, is sentenced to some kind of punishment, compensation, or other form of sanction" (Ross, 1975, p.13). It is in this sense that accountability or answerability is central to the legal analysis of responsibility. A characteristic of being held responsible is what Hart (1948/49) terms defeasibility, which is related to the problem of identifying how and to what extent the legal claim of the litigating party can be upheld. As Feinberg (1969) puts it, "Defeasibility, then ... is closely associated with the legal notion of a prima facie case: 'A litigating party is said to have a prima facie case when the evidence in his favour is sufficiently strong for his opponent to be called upon to answer it. A prima facie case, then, is one which is established by sufficient evidence, and can be overthrown only by rebutting evidence adduced on the other side'" (p. 96). Hart's use of the concept of defeasibility arises in the context of his distinction between descriptive and ascriptive sentences in ordinary language analyses of sentences pertaining to human action. He points out that sentences such as, "He did it", are not descriptive but ascriptive, in that "...their principal function is ... quite literally to ascribe responsibility for actions" (Hart, 1948/49, p. 145). Hart goes on to argue that such ascriptions bear some resemblances to formal claims made in legal contexts. Defeasibility refers to the fact that such claims can be challenged and defeated, either by denying the factual basis of the claim, or by pleading that the claim should not succeed in the present case because recognized exceptions (e.g. provocation, duress) are brought into play by the circumstances of the case. Thus the claim 'He hit her' can be challenged by denying the physical facts, or by pleading self-defence. These two ways of challenging the claim parallel the manner in which defeasible legal utterances can be challenged, according to Hart (1948/49).* If the accusations or charges are not rebutted they carry liability to punishment, blame, or other negative sanctions.

---

* It should however be pointed out that in his more recent considerations on the subject of defeasibility, Hart (1968) suggests that "...the main contentions [of his 1948/49 paper in which the idea of defeasibility was developed] no longer seem to me defensible"(p. v).

Thus, the first step consists in establishing who is responsible, i.e., identifying the person who through his/her action or omission has effected the reprehensible act. Once this is established, the issue becomes one of whether the person in question fulfils the necessary and sufficient criteria for sanctioning. In English criminal law, this entails a twofold decision, namely: (a) establishing whether or not the person in question fulfils the objective criteria or conditions for violation, or objectively illegal actions (*actus reus*); and (b) establishing whether or not the person fulfils certain subjective criteria or conditions (*mens rea*). This latter set of conditions refers to the mental or psychological state of the defendant, and is concerned with whether or not the state of the person at the time of the incident in question departed from that of a 'normal adult'. Thus, in Hart's (1968, p. 277ff) terms, the issue is one of '*capacity responsibility*'. It is in this context that the term 'responsible for his/her actions' arises and the basic referents are complex psychological characteristics of persons. With reference to *mens rea*, Hart mentions that it is not only the above mentioned psychological conditions that are pertinent. There is yet a further set of conditions that has to be considered. This concerns the presence or absence of knowledge or intention. Whereas the former has to do with 'imputability', the latter has to do with 'fault'. Subjective conditions, in this second sense, refer to the establishment of *intent/intention* on the part of the agent, although *negligence* alone may sometimes be sufficient to establish this condition. The concept of guilt is thus relevant to the concept of responsibility, since if the conditions of responsibility are fulfilled, then guilt and thus liability are established. Guilt in this context obviously does not refer to an emotional state of the agent, although it may coincide with such a state.

Two further criteria for responsibility are raised by Hart (1968), namely: "causal or other forms of connexion between act and harm" and "personal relationships rendering one man liable to be punished or to pay for the acts of the another" (pp. 217-218). The former refers to the establishment of some form of connection between the act and the harmful outcome, although this need not be a causal relationship. This basically means establishing whether or not the action is linked to the agent and not to accidental features of the situation.* The latter

* It should be noted however that one of the central questions in linking the act with the undesirable outcome concerns the *boundaries* of the causal link. To illustrate, consider an example raised by Feinberg (1969). "A boozy pedestrian on a dark and rainy night steps into the path of a speeding careless motorist and is killed. What caused this regrettable accident? Since liabilities

criterion refers to a minimum condition required for liability for punishment, namely that the person to be punished should him/herself have done the reprimandable act. However, there are exceptions to this second criterion, particularly in cases of *role responsibility*, or *vicarious responsibility*, both of which are discussed further below.

It can be seen that there are diverse criteria for the establishment of 'legal-liability responsibility'. Of these Hart (1968) remarks that "the most prominent consist of certain mental elements, but there are also causal or other connexions between a person and harm, or the presence of some relationship, such as that of master and servant, between different persons. It is natural to ask why these very diverse conditions are singled out as criteria of responsibility, and so are within the scope of questions about responsibility, as distinct from the wider question concerning liability for punishment. I think that the following somewhat Cartesian figure may explain this fact. If we conceive of a person as an embodied mind and will, we may draw a distinction between two questions concerning the conditions of liability and punishment. The first question is what general types of outer condition (*actus reus*) or what sorts of harm are required for liability? The second question is how closely connected with such conduct or such harm must the embodied mind or will of an individual person be to render him liable for punishment? Or, as some would put it, to what extent must the embodied mind or will be the author of the conduct or the harm in order to render him liable? Is it enough that the person made the appropriate bodily movements? Or is it required that he did so when possessed of a certain capacity of control and with a certain knowledge or intention? Or that he caused the harm or stood in some other relationship to it, or to the actual doer of the deed?" (Hart, 1968, pp.221-222).

This provides an overview of the conditions or criteria of responsibility, and summarizes the key distinctions made in legal analysis. A more precise rendering of what it means to say that somebody is responsible for an action requires an analysis of the second

---

are at stake, we can expect the rival attorneys to give conflicting answers. But more than civil liability is involved. A reformer argues that the liquor laws are the cause, claiming that as long as liquor is sold in that region we can expect to have so many deaths a year. From traffic engineers, city planners, and educators we can still expect different answers; and in a sense they might all be right, if they named genuine 'causal factors'"(pp.114-115). The point is that not only is causality relative; but so also are the boundaries of a causal link. Establishing such boundaries involves selection of one or more causes from a number of likely candidates.

aspect of responsibility that arises from the distinction mentioned at the beginning of this section. This concerns the *meaning* of the concept of responsibility. As established earlier, responsibility in judicial usage refers to 'something one has for something to someone'. In the judicial context, the 'something' may be a theft or a murder; in the everyday context, it may be a lie or falling asleep during a lecture. In the judicial context, the 'someone' to whom one is responsible is a court of law; in the everyday context the 'court' may be one's conscience or a classroom. In both legal and moral judgments, the judgment is the outcome of a 'trial'. Within the context of a trial the issue is to decide whether the defendant can offer testimony that establishes his/her innocence for the violation in question. In this context responsibility as a concept can acquire two meanings (cf. Ross, 1975, p. 17 ff), which correspond to the two steps in the trial: (a) *accusation*, i.e., being the person who can rightfully be accused (bearing responsibility for the act); and (b) *judgment*, i.e. being the person who can rightfully be sentenced once the condition of guilt is established (being responsible for the act). Bearing responsibility for the act refers to accountability/answerability, which can be for one's own actions — or indeed for the conduct of others, which is best described as *vicarious responsibility*. *Role responsibility* can be seen as a special case of vicarious responsibility, in which the person is answerable for the actions of others by virtue of his/her role; thus managers are accountable for the actions of subordinates, editors are responsible for what appears in their journals, captains of ships are responsible for their passengers, and so on. In each case, an individual bears responsiblity for actions which are often executed by others. Being responsible for an act carries different meanings, depending on that for which one is responsible. For example, an individual can be responsible for a murder (i.e., guilty of murder), or be responsible for the failure to achieve a goal. In the second case the individual might be responsible for the actions of others and therefore liable for the outcomes of their actions. A further complication arises from the fact that the meanings of responsibility can shift within a particular case. For example, 'Eichmann was responsible for the death of 2 million Jews', can mean that Eichmann was responsible for the carrying out of orders for and therefore accountable to Hitler, or more obviously that he fulfilled the conditions required to establish his guilt for the death of 2 million people. Many further examples could be cited (cf. Ross, 1975). What this means is that the concept of responsibility in the sense of 'being responsible for' acquires distinctly different connotations depending on the nature of the violation under consideration. Thus responsibility as liability, i.e., 'somebody is responsible for something to someone' refers broadly to the conditions, subjective and objective, which are jointly necessary and sufficient for the fulfilment of conviction and sentencing. These conditions are defined with reference to a given legal system. It should be noted that the connection between the conditions (i.e., the actions, facts) and the legal consequences which established the second meaning of responsibility is not a 'natural' one, in that it is neither causal nor logical, "but exists only by virtue of the legal rule in that the facts are judged on the basis of legal rules" (Ross, 1975, p.21). In this sense, then, responsibility is a legal judgment, the judgment occurring at the conclusion of an inference: given certain established facts about the particular act in question, and given the legal rules that prevail, it follows that the person is punishable. Ross notes some further implications of this inference which bear upon the different ways in which the concept of responsibility is used in a legal context and which are therefore relevant to understanding its everyday usage. The pronouncement of responsibility can function as a demand or an assertion. How either is used depends on that aspect of the social event that is being referred to, either the nature of the circumstances, or the nature of the consequences. Thus it has to be concluded that the concept of responsibility does not have unambiguous semantic references. This however does not mean that the concept is vacuous. The function of responsibility is to express the connection between the conditioning facts and conditioned consequences of the act in question. Thus, one could conclude on the basis of the present analysis that there exist a number of formalized rules which establish a connection between specfic acts (or their omission), given that they are violations, and specific conditions or consequences of these acts. When these rules are applied in such a way as to pronounce the agent guilty, then one speaks of the agent *being responsible for* the act. A different set of conditions results in the actor bearing responsibility for the act, i.e., being accountable or answerable for the act. The specific ways in which the concept of responsibility is used in legal contexts therefore varies; what is constant across events and contexts is that responsibility refers to the relationship between an act, its circumstances and its consequences.

Finally, let us consider the difference between legal and moral responsibility. In general, legal philosophers do not see these two concepts as distinct from each other. However, they do differ in terms of the sanctions that are applied if the actor in question is found guilty. "The idea of moral responsibility, no less than that of legal responsibility, is an expression of a normative demand for the tying of guilt to the consequences of guilt, the 'punishment' which here is called 'disapproval'" (Ross, 1975, p. 25). In the case of legal responsibility in criminal law, by contrast, conviction results in a sentence. Conviction is an act through which guilt is established *and* the punishment demanded in law is invoked.

The foregoing is just a brief analysis of some of those aspects of legal philosophy which are particularly relevant to the way in which responsibility may be conceptualized in social psychology as we shall hope to show in the following section. There are other detailed aspects of legal-philosophical analysis, for example examinations of causality (cf. Hart & Honoré, 1959), which may also be regarded as relevant, and some of these will be introduced in section 4.3.3.. We shall now return to Heider's model of the attribution of responsibility and examine the way in which it has been developed by Hamilton (1978).

4.2.3. HAMILTON'S (1978) EXTENSION OF HEIDER'S MODEL

Hamilton (1978) defines responsibility as a "decision about liability for sanctions based on a rule" (p.316). She thus regards the attribution of responsibility as a judgmental process. The elements which enter this judgmental process are, in her view, the responsibility rules, the deeds of the actor, and the expectations that others have about what the actor should do. The expectations that others have are defined as the actor's 'social role', and this is regarded as an essential component in the attribution of responsibility.

Hamilton proceeds by reinterpreting Heider's (1958) levels of responsibility, making use of legal and philosophy of language analyses of the concept of responsibility. Heiderian levels are regarded as analogues of legal categories, or legal responsibility rules. Thus, the first level of "association responsibility"* is seen as an analogue of "vicarious liability rules", e.g. a publican or bar-owner being responsible for the sale of alcoholic beverages to minors on his or her premises, whether or not he/she has personal knowledge of, or has

---

* Hamilton follows Shaw & Sulzer's (1964) terminology when referring to the five Heiderian levels.

consented to, the sale. The second level, "commission responsibility", is regarded as an analogue of "strict liability rules", e.g. the liability of a company for accidents that may befall its employees in the conduct of their duties of employment. The third level, "forseeability responsibility" is seen as related to negligence in criminal and civil statutes. The fourth level, "intention responsibility" is regarded as analogous to "full responsibility", as in the case of criminal responsibility for an intended act. Finally, the fifth level, "justification" is regarded as a mixture of mitigation, justification and excuse. The importance of drawing these analogies is that, in Hamilton's view, they clarify the fact that these different legal categories involve distinct rules for attributing responsibility; such judgments do not correspond to different degrees of responsibility attribution or to developmental differences in responsibility attribution. Hamilton points out that, in terms of legal rules, one can be held fully responsible at each of Heider's levels. Hamilton's reworking of Heider's model has important implications. First of all, it points out that there are different rules by which responsibility is judged. This implies, secondly, that the meanings of responsibility vary as a consequence of which rule is applied in a particular context. Third, it is important to note that not every rule is applicable to every person. For example, the rule of association can only be applied to incumbents of particular roles, e.g. those roles which were referred to in the previous section in connection with 'vicarious responsibility'. However, 'intention responsibility' can be applied to every adult. The intermediate rules between association and intention imply a differential weighting of role and responsibility for the judgmental process.

After clarifying the different responsibility rules, Hamilton examines the concept of *role* in relation to the attribution literature, where the concept of role has featured most explicitly in Jones' work (e.g. Jones & Davis, 1965; Jones & McGillis, 1976). She distinguishes her use of role from that of attribution theorists in that roles are, in her view, not external forces determining action, but are normative, i.e. guides to what one *ought* to do. As such they are neither internal nor external forces shaping the agent's actions. She criticises the distinctions drawn by attribution theorists between external and internal attribution in relation to roles on the grounds that "...what is missing from the view of role as an external force is precisely what makes us fully human: society acting *in* us, as well as on us" (Hamilton, 1978, p. 321). Having argued that the external-internal attribution dichotomy is not a useful one in this context, Hamilton goes on to examine the possible *differences in sanctioning rules for occupants of different roles*. This involves considering three meanings of responsibility and their relation to different social roles in authority hierarchies. The three meanings referred to are: (a) diffuse obligation to act; (b) reliable performance in role; and (c) blame (liability) for rule-breaking. Thus, higher prestige job occupants are judged on the basis of their fulfilment of diffuse and internalized obligations to act and oversee other persons' actions. This implies that they will be adjudicated differently from those who occupy low prestige jobs and who are expected to comply with minimal job requirements. Lower status persons will be punished for breaking rules, i.e. non-compliance with the set standards. This type of social expectation is associated with reliable performance and this is therefore the criterion by which their acts will be judged. Hamilton comments that: "It is typically superiors in authority hierarchies who can be treated legally according to vicarious liability doctrines, the Association responsibility of the legal world. Such superiors are in a sense held to more 'primitive' Heiderian standards. But this obviously does not mean that society is less moral in the way it treats superiors. Instead, it means that society is responsive to the fact that different roles may necessitate different standards of accountability" (Hamilton, 1978, p. 322). It seems to us to be rather unfortunate that these examples employed by Hamilton convey the impression of an external and determinate social structure, in which fixed rules are followed in adjuicating responsibility, for this tends to conflict with her observations on the concept of role. The major contribution of her work lies, in our view, in Hamilton's argument that the rules of responsibility that are invoked in decisions about liability for sanctions will vary as a function of perceived authority relationships, the social context within which the 'faulty action' has taken place, and those who act as a 'court'. Authority relationships and the types of role responsibility may vary for one person across the variety of social situations which he/she is likely to enter. In this sense, the attribution of responsibility involves the invocation of different rules for judging liability for sanction, and the meanings of responsibility will therefore vary from one context to another, as well as being a function of the perceived relationships between those involved. The importance of these considerations for the social psychological literature is undeniable, particularly in view of the fact that responsibility has not been clearly conceptualized within social psychology, as we shall see in the section on defensive attribution and responsibility.One possible problem with Hamilton's work is that social psychologists who seek to come to grips with the differential use of responsibility rules in experimental contexts could simply interpret it in terms of a set of independent variables. The danger of this happening is enhanced by Hamilton's implicit treatment of social structure as a static 'given'.

The shortcomings of the social psychological literature on responsibilty attribution stem mainly from the decontextualized pursuit of a concept which has been (and in a variety of quarters still is) regarded as a unitary concept that can be isolated for the purposes of experimentation. Any analysis of responsibility, such as the one provided by Hamilton (1978), which emphasizes the contribution made by social context to the responsibility ascription process, must be a step in the right direction.

Now, we shall examine the second major trend in the social psychological literature on responsibility attribution, namely the experimental work on 'defensive attribution'. There is no shortage of reviews of this literature (cf. Burger, 1981; Fincham & Jaspars, 1980; Fishbein & Ajzen, 1973; Vidmar & Crinklaw, 1974), so no attempt to provide a comprehensive review will be made here. Rather, our discussion will consist of a resumé of the central propositions which have been advanced in relation to defensive attribution and an analysis of the main shortcomings of the work in this field.

4.2.4. RESPONSIBILITY AND DEFENSIVE ATTRIBUTION

The second line of social psychological work on responsibility ascription is generally referred to as "defensive attribution" or the "accident research paradigm", and originated in Walster's (1966) study of observers' attributions of responsibility for an accident. The basic proposition guiding this work is that the degree of responsibility attributed to an actor who is involved in an accident is a function of the severity of the consequences of the accident: the more severe the consequences of an accident, the greater the responsibility attributed to the actor will be. This proposition rests on a general assumption, termed "defensive attribution" (Shaver, 1970b), which accounts for the aforementioned relationship between accident severity and responsibility assignment in the following terms. People find it threatening to think that chance happenings with drastic consequences might happen to *anybody*, because *anybody* obviously includes them.

They therefore attribute more responsibility to the person involved in such accidents. By assigning responsibility for the accident specifically to the person involved, they are able to discount or diminish the possibility that a similar accident may befall themselves. The findings of Walster's (1966) study supported this basic proposition, in that subjects who heard a description of an accident with severe consequences attributed more responsibility to the actor than did those subjects who heard a description of a similar accident in which the consequences were mild.

The research enterprise which evolved from Walster's (1966) study yielded a series of experimental studies, most of which failed to replicate the predicted relationship between accident severity and attributed responsibility. Burger (1981), in his meta-analysis of this literature, identified "... 22 studies in 21 different articles that included a manipulation of accident severity and reported outcomes for a measure that assessed the extent to which the perpetrator was responsible for the accident" (p.499). Of these *published* studies, only six found any evidence of a significant effect of outcome severity on responsibility attribution. In spite of this unpromising track-record, there are still those (e.g. Burger, 1981) who see value in the defensive attribution hypothesis. Others are more sceptical. An early critical note was struck by Fishbein and Ajzen (1973, pp.148-149) who drew attention to the fact that even Walster's (1966) results, generally regarded as supportive of her hypothesis, are somewhat equivocal on closer inspection. More recently, Arkkelin et al. (1979) reported four experiments which carefully examined the informational cue-value of the consequences of an accident for responsibility attributions. They found that whereas information cues such as speeding and the condition of the car's brakes are utilized by subjects in responsibility attribution, severity of consequences for a victim are generally *not* employed by subjects in making attributional inferences of responsibility for the accident. Such findings cast considerable doubt on the basic premises underlying a major proportion of the work in this field of responsibility attribution.

Despite clear reservations about the conceptual foundations of this research (cf. Fishbein & Ajzen, 1973; Vidmar & Crinklaw, 1974) the defensive attribution hypothesis has retained its appeal to researchers, with the result that numerous studies have accumulated over the years. In the most recent critical review of this area, Fincham and Jaspars (1980) conclude that "as yet no coherent conception of defensive attribution has emerged" (p.94), and contend that the conceptual foundations of this research remain extremely weak. The research strategy which has sustained defensive attribution research can be called a 'variable enrichment strategy', involving the ad hoc inclusion of additional factors such as *relevance* (e.g. Chaikin & Darley, 1973; Lowe & Medway, 1976), *likelihood of the accident* (Wortman & Linder, 1973), *personal and situational similarity* (e.g. Chaikin & Darley, 1973; McKillip & Posovac, 1975; Shaver, 1970b; Shaw & McMartin, 1973), *outcome valence* (e.g. Medway & Lowe, 1975; Reisman & Schopler, 1973), *attractiveness of actor or victim* (Landy & Aronson, 1969; Shepard & Bagley, 1970), and so on. 'Variable enrichment strategies' proceed by retaining the central hypothesis, despite the absence of empirical support for it and invoke progressively more circumscribed conditions under which the hypothesis holds, even though the variables which are introduced to buttress the central hypothesis may be completely tangential to the explanation of the phenomenon in question. This variable enrichment strategy has parallels with the "secondary elaborations" discussed by Evans-Pritchard (1937) in relation to Azande magic. Such a strategy is amply demonstrated by the history of research on accidents and responsibility attribution, for the concept of defensive attribution has been jealously retained despite the lack, from the very beginnings of this research enterprise, of any solid evidence for its existence.

To see how it has been possible for such a poorly supported hypothesis to be retained, and to illustrate the sorts of conceptual difficulties that arise, we shall briefly chart the history of one of the more prominent variable enrichment strategies that has been deployed. This strategy was introduced by Shaver (1970b; Shaver & Carroll, 1970), and is still regarded as an important explanatory concept in this field (cf. Burger, 1981). It was Walster's (1967) failure to replicate the findings of her earlier study (Walster, 1966) that led to the introduction of modifications to the orginal hypothesis. In order to explain the puzzling non-replication in Walster's (1977) second study, Shaver (1970b) proposed that the perceived situational and personal relevance (similarity) of the accident were factors requiring closer attention. He suggested that the accident situation should be relevant to subjects, i.e. be drawn from their everyday experience. Given this proviso, the nature of the defensive attribution hypothesis is modified, such that *high* responsibility is attributed to the perpetrator of the accident if he/she is highly *dissimilar* to the subject, and *low* responsibility is attributed to the perpetrator if the perceived similarity between perpetrator and subject is *high*. Thus, the greater the similarity between perpetrator and subject, the more likely it is that the accident will be attributed to chance factors. Several studies were conducted in order to examine this particular refinement of Walster's (1966) hypothesis (e.g. Chaikin & Darley, 1973; Lowe & Medway, 1976; McKillip & Posovac, 1972, 1975; Pliner & Cappell, 1977; Shaw & McMartin, 1977; Shaver, 1970a, b).

One of the major problems afflicting this research was pointed out by Vidmar and Crinklaw (1974), who noted that "All of these versions [of the defensive attribution hypothesis] suffer from the very serious flaw that they do not provide any rationale that predicts whose fate subjects will identify with when both a perpetrator and a victim are involved in an accident"(p. 114). Although some of the reported research in the period between 1974 and 1980 is supportive of Shaver's version of the defensive attribution hypothesis, the hypothesis itself contains "fundamental internal contradictions", as pointed out by Fincham and Jaspars (1980). The problem identified by them arises when the perpetrator and the victim are one and the same person, as indeed they are in numerous studies. Let us review Shaver's arguments in greater detail. Perceived similarity (personal relevance) is held to be central in mediating defensive attribution. The direction of defensive attribution is such that severe consequences result in the attribution of greater responsibility when the subject is dissimilar to the perpetrator, but less responsibility is attributed when the subject is similar to the perpetrator. However, when the subject identifies with the *victim*, rather than the perpetrator, then perceived similarity results in different attributions. Whereas attributions to *chance* are preferred when the subject identifies with the *perpetrator*, identification with the *victim* leads the subject to attribute *more responsibility* to the perpetrator, because in this case attribution to chance threatens the subject. Let us now consider the conceptual dilemma pointed out by Fincham and Jaspars (1980): What happens when perpetrator and victim are one and the same person, as is the case in a number of studies in this field? Fincham and Jaspars comment that: "According to Shaver's reasoning the perceiver as possible perpetrator/victim should both decrease and increase attributed responsibility, respectively. However, Shaver's (1970b) concluding suggestion that 'avoidance of blame for an accidental occurrence is more important than avoidance of the outcome itself' (p.112) seems to resolve the dilemma. This would mean that in the case of perpetrator/victim, subjects presumably relinquish their perceived control over the event by denying responsibility and hence allow that the misfortune could befall them again. This threatening thought, which usually motivates subjects to assume responsibility, is now tolerated because of their motivation to avoid blame. No justification is given for this crucial assumption and one can imagine many instances where the reverse might apply. The question now becomes: At what point does the threat of the damage recurring begin to exceed the need to avoid blame? This question would be extremely difficult to resolve, and indeed defensive attribution research does not have a good track record when it comes to a priori specifications of crucial parameters" (Fincham & Jaspars, 1980, pp. 87-88).

Another type of problem that arises in connection with defensive attribution research concerns the ambiguity of the dependent measures employed. It has been pointed out that responses on the dependent variable of responsibility may be influenced by both the contextual (i.e. stimulus) factors and the level at which the subject responds. Thus the circumstances of the accident may suggest that the actor was simply associated with the act in a general way, or that he/she was instrumental in producing the effects but could not have foreseen them, and so on. Equally, subjects may differ in their interpretation of a question such as "Is the actor responsible for the accident?", in that some subjects may construe this as a question of association, others a question about commission, and so on. It is therefore difficult to ascertain the meaning of responses unless these two variables of 'stimulus level' and 'response level' are experimentally separated. Despite repeated criticism (e.g. Fishbein & Ajzen, 1973; Vidmar & Crinklaw, 1974), these factors have remained confounded in most experimental designs. Furthermore, the concepts of blame, responsibility, causality, punishment, etc. have been used without any clear notions about either the relationships between them, or the different meanings that such concepts acquire as a function of the varied social contexts within which they are employed. Typically, the use of these concepts has been guided by intuitive notions entertained by the respective researchers and regarded as interchangeable between the different experimental settings within which they were assessed. As was mentioned in discussing both the legal-philosophical analyses of the conditions and meanings of responsibility and Hamilton's (1978) work, the meaning of responsibility depends very closely on the social context within which it is employed. Social psychological work has not yet taken any account of this. Thus, the concept of responsibility as employed by social psychologists relies mainly on the meanings that the researchers have implicitly attached to it, either in their operationalizations or in their discussions of the concept. A final restrictive stipulation that we would like to raise concerns the very notion of 'defensive attribution'. There is, of course, no direct evidence that defensive attribution is a process which mediates attributions of responsibility. Accordingly, the value of this construct resides exclusively in its ability to bring order into the relationships between stimuli and responses. It is, in short, an hypothetical construct. Such is the dominance of the concept of defensive attribution, however, that researchers tend to invoke it as if its status were unquestioned. This type of approach tends to confound pure conjecture with the description of real phenomena, but is typical of a general class of dilemmas in social psychology (cf. Semin & Manstead, 1979, p. 195 ff).

In conclusion, we concur with Fincham and Jaspars' observation that: "The continued popularity of defensive attribution research is perhaps surprising in view of the increasing number of constraints imposed on the hypothesis, which suggest that such defensive attributions are indeed rare. Far more worrying, however, is the uneven growth of data collection and conceptual development, since defensive attribution research has proceeded in an ad hoc manner without any attempted theoretical integration of various hypotheses and findings" (1980, p. 86).

4.3. Conceptions of responsibility and its attribution: a reappraisal

4.3.1. ACCOUNTABILITY, RESPONSIBILITY AND ATTRIBUTION

In order to reappraise the diverse but ultimately related ideas that have been articulated in the social psychological literature on the attribution of responsibility, we need to return to the general theme of the book, the accountability of conduct. It has been argued that a distinctive feature of social interaction is that it is reflexively monitored. This human propensity, reflexivity, means that actors monitor not only their own actions, i.e. become objects to themselves, but also the actions of others. This unique character of the actor is a prerequisite for the possession of self (cf. Mead, 1934), and is directly related to the accountability of conduct. In the course of their daily lives actors produce coordinated and well regulated activities: they engage in diverse social practices, design action plans and so on. For these they have reasons. That is, when and if asked, they can proffer their reasons for these activities. Generally, of course, they are not asked for their reasons because most of their activities proceed unproblematically. It is in *problematic* contexts, i.e. when routine expectations are violated, that both the reflexive monitoring of conduct and accounting practices become manifest, for it is here that questions about conduct are implicitly or explicitly raised. What is it that triggers such questions? The simple answer is that such questions are posed when there is a mismatch between expectations and action; that is, there is some disjunction between conduct, on the one hand, and routine expectations or moral standards, on the other. That it is possible to pose these questions about conduct is based on an implicit premise. This is that actors are agents of their actions, i.e. they are *responsible* for their actions. They can be questioned because they are *capable* of providing *reasons* for their conduct. This is the broader, implicit aspect of the term responsibility, which could be paraphrased as *agency* for actions. It is therefore not surprising that Heider (1944), in attempting to establish the distinction between personal and impersonal causation, quotes Fauconnet (1928): "There exists a causality peculiar to man, different from the causality which connects natural phenomena. Man is, in a certain sense, a first cause, if not of the physical movements which constitute his acts, at least of their moral quality...From this perfect causality originates his responsibility..." (p.277, quoted by Heider, 1944, p. 360). In similar vein, Shotter (1981) argues that: "Being autonomous means being the author of one's actions... Thus, in our ordinary, everyday, common-sense view of people as autonomous, we assume people know how *to make* their actions conform to something in their common-sense, and furthermore, we also assume that they are able, potentially at least, to report upon, or to account for, how they made themselves so conform. In a moral world, self-expression and accountability are inextricably interlinked" (p.279).

One can argue from a variety of perspectives that the accountability of conduct constitutes the basis of social and moral order. These perspectives are intimately intertwined. One form of this argument is found in the view expressed above, i.e. that actors have agency and therefore have reasons for their actions, reasons which they can be called on to articulate (cf. Fauconnet, 1928; Gauld & Shotter, 1977; Giddens, 1976; Heider, 1944; Mead, 1934, Shotter, 1981; *inter alia*). Another form of the argument proceeds from the premise that *social* life could not exist without some degree of regularity. This regularity is provided by shared rules, conventions, and social practices, which rely on consensual understandings in everyday life and through which activities in everyday life are coordinated and judged to be acceptable or unacceptable (cf. Chapter 1). This line of argument is related directly to the idea of accountability. That we are accountable and responsible for our actions is an implicit assumption which guides our everyday activities and the way that these are monitored by ourselves and others. Whichever form the argument takes, the interface between accountability and social order raises two questions of fundamental importance to social psychology: first, what are the origins of socio-cultural attributions in general? And secondly, how is responsibility, in the particular sense of liability for sanction, ascribed to others?

The first of these two questions will not be dealt with at any length here, mainly because it extends beyond the limits of our present brief but also partly because some of the issues entailed by this question have already been considered in the course of Chapter 1. That most conduct is implicitly accountable but passes off without being questioned means that it follows taken-for-granted social practices and is therefore *meaningful*. The interpretation of social interaction involves the ascription of rules for action and this, in turn, implies that the recognition of action as intelligible and warrantable consists in assigning *identity* to particular sequences. As argued by Blum and McHugh (1971) this involves the 'ascription of social motives'. The agent is regarded as autonomous and is assumed to be the the architect of his/her actions. The ascription of motives to actions also means that these actors are treated as persons with identities. Thus the interpretation of social interaction through the ascription of motives invokes the concepts of identity and agency. This reveals the intimate connections between the interpretation of actions, the ascription of social motives (i.e. socio-cultural attributions), and responsibility for actions (whether or not they are called into question). As Shotter (1981) argues: "...the idea of a moral order is implied in the concept of personhood; for only within a relatively stable social order is the development of a conferred social competence, and thus autonomous and responsible personhood, possible" (p.281). Thus the analysis of responsibility in its more general sense elucidates the relations between several concepts which are considered in the course of the present volume. The interpretation of social action entails the ascription of social motives, thereby linking interpretation with socio-cultural attributions. The ascription of social motives entails the identification of actions as authored by particular actors. It is therefore not surprising to find that when conduct is called into question as a result of its disjunction with expectations, the issue of *identity* management becomes prominent, as discussed in Chapter 2. In order to manage threatened identities, actors attempt, through motive talk, to make sense of questionable conduct, as discussed in Chapter 3.

Thus the examination of what it means to say that someone is responsible for his or her actions leads one to consider the connections between social order, identities and socio-cultural attributions. Addressing these issues amounts to a pursuit of objectives similar to those of attribution theorists, but without divorcing the subject matter from its social context. Examining the relationships between socio-cultural attribution and social order and control calls for a social psychology of how people explain, understand and interpret their social reality and thereby contribute to what is thought of as society. Among many other things, such an examination would have to consider the extent to which the accountability of conduct represents a sufficient or necessary basis for social existence, i.e. it would entail an analysis of the ontological status of the accountability of conduct. Such an analysis will be provided in Chapter 5. In the meantime, we shall return to a more specific aspect of responsibility attribution. In considering the antecedents and consequences of responsibility ascription we shall now be concerned specifically with the attribution of liability for social sanctions which arises from the infraction of codes, standards or rules of conduct. In keeping with Hamilton (1978), we shall follow the idea that responsibility attribution is a decision about liability for sanction resulting from the application of certain rules. Before considering the nature of these rules, we shall examine the conditions which precipitate their application.

4.3.2. THE INSTIGATION OF RESPONSIBILITY ATTRIBUTION

It is argued that the following are distinctive features of situations in which the attribution of responsibility for undesirable outcomes is instigated: 1. The outcome is defined as undesirable because it involves the infraction of some norm or rule that is taken seriously; 2. It is witnessed (directly or indirectly) by one or more persons; 3. These witnesses entertain some notion of a connection between one or more agents and the outcome; 4. The agents who *might* be regarded as responsible for the undesirable outcome are assumed by the witnesses to possess some knowledge of whatever norm or rule has been violated. These we submit are the invariant properties of situations in which people make decisions about liability for social sanctions. The nature of the decision depends on two classes of rule which are applied; *connection rules* which establish the nature of the link betwen the agent(s) and the undesirable outcome; and *capacity rules* which establish whether or not the agent has 'normal' capacities, the most basic of which is the ability to understand what conduct is required by the standard in question.

These then are the distinctive features of situations in which questions are raised about responsibility for outcomes arising from *others'* actions. What, if any, are the differences between these features and those which characterize situations in which questions are instigated about responsibility for the undesirable outcomes of *one's own* actions. Of the four features mentioned above, only the second is clearly unnecessary; one can obviously raise questions about one's responsibility for the outcomes of one's own actions without these outcomes having been witnessed by others. For example, if a parent has been saving money in order to buy a Christmas present for his or her child, and through carelessness mislays the money, or through recklessness gambles the money away, the parent might well regard him or herself as responsible for the loss of the money, even if nobody else was aware of either the intention to buy the present or the loss of the money.

4.3.3. RESPONSIBILITY RULES

Whether questions of responsibility for outcomes are raised in relation to one's own conduct or that of another, we have to consider how answers to such questions are reached. In this connection, legal analyses of responsibility ascription can be drawn upon to assist a social psychological analysis. Thus, it is assumed that the function of responsibility ascription is to express a connection between individuals, deeds, and undesirable outcomes. Responsibility then can be seen as referring to a series of rules which enable one to make inferences and judgments about the applicability or inapplicability of social sanctions.

The transition from bearing responsibility for an act to being responsible for the outcome of an act is achieved, according to legal analyses of responsibility, by the application of a set of rules. Which rule is invoked depends partly on the social context. In an idealized analysis, there is a a series of rules which are dependent on the nature of the interaction in progress, the perceived relationship between the participants, the type of act or omission in question, the circumstances of the action, and so on. The rules that are applied to link the deed to a judgment of liability are manifold. Legal analysis suggests that both *objective criteria*, concerning the external circumstances of the violation and *subjective criteria*, concerning the agent's state of mind at the time of the violation, need to be satisfied.*

The satisfaction of the first set of criteria is achieved by the application of *connection rules*. In legal philosophical analyses connection rules are exemplified by role responsibility, causal responsibility, and legal liability responsibility (cf. Hart, 1968; Hart & Honoré, 1959). It is worth noting that these rules do not always require the establishment of a causal link betwen an agent, his or her deed and the undesirable outcome (e.g. role responsibility and vicarious responsibility rules). Even where this link is established by invoking a causal analysis, the nature of this analysis differs markedly from philosophical and scientific conceptions of causality. Hart and Honoré (1959) argue that the analysis of causality in the context of judgments of legal responsibility involves the identification of unique circumstances and events and the establishment that the outcomes in question resulted from the presence of those unique circumstances and events. Only those conditions that are necessary for the occurrence of an act (or its omission) are identified. Thus, the concept of causality in this context is quite different from the Humean conception of causality and therefore from causality as used in mainstream theories of attribution (e.g. Kelley, 1967, 1973). The point made by Hart and Honoré (1959) in this connection is that the type of causality revealed by the application of, for example, Mill's (1848) Method of Difference is the type of causal connection which can be formulated as a general law (e.g. the presence of oxygen is

---

* Of course in the case of strict liability questions about subjective criteria are not raised.

necessary for fire to occur). The argument is that such general laws do not specify which of all those conditions that are necessary for an event to occur is *the* cause on any particular occasion. Thus, it is of little consequence to the lawyer or indeed the layperson who is dealing with a case of arson to assert that the cause of fire was the presence of oxygen. Instead, Hart and Honoré (1959) regard a cause, in the legal context, as an extraordinary event, something which stands out against the backdrop of routine activity and results in harmful consequences. Causal attribution, in this context, is the process of establishing a path connecting an abnormal or extraordinary condition or event (e.g. the spilling of paraffin or the dropping of a lit cigarette) with the event or outcome in question.*

The satisfaction of the subjective criteria for judgment of liability is achieved by the application of *capacity rules*. As Hart (1968) points out "...the expression 'he is responsible for his actions' is used to assert that a person has certain normal capacities... The capacities in question are those of understanding, reasoning, and control of conduct: The ability to understand what conduct legal rules or morality require, to deliberate and reach decisions concerning these requirements, and to conform to decisions when made. Because 'responsible for his actions' in this sense refers not to a legal status but to certain complex psychological characteristics of persons, a person's responsibility for his action may intelligibly said to be 'diminished' or 'impaired' as well as altogether absent, and persons may be said to be 'suffering from diminished responsibility' much as a wounded man may be said to be suffering from a diminished capacity to control the movements of his limbs" (Hart, 1968, pp. 227-228).†

As noted above, legal analyses suggest that judgments of liability for sanction depend upon the satisfaction of both objective and subjective criteria. In other words, both connection rules and capacity rules are necessary to establish the applicability or inapplicability of social sanctions. It is not sufficient for an agent to be causally or otherwise connected to the harmful or undesirable consequence of deeds. Before social sanctions are applied that agent must be seen as having capacities of understanding, reasoning and control. Because

* The differences between causal analyses in everyday life and the type of causal analysis imputed to laypersons by the principal attribution theories are discussed by Fincham and Jaspars (1980), who draw on Hart and Honoré's (1959) work.

† cf. M'Naghten Rules formulated by the Judges of the House of Lords, 1843.

capacity rules are necessary to the making of decisions about
responsibility they can, in effect, override established connections
between an agent and an outcome.

Unlike the features which instigate questions about responsibility
for outcomes, these rules for ascertaining liability for social sanction
are cultural products. In other words, the means by which persons are
identified as responsible for undesirable events will vary across
temporal and cultural contexts. The most clearcut examples of such
variation are provided by observations documenting responsibility
rules in other cultures. Among the Azande, for example, witchcraft
theory and poison ordeals are the means by which questions of guilt
and innocence for undesirable outcomes are settled. Thus a poison
ordeal administered to a 'witch' accused of killing someone who has
died enables the detection of guilt by killing the guilty witch. "The
poison-ordeal is administered, as a branch of the judiciary, by the
prince. Some people could come through the ordeal unharmed, others
succumbed. The death of witches in the ordeal upheld the belief in
witchcraft and in the efficacy of the ordeal. Moreover, the social
demand for justice and vengence were satisfied" (Douglas, 1980, p.
53). Quite different responsibility rules were to be found among the
Ainu of Japan. Justice was obtained among these "hairy aborigines of
Japan" (Batchelor, 1892) on the basis of responsibility rules including
the following: "[The] hot water ordeal [which] consisted in making an
accused person thrust his arm or leg into a pan of boiling water. If
afraid to undergo this test, the guilt of the subject was assumed; or if,
when the arm was thrust into the water it was scalded, guilt was
supposed to be proved. A person was only declared innocent if the arm
came out uninjured. [Or]...The hot iron or stone ordeal. This consisted
in merely placing a piece of hot iron or a heated stone in the palm of the
hand, and keeping it there until confession was made. Of course, if the
heated instrument did not burn the hand, a person's innocence was
fully established....[or]...'The cup ordeal'. This consisted in causing a
person to drink a cup of water. When this was done, he was made to
throw the cup behind him, over his head. If the cup lighted the right
way upwards, the innocence of the individual was supposed to be
established; if otherwise, he was proved guilty" (Batchelor, 1892, pp.
135 - 137).

Such illustrations of responsibility rules in other cultures can only
reinforce the conclusion that questions of responsibility are settled by
the application of rules to establish relationships between agent(s),

acts, circumstances, and harmful or undesirable consequences. The distinction introduced earlier between connection rules and capacity rules would seem, on the basis of a cursory comparison with responsibility rules employed in other cultures, to be particularly characteristic of Western culture. A possible reason for the cultural specificity of this distinction is provided by Hart (1968, p. 221), in relation to the distinction between *mens rea* and *actus reus*. He suggests that this distinction can be found in the Cartesian dualism between body and mind, a distinction which has had a profound influence on Western thinking. It is concluded that responsibility judgments are made in accordance with culturally specific rules which are employed within the context of transgressions.

4.3.4. IMPLICATIONS FOR SOCIAL PSYCHOLOGY

In this concluding section we shall consider the implications for social psychology of conceptualizing responsibility as a decision about liability for sanction. At the outset it should be emphasized that different objectives can be pursued through the study of responsibility attribution. These objectives might range from trying to understand the interplay between motivational and cognitive processes, through the way in which social-cognitive development enables responsibility attribution to be made in an increasingly differentiated fashion, to the cataloguing of the means by which responsibility attributions are made in particular cultures and subcultures.

We shall begin by considering the implications of a rule-based conception of responsibility for one of the major strands of social psychological research, i.e. defensive attribution. The implicit objective of this research would seem to be the examination of how personal needs or motivations 'distort' the way in which responsibility is ascribed. Thus the attribution of responsibility is in fact incidental to the underlying objective of such research, namely the demonstration that the human psyche is irrational. However, the achievement of this objective requires as a first step the identification of those responsibility rules that would be applied to the scenarios employed in the experimental research, if biasing factors did not intrude. Motivational factors might affect decisions about liability for sanction in any of three ways. First, it might be that responsibility rules are invoked in situations where questions of responsibility would not normally arise. Second, it might be that no responsibility rules are invoked in situations which would normally give rise to decisions about sanctions. Finally, it might be that motivational factors produce a change in the type of responsibility rule applied in reaching a decision about liability for sanction. Thus, if the fundamental objective of defensive attribution research is to uncover the modifications of social judgments produced by motivational factors, then a clear understanding of the rules that mediate such judgments in the absence of bias is a prerequisite. Only then can one consider whether and how the personal needs of the perceiver result in the invocation of different responsibility rules.

Other objectives that might be pursued in studying the attribution of responsibility are more directly concerned with attempting to understand how responsibility ascriptions are made. If one begins with a conception of responsibility as a rule-based decision about liability for sanction, then one plausible line of social psychological research on responsibility ascription would involve the systematic cataloguing of responsibility rules. It seems likely that the types of responsibility rules employed in the everyday interpretation of situations involving undesirable outcomes will vary as a function of the cultural context, the developmental status of the perceiver, the relative power and status of the agent and the perceiver, and so on. Systematic research of this type would lead us to a more precise understanding of how settings, persons, rules and relationships jointly determine the set of sanctioning rules which serve as a basis for perceivers' everyday reactions to undesirable outcomes.

Another plausible line of research on responsibility ascription suggested by a rule-based conception of responsibility would be to inquire into the way in which responsibility rules are learned and utilized by children. Of course, there already exists much theory and research concerned with the development of moral reasoning (e.g. Kohlberg, 1969, 1976). The cognitive-developmental theory which tends to dominate such research regards the development of moral reasoning as the product of intellectual growth. As Emler and Hogan (1981) put it, "Moral reasoning is seen as self-contained, as independent of social and cultural pressures, as obeying its own internal laws of development. The direction and pattern of development are thus dictated by dynamics inherent in psychological functioning" (p. 310). We concur with Emler and Hogan's argument that this cognitive-developmental approach underestimates the importance of the cultural context in which moral concepts are acquired. The 'role-theoretical' view of socialization advocated by Emler and Hogan

(1981) involves the adoption of a sociology of knowledge perspective on the acquisition of moral, legal, and judicial concepts and attitudes. With regard to responsibility ascription, such an approach would entail the examination of how children's and adolescents' knowledge and use of responsibility rules change as a function of the structure of the interpersonal relationships they experience. Although Emler and Hogan are not directly concerned with developmental changes in knowledge and use of *responsibility rules*, their observations on the interplay between social experience and attitudes to law and justice are suggestive of the directions which could be taken by social-developmental research. They argue that "Little children are largely involved in authoritarian or asymmetrical relationships, and their attitudes are correspondingly authoritarian. Adolescents are involved in egalitarian role relationships. Adults are involved in bureaucratic organizations and their attitudes are characteristically different from those of children and adolescents" (p. 314). Emler and Hogan's emphasis on the impact of subjectively experienced role relationships on individuals' attitudes to legal and judicial issues complements Hamilton's (1978) insistence that roles are "...normative contexts that determine the standards of accountability of the actor" (p.326). Just as decisions about liability for sanction may vary as a function of the role relationships of those to whom responsibility is ascribed, so the types of rules which shape the decision-making process may vary as a function of the role relationships of those who make decisions about responsibility for undesirable outcomes.

Having outlined some of the positive implications for research on conceptualizing everyday responsibility ascription as a rule-based decision-making process, the outcome of which is the application of a social sanction, we shall now consider two dangers which may arise from such a conceptualization. Both of these stem from the fact that social psychological analyses of responsibility attribution that seek to incorporate legal-philosophical concepts are, necessarily, *idealised* analyses. One danger arising from such idealised analyses of responsibility attribution is that human beings are cast in the role of intuitive lawyers, in just the same way that attribution theoretical treatments — because they are idealized abstractions deriving from a scientific frame of reference — cast human beings in the role of intuitive experimenters and/or statisticians. Thus the adoption of a conceptualization of responsibility as a judgment made according to certain rules runs the risk of substituting one set of normative models of human beings for another. The problem is that *any* normative model of human psychological functioning runs the risk of obscuring the very phenomena it seeks to explain, because it has a logic of its own against which common-sense is assessed. Rather than helping us to *understand* common-sense, such metaphors can become benchmarks for the *evaluation* of common-sense.

The second danger that arises from an idealized analysis of responsibility attribution is that it will represent statically what is in reality a dynamic process. Given the occurrence of an undesirable event for which someone *might* be responsible, one particular responsibility rule may be seen as being cued by certain features of the undesirable outome, the context in which it occurs, the statuses of the interactants involved, and so on; this responsibility rule is applied, and results in a decision about the liability of one or more individuals for social sanctioning. Such a representation of the responsibility ascription process tends to gloss over the *negotiated* aspect of responsibility. As Scheff (1968) has argued, "...the assessment of responsibility always includes a process of negotiation" (p.5). In other words, perceivers do not typically arrive at responsibility judgments concerning the undesirable outcome of another's actions without hearing what this person has to say about the outcome. Questions about motives are posed, in the form of challenges or inquiries about conduct, and the actor to whom such questions are addressed typically has the opportunity to provide an apology, excuse, or justification for the undesirable outcome. This process of questioning and responding, or motive talk as it was characterized in Chapter 3, amounts to a negotiation of responsibility.

In conclusion, it is clear that the analysis of the attribution of responsibility takes on a different complexion and proceeds in different directions, depending upon the objective that is being pursued. These objectives might be to demonstrate how the use of responsibility rules is modified by affective or motivational factors; to show how knowledge and use of responsibility rules changes as a function of the social-developmental process; to devise taxonomies of responsibility rules, and to document how these vary as a function of the types of situations in which untoward events occur, and the perceived relationship between interactants in such situations; to study how liability for sanctions is negotiated as part of an ongoing interpretative process; and so on. In pursuing any of these objectives it should not be forgotten that what is involved is the use of connection rules which link agents, acts and undesirable consequences. The particular nature of these rules will obviously vary across cultural contexts; however, the presence of such rules, regardless of cultural idiosyncracies, is essential to the establishment and maintenance of social and moral order, and on this basis we anticipate that they will be found in *any* human society.

5

The epistemological foundations of accountability of conduct

5.1. Introduction

In the course of the last three chapters we have been concerned with an examination of the social practices employed in the regulative interpretation of actual or potential fractures of social interaction. These practices, which have been subsumed here under the general title of accountability of conduct, can also be seen as constituting typical subject matter for research into social cognition. A characteristic feature of the work we have reported so far is that it addresses the general issue of accountability from both traditions of social psychology: the 'sociological' and the 'psychological'.

Our aim in this final chapter is to evaluate the epistemological status of this work, and examine the possibility of locating this work within a broader epistemological perspective. By this is not meant an evaluation of the theoretical status of the individual issues we have addressed so far, under the management of social identity, motive talk, and attribution of responsibility, for we have attempted to address the specific theoretical problems involved in these areas within the respective chapters. Rather our concern here is with the general status of the work reported in these chapters, taken as a whole. This concern is stimulated by some general criticisms that can be and often are raised about the type of work we have discussed so far.

The first type of criticism concerns the cultural relativism of the research topics. All the work that we have presented under the rubric 'accountability of conduct' is subject to the limitation that it is conducted and presented within the confines of a predominantly Anglo-Saxon culture and is strongly influenced by that cultural context in its generation of synthetic or classificatory schemes, and in the generation of particular models concerning the ascription of responsibility, intentions, motives, and so on. The culture-bounded-ness of this research enterprise raises the question of the extent to which claims for the generality of the relevant theories or models can be made, if at all. If any claim to generality is to be maintained, either with respect to the content matter or the postulated inter-pretative processes involved, then one must consider which aspects of this knowledge have a claim to cross-cultural generality, and why this is so. Related to this cultural relativism problem is the question of the historical boundedness of such knowledge (cf. Gergen, 1973). Indeed, there is as much evidence concerning *transhistorical* vari-ations in numerous social practices (cf. Elias, 1977) as there is concerning *cross-cultural* variations in accounting practices (cf. Roberts, 1979).

We shall begin by examining in some detail the rationale for these limitations. Since the issues are concerned with the limitation of the generality of any statement that can be made on accountability we have termed this section 'the restrictive perspective on accountability'. Next we shall examine a counterargument, which we have termed 'the integrative perspective on accountability'. Within this latter section, two different but interrelated arguments will be presented. The first arises out of an examination of the ontological foundation of accountability, and rests on the the assumption that the human species has a reflexive propensity. This argument admits that accountability is a human artifact, along with social rules and conventions. However, it is argued in addition that while such human artifacts may be culturally relative in their expression, their existence in some form is an essential and inescapable feature of human coexistence, and a necessary condition for the creation of a mutually shared reality. The second argument proposes that society and social order as historically permanent phenomena could not be maintained without accountability prac-tices. We shall therefore go on to examine the generic premises of accountability across cultures and emphasize the similarities of these practices in terms of their functions, rather than the differences that are apparent in the content of the different practices.

5.2. The restrictive perspective on accountability

The main limitations on the epistemological status of the work we have examined in the previous three chapters arise out of the historically and culturally bounded perspective entailed in the theory and research in these areas. Such limitations as pertain to social psychological work in general have already been the focus of considerable debate, mainly initiated by Gergen's provocative contention that "In essence, the study of social psychology is primarily an historical undertaking"(1973, p.316). The ensuing discussion (cf. Buss, 1975, 1979; Manis, 1975; *Personality and Social Psychology Bulletin,* 1976,**2**; Schlenker, 1974; Thorngate, 1975; Triandis, 1978; *inter alia*) is particularly relevant to the critical appraisal of the epistemological status of social psychological knowledge in general and the work reviewed in the three previous chapters in particular.

Gergen (1973) develops two central lines of argument in support of his thesis. The first of these is concerned with "the impact of science on social behaviour", and the second with historical and cultural change. In analysing the interplay between scientific knowledge, social knowledge and behaviour Gergen advances three interrelated arguments. Each of these, in our view, can be seen as arising from the potentially reflexive relationship between human beings and the nature of social psychological knowledge. The main contention is that the documentation and availability of social psychological knowledge contains the potential of being invalidated or eradicated through self-fulfilling or self-frustrating hypotheses that people may entertain when they engage in action which they identify as belonging to a domain relevant to that knowledge. If the knowledge is assimilated reactively on a widespread basis, then the original phenomenon may disappear completely. In considering the implications of historical and cultural change for social psychological theory, Gergen argues that the 'facts' of social behaviour are based on propensities which change as a function of time and circumstance. Thus, the status of social psychological knowledge is such that it is historically and culturally bound and cannot have any claims to universality. Purely to illustrate this point, we shall refer to the classic conformity studies conducted by Asch (1956). If subjects were not naive about the experimental manipulation (namely, all of the 'subjects' bar one are confederates of the experimenter and on specific trials make unanimous but patently incorrect perceptual judgments), then the probability of compliant behaviour would diminish considerably, if not completely. If this knowledge were culturally shared, then the phenomenon would not be demonstrable in the first instance. Perrin and Spencer (1981) argue for example, that "...the social and cultural conditions obtained in the USA and to a lesser extent in Europe, in the 1950s and 1960s were contributory rather than incidental to the demonstration of the Asch effect"; and also that "...the 'Asch Effect' should be seen as a product of definable social and cultural conditions"(1981,p.205). Their study demonstrates the complete absence of the conformity effect among British university students. In Gergen's words this can be seen as a result of the fact that "...sophistication as to behavioural principles liberates one from their behavioural implications"(1973,p.312).

Gergen (1973) specifies the reasons why such sophistication can effect 'liberation' in the following two arguments. First, he maintains that a considerable range of psychological theorizing has an evaluative and therefore prescriptive bias, distinguishing between positive and negative types of behaviour. That this type of bias is widespread and often not even acknowledged is demonstrated in Semin's critique of attribution theory (Semin, 1980, 1981a; see Chapter 1). Second Gergen argues that in present societies the highly valued uniqueness of individuals leads people to "...strive to invalidate theories that ensnare us in an impersonal way"(Gergen, 1973, p.314). These two arguments are suggestive of the kinds of limits on the status of social psychological knowledge that arise as a consequence of its availability. However, changes in cultural forms of conduct themselves may and do lead to a change in the types of behaviour examined in social psychology, for which there is no immediate and obvious provision.

Critics of Gergen's position have developed different lines of attack. One of the best known strategies consists in questioning Gergen's conception of science. A typical example of this view is Schlenker's (1974) critique, the hub of which is that Gergen's account is a demonstration of his 'misconception of science'. At the basis of Schlenker's critique is a conception of science anchored in a positivistic philosophy. It is assumed that models such as the deductive nomological and the inductive statistical provide adequate means for ascertaining the generality and universality of social psychological knowledge, however much the present status of such knowledge may be temporarily hampered by its relative 'youth'. Such lines of argument (Manis, 1975; Schlenker, 1976,) are so out of line with present-day thinking about the adequacy of such models not only for the social sciences (Giddens, 1974; Harré & Secord, 1972; Keat & Urry, 1975) but also for the natural sciences (Feyerabend, 1962, 1972; Lakatos, 1970), that we shall not pursue here the relative merits or demerits of such critical contentions. The sources referred to above provide detailed discussions of the issues involved.

A different, in part apparently sympathetic response to Gergen's position is advanced by cross-culturally inclined social psychologists. Triandis' (1978) paper is probably the most typical of this alternative. His definition of a universal is a "...psychological process or relationship which occurs in all cultures"(Triandis, 1978, p.1). Acknowledging that this is a somewhat loose definition due to the present state of research, Triandis nevertheless proceeds to outline a position from which such 'processes' or 'relationships' may be identified. He concurs with Gergen only to the extent that social psychological and personality work have preferentially proceeded with "relatively concrete constructs", mainly, in his view, because more abstract constructs lend themselves less easily to measurement.* While concrete constructs are more easily operationalizable, they are also more likely to be limited with respect to their external validity and, therefore, subject to the criticisms advanced by Gergen. Gergen would not agree with this argument, but this point will be taken up in detail below.

In sketching a blueprint of a universalistic theory of social behaviour, Triandis begins with the following premise: "A general theory of social behaviour, applicable to all situations (across time and place), requires the identification of those fundamental constructs which are likely to maintain the same meaning across time and place. Such fundamental constructs would function as anchors and provide standard measurements for constructs that vary in meaning across time and place" (Triandis, 1978, p.5). He then embarks on a search for universal constructs which have invariable meanings across cultures in order to be able to correlate variable constructs with these invariable ones. In order to identify these universal constructs an

---

* Aside from suggesting that Triandis subscribes to a positivistic view of science, this remark puts him in good company. Hempel (1958), for example, notes that: "It is a remarkable fact ...that the greatest advances in scientific systematization have not been accomplished by means of laws referring explicitly to *observables*, i.e. to things and events which are ascertainable by direct observation, but rather by means of laws that speak of various *hypothetical, or theoretical, entities*, i.e. presumptive objects, events and attributes which cannot be perceived or otherwise directly observed by us"(p.177). If Triandis were to adopt a different scientific position, for example realism, then the problem he notes, namely measurement of abstract constructs, would hardly constitute a problem (cf. Harré, 1970).

analysis "at a very abstract level" is offered. For this Triandis employs the S-R 'paradigm', with the attendant 'mediational processes' (O) located "somewhere between the S and the R". Triandis limits the domain of his concern to other people, the actions of these people directed towards the individual, and the individual's responses, designating the behaviour involved as interpersonal. He then proceeds to a classification of various prospective psychological and anthropological terms which are to have claims on universality. These are grouped into three, namely:(1) stimulus universals (attributes of persons — e.g. age, sex, personal names, status; inferred attributes of persons — e.g. goals, etiquette, conformity, norms, roles, ethics, values; stimulus person's behaviour towards the person — e.g. kissing, sexual intercourse, avoiding, obeying, gesturing, gift giving, etc.); (2) process universals (e.g. reciprocity, equity, cognitive consistency, social comparison, etc.); and finally (3) response universals (four universal dimensions, i.e., association-dissociation; superordination-subordination, intimacy-formality; covert-overt behaviour). While there appear to be some contradictions in the brief rationales presented for the inclusion of certain instances [e.g. "... *cognitive consistency* is probably universal, though cultures may differ in the degree to which inconsistency is noxious. For example, Thai experts doubt that cognitive dissonance is of significance in Thailand"(Triandis, 1978, p.5)] and although the listing of the instances of psychological universals sometimes appears to be rather indiscriminate, these shortcomings are not relevant to our present concerns. Instead we need to examine critically the basic premise underlying the possibility of a 'universal theory of social behaviour'.

It is contended that this premise contains within it the major shortcoming of this approach. The contentious statement in the premise is the "need to identify those fundamental constructs which are likely to maintain the same meaning across time and place" (Triandis, 1978, p 5). One rather obvious and fundamental objection to this statement is that even the professionals in this area would fail to reach agreement about the use of these constructs. This requires no elaboration. A different type of objection is that there is an ambiguity contained in the referent of the notion of meaning invariance. It is not clear whether this referent is to be the Western psychologist or indigenous members of other cultures. The notion of meaning invariance may represent an impossible goal, regardless of the perspective from which meaning invariance is assessed. As Winch puts it, "To give an account of the meaning of a word is to describe how it is used: and to describe how it is used is to describe the social intercourse into which it enters" (1958, p. 123). Thus, *the meanings of constructs are determined by their linguistic and pragmatic contexts*. As Douglas (1971) argues: "There are at least two important kind of contexts that determine meanings:(1) the *linguistic context* (which may or may not be independent of the second kind), and (2) the *practical* (use) *context*. Meanings are dependent on the linguistic context when they are (partially) determined for the members by other linguistic items or properties that occur in the same situation, such as the same text. They are dependent on the practical context when they are determined for the members by other non-linguistic aspects of the situation in which they occur. The practical or use context consists primarily of such things as the time and place in which they occur and the knowledge that is taken for granted about the persons involved" (Douglas, 1971,p.38). The practical determination of the meaning of any construct is referred to as its indexicality (cf. Bar-Hillel, 1954; Pierce, 1933; Russell, 1940). The point is that all symbolic forms contain a fringe of incompleteness that must be filled in with reference to practical contexts (cf. Garfinkel & Sacks, 1970, pp.348-350). For this reason alone, the notion of a cross-cultural meaning invariance of constructs is a contradiction in terms.

If, however, Triandis is referring to a meaning invariance arrived at through measurement procedures then other substantial problems arise. The most important of these is that the meanings of meas-urement terms depend on the theoretical terms which are employed in constructing them. Thus, "... it is not possible to provide descriptions of what we observe that are totally free of any conceptual and theoretical implications and assumptions" (Keat & Urry, 1975, p.52). This argument is related to that concerning the incompleteness of meaning without reference to a context. The context in this case is implicitly contained in the measurement procedures and the under-lying theory, which are imposed on the relative meanings of constructs existing in different cultures and thus distort their original contextual meanings. In other words, constructs developed in a particular community are imposed upon the constructs of different cultures. That we are prone to do this even within our culture is demonstrated in Chapter 1 in connection with attribution theory. If we wish to understand the concepts and constructs in other cultures and examine their comparability to constructs and concepts in our own culture then we must examine their actual use in the respective cultures. Imposing our own measurement standards with the aim of discovering "invariant" meanings essentially involves the imposition of a context developed in one community (e.g. Western psychological techniques) to constructs removed from their own contexts of use (cf. Winch, 1970).

The present state of the debate initiated by Gergen's (1973) paper (cf. *Personality and Social Psychology Bulletin*, 1976, **2**) suggests that the transitoriness of social psychological knowledge is an inescapable aspect of the type of knowledge accumulated by social psychologists, including the material which forms the subject of the present volume. In particular, the concepts and findings discussed in Chapters 2, 3, and 4 would appear to be subject to this historical limitation, insofar as nearly all of the analytic work in the area of accountability has been based on the examination of socio-culturally and historically determinate patterns. However, in the section that follows we shall consider another approach which, by examining the basic premise underlying Gergen's (1973, 1976) argument in more detail, provides a way in which knowledge about the accountability of human conduct can be regarded as less constrained by temporal or cultural factors. In considering this approach we do not seek to establish a universalistic position, in which universality is construed as a formulation which regards human behavioural manifestations or presumed processes as universal in one form or another. The search for human universals either in terms of manifest response or in terms of stimulus categories seems to be an impossible endeavour.

5.3. The integrative perspective on accountability

Gergen's critique of social psychological knowledge in general (and, by implication, of the work on accountability of conduct in particular) relies primarily on a specific premise. Knowledge produced in social psychology "...does not *generally* transcend its historical boundaries" (Gergen, 1973, p. 310, emphasis ours) mainly because of the reflexive relationship between human beings and social psychological knowledge. This statement can mean either of the following. First, the transhistorical status of knowledge holds only for particular types of knowledge produced in social psychology. Consistent with this,

Gergen does seem to make a distinction between the "body and the mind" as Schlenker (1974) puts it, whereby processes are implicitly regarded as more universal the more biologically rooted they are. A second possible meaning is that social psychologists have in general not been sensitive to the ethnocentrism and chronocentrism that permeate their endeavours. While this leaves open the possibility that there are aspects of human social life which are not subject to these restrictions, Gergen's statements do not make clear what these possibilities might be. This statement, as we shall argue, is founded on the premise that the relationship between human beings and the nature of knowledge produced in social psychology is generally a reflexive one, leading to a change in the behaviours that are the subject of this knowledge. Gergen extends his argument one step further, when he discusses the potential for a 'psychology of enlightenment' which he regards as a 'theory of reactions to theory', and dismisses this option on the same grounds, i.e. that this knowledge is also reflexive in nature. This is the point at which, in our view, Gergen's argument does not go far enough. The reason for this is that Gergen's conceptualization of social psychology is based on a premise which acknowledges current modes of theorizing as the only possible modes. Such theorizing and its associated research is exclusively concerned with manifest social behaviours and/or operationalizable entities. Thus, Gergen sees any metatheory about how people react to knowledge of theories as being cast in the same conceptual mould as the theories themselves. Viewing social psychology simply in terms of current practice leads inevitably to Gergen's conclusion that a "psychology of enlightenment effects" fails due to the problem of infinite regress. Gergen asserts that "A psychology of enlightenment effects is subject to the same historical limitations as other theories of social psychology" (1973, p. 315). If one accepts Gergen's premise and the conclusion that necessarily follows, one shares with him the danger of espousing a logically absurd position, one which could be called 'absolute relativism'. This can be defined as a position which contends that all knowledge is relative, *except the contention that 'all knowledge is relative'*, which is considered *absolutely* true, for all times and all places. The absurdity of this position is captured by Trigg (1973): "If someone declares that truth is not objective but only relative to societies, he may very well claim 'there is no such thing as "objective truth"', or 'truth is relative to societies'. Both assertions, however, clearly purport to be objectively true, and are intended as truths about all societies" (pp. 2-3).

In our view, Gergen's argument depends upon the supposed consequences of a general human propensity, reflexivity. Below we shall develop a counterargument to the view that examinations of human social existence are necessarily ethno- and chronocentric. We shall argue with Winch (1970) that "...the very conception of human life involves certain fundamental notions"(p. 107), which Winch calls limiting notions, such as birth, death, sexual relationships and so on. Winch goes on to argue that: "The specific forms which these concepts take, the particular institutions in which they are expressed, vary considerably from one society to another; but their central position within a society's institutions is and must be a constant factor" (Winch, 1970, p. 107). Winch does not pursue this idea of limiting notions beyond noting that they are important features of any human society and suggesting that any attempts to understand the lives of other societies may most fruitfully proceed by examining the forms that such limiting notions take in different societies. We shall argue that reflexivity is just such a fundamental notion although to consider it as limiting may be somewhat misleading. The particular way in which we develop our argument treats these fundamental notions as integrative ones, around which cultural practices evolve and develop, lending structure to human social existence.

5.3.1. THE ONTOLOGICAL FOUNDATION OF ACCOUNTABILITY

This section on human reflexivity and its relation to the issue of social order and control is not really a digression from our main theme of accountability of social conduct but rather a presentation of the ontological foundation of and rationale for accountability in relation to the general issue of social control and order. Reflexivity as a unique propensity of man is a relatively new idea, the beginnings of which are to be found around the turn of the present century. The idea of reflexivity presented a unique change in the conceptions of man's nature. Until the 17th century prevalent views of man were bound by scholastic philosophy and the question 'What is the nature of man?' was answered in terms of his relation to God, and the Act of Creation. God, according to this view, created man by combining a material body and an immortal soul. Thus, the origin myth suggests that all human beings stem bodily from Adam and Eve, but are endowed by God with an immortal and unique soul. Descartes enabled philosophy to be emancipated from theology by defining the human body as any other body in the sense of the then newly discovered natural sciences, namely a material body. The distinctive feature of this body in contrast to others was that it was a machine embodied with a soul. Thus, the question 'What is the nature of man?' was given the answer a 'machine with a soul' which Ryle refers to as the "dogma of the Ghost in the machine". Ryle summarizes this dogma, which still prevails in some form or another among theorists and laymen alike, in the following manner:

> The official doctrine, which hails chiefly from Descartes, is something like this. With the doubtful exceptions of idiots and infants in arms every human being has both a body and a mind. Some would prefer to say that every human being is both a body and a mind. His body and mind are ordinarily harnessed together, but after the death of the body his mind may continue to exist and function.
>
> Human bodies are in space and are subject to the mechanical laws which govern all bodies in space. Bodily processes and states can be inspected by external observers. So a man's bodily life is as much a public affair as are the lives of animals and reptiles and even as the careers of trees, crystals and planets.
>
> But minds are not in space, nor are their operations subject to mechanical laws. The workings of one mind are not witnessable by other observers; its career is private. Only I can take cognizance of the states and processes of my own mind. A person therefore lives through two collateral histories, one consisting of what happens in and to his body, the other consisting of what happens in and to his mind. The first is public, the second private (Ryle, 1949, p.13).

Since it is not directly relevant to our general argument we shall not concern ourselves either with Ryle's critique of this dogma or with the immense difficulties adherents of this view have had and continue to have in reconciling the interactions between the body and the mind. The relevant point in the present context is that this was and is a very successful dogma which has lasted over 400 years and still lingers on with some force (cf. Gehlen, 1957). It is within the context of the particular critique of this dogma by American pragmatists, e.g. Pierce, James, Dewey, and by continental philosophical anthropologists, e.g. Scheler, Gehlen, that the reflexive nature of man was acknowledged and became a main theme in instancing the unique nature of man in contrast to the lower species. In 1928, Max Scheler, in his book *Die Stellung des Menschen im Kosmos*, tackled the question of the nature of man. The unusual quality of this work is that this question was addressed without reference to a comparison between God and man.

The distinct quality of Man was examined by Scheler by means of a comparison with the lower species. This meant however that what was until then regarded as the privileged domain of biologists, physiologists and physicians was to be incorporated into a 'philosophical question': Scheler's argument was that all those human qualities such as intelligence, memory, ability to discriminate and decide, to use instruments, etc. were qualities which distinguished human beings from the lower species only in degree and not in principle. The distinctive and unique feature of human beings, according to Scheler, is that they possess a "Geist", a propensity which in his view is opposed to life. This conclusion was derived from the following reasoning. A creature who has Geist is not directly channelled by his biological drives, he does not respond to his environment and its contingencies in a direct and determinate way as an animal does. Man is able to make his own *world*, by making the environment an object, and thus by distancing and detaching himself from it. This objectivity, this internal freedom, or in the present terminology, this reflexive propensity, through which action and knowledge can become object was the specifically and distinctly human feature. This meant that action and knowledge could be directed such that they were not serving an obviously biological interest. This view suggests that man has an *indeterminate* nature in contrast to the lower species. Thus, Scheler concluded that man has a *world* and not an *environment*, a sphere of things around himself. He can make himself object to himself and thus became self-conscious. This ability to become self-conscious, self-aware, to distance himself from himself reflectively, enables him to negate particular expressions of himself, repress impulses and drives, and modify their expressions. The Geist, then, according to Scheler, obtained its energy precisely through its possibility of negating. Within this context it is thus not surprizing that Scheler came to the conclusion that Geist was opposed to life. Scheler himself is criticised for not providing a proper solution to the mind-body problem and, indeed, for complicating it even further (cf. Gehlen, 1957). However, what is relevant in our context is the central theme that he developed, namely the notion of reflexivity subsumed under the term "Geist". This theme not only influenced the development of philosophical anthropology on the continent but also led to the development of a phenomenological biology (cf. v. Uexkull, 1921, 1958) and a comparative psychology (cf. Buytendijk, 1958) which has had no parallel in the Anglo-Saxon literature until recently (cf. Crook,

1980). An idea similar to that of the reflexivity of Man was developed by the American pragmatists in their rejection of Cartesian dualism and the most important example of this idea within social psychology is found in the social behaviourism of G. H. Mead and his conceptions of the mind and the self, with its two phases of the I and the Me.

All these new approaches actually enabled a particular view of Man to be advanced which suggested that he is the most *seducible* and *malleable* of all creatures. Therein lay the key to understanding the great diversity of cultures across time and space. The malleability theme, or man's seduceability was to be developed as a consequence of his reflexivity and the resulting ability to detach himself from the immediate context. However, the theme itself is not particularly new and was, for example, already present in the 15th century. It was not, of course, developed from the notion of reflexivity but rather within theological reasoning. Pico de Mirandola's discourse "On the Dignity of Man", written in 1487, provides a testimony to this. He posed the same question addressed by Scheler, namely: What constitutes the 'outstandingness' of Man? The answer is related to the story of Creation. After God created the world, He found that there was nobody to admire His work. And He created Man to appreciate his work, but had no archetypes for this. At this point let us follow Pico de Mirandola:

> At last the best of artisans ordained that that creature to whom He had been able to give nothing proper of himself should have joint possession of whatever had been peculiar to each of the different kinds of being. He therefore took man as a creature of indeterminate nature and, assigning him a place in the middle of the world, addressed him thus:
> Neither a fixed abode nor a form that is thine alone nor any function peculiar to thyself have we given thee, Adam, to the end that according to thy longing and according to thy judgment thou mayest have and possess what abode, what form and what functions thou thyself shalt desire. The nature of all other beings is limited and constrained within the bounds of laws prescribed by Us. Thou, constrained by no limits, in accordance with thine own free will, in whose hand We have placed thee, shalt ordain for thyself the limits of thy nature. We have set thee at the world's centre that thou mayest from thence more easily observe whatever is in the world. We have made thee neither of heaven nor of earth, neither mortal nor immortal, so that with freedom of choice and with honour, as though the maker and molder of thyself, thou mayest fashion thyself in whatever shape thou shalt prefer (In Fromm & Xiram, 1969, p. 103)

Captured in this passage is the same notion that malleability and seduceability are peculiar to human nature that was made possible through the reflexivity theme developed during the late 19th century and early 20th century.

Employing the interrelated themes of reflexivity and malleability or seducibility of human nature, Gehlen (1957) constructs a general argument about the ontological foundations of social institutions and thus those of social order and control. In his argument Gehlen attempts to link the biological perspective on the human species with a historico-cultural one, through conceiving of human society and existence as based on action. On the basis of existing zoological (Portmann, 1951; 1962; Storch,1948), biological (v.Uexkull,1921, 1958) and comparative psychological (Buytendijk, 1958) work, he argues that the human species is poorly endowed with instinctual equipment when compared with the lower species. This is manifest in at least two distinct ways. The first is the extended period of development and dependency that the human neonate has until it can reach a self-supporting existence. This prolonged dependency is unique to the human species. Second, he suggests considering a thought experiment. If humans were stripped of all their artifacts they would not be able to survive. This, Gehlen argues, is mainly due to a deficiency in their biological make-up. In other words, human beings are not instinctually endowed with determinate forms of adaptive equipment; thus Gehlen's argument is that there is a general instinctual deficiency of the human species if one compares it with the lower species. However, these deficiencies are compensated by the ability of human beings to change the nature they confront such that it serves their life purposes, irrespective of whatever form this nature may take. Thus, the environment that surrounds all societies consists of a nature, reshaped and reformed through intelligent action to fit the needs of the particular community in question. The particular cultures themselves are communities with specifically developed cultural artifacts allowing their own social existence to be optimally suited to cope with the ecological conditions within which they find themselves (cf. Harris, 1978). Human social life is influenced by the practical problems of earthly existence as they are presented within distinct ecological conditions, but the important point is that the relationship between the human species and ecological conditions is an indeterminate one, in that the adaptive relationships that human beings will develop in specific ecological conditions are not fixed in advance. The particular cultural forms that will develop are open ended. However, this also means that the relations between one human being and another are equally open and malleable. In other words human relationships, according to Gehlen, are of an indeterminate form. It is within the context of these latter considerations that Gehlen develops the argument that social institutions in the broadest sense are central human artifacts which establish the pillars for social coexistence. Thus, institutions such as religion, the legal system, conventions of hierarchy, rules and conventions for action, and the most important of all institutions, language, become central artifacts of the human species in that they represent the means by which individual subjectivity is transcended and social coexistence with a mutually shared reality and history is created. Indeed, if there were no such mutual conventions and rules it would be impossible to share a joint reality. Were it possible to conceive of a state in which all institutions of a community were completely destroyed, then, Gehlen argues, chaos would reign, and all intersubjectivity (that is, the sense of a jointly shared reality) would disappear. Social coexistence would be impossible. By definition that state of affairs is beyond demonstration, but made plausible by the documented disastrous effects of the destruction of only one central institution such as employment. This was for example the major finding of the classic work by Jahoda, Lazarsfeld and Zeisel(1933) which shows that severe economic depression results in the destruction of a central social institution, namely work, leading to a loss of sense of reality in the particular individuals and community concerned.

5.3.2. THE CULTURE-CONDUCT INTERFACE

A general social psychological approach to the issue of culture and social order has not been forthcoming with the exception of the psychodynamic approach (cf. Bocock, 1976; Badcock 1981; Brown, 1959; Freud, 1930, 1974) which has influenced both sociological thinking on this problem (cf. Parsons,1952) and anthropological approaches to understanding culture and custom (cf. Fortes, 1977). In social psychology this problem has not been a live one, and there exists to our knowledge no contemporary research addressing it.* This is partly

---

* Although research on conformity and group pressure can be regarded as addressing the issue of social order, it does so in a highly decontextualized fashion. Conformity is examined as an exclusively intra-group phenomenon and the relationship between the group and society overlooked.

due to the fact that social order and control have been regarded predominantly as sociological prerogatives. Moreover those formulations that exist have by and large been influenced by the Hobbesian conception that regards social order as external to individual members of society. This is apparent in the work of Durkheim (1895), Ross (1901) and Parsons (1951). Such formulations of the problem make it inaccessible to psychological thinking because they suggest that individuals cannot modify or influence the fundamentals of social order. The governing theme is that society presents an 'inhibiting environment' as Giddens (1976) puts it in relation to early Durkheimian thinking on this subject. A dichotomy between individual and society is assumed. The gist of these conceptions has its origins in the notion that 'society', regarded as a somewhat separate entity, has to control the 'animal nature' of man.This is evident, for example, in Durkheim's notion of the *conscience collective*.

However, the view of society as expounded in the 'interpretative sociologies' (cf. Giddens, 1974), and exemplified particularly in the ethnomethodological tradition (e.g. Garfinkel, 1967; Garfinkel & Sacks, 1970),carries two implications. First, such approaches allow one to construe the 'external and constraining reality' as a product of the continued social practices of its members, and bracket an institutional analysis in favour of an analysis of action.In other words, they regard social order as the result of 'ceaseless reality work' (cf. Mehan & Wood, 1975). Second,such approaches permit the development of a social psychological perspective on the problem of social order and control, although this may not have been the original intention or aspiration of Garfinkel (cf. however, Mehan & Wood, 1975). The broad theoretical framework offered in the first chapter and the specific theme of the book, namely the processes and social practices through which individuals avoid, prevent, negotiate and normalize fractured social interaction, presents us with the possibility of providing a social psychological analysis of the issues of social order and social control.

The affinity of the particular topic of the social practices surrounding potentially or actually fractured social interaction to the more general problem of conduct and culture, and thus to social order, has been noted by others (e.g. Blumstein, 1974; Hewitt & Hall, 1973; Stokes & Hewitt, 1976; *inter alia*). Referring collectively to such social practices as those addressed in the present volume, Stokes and Hewitt (1976) suggest the term "aligning actions". They also employ this term explicitly in a second context, aside from their immediate reference to the aligning of fractured social interaction. This second usage allows them to regard such actions as playing "...a major part in sustaining a relationship between *culture* and *conduct*, in maintaining an alignment between the two in the face of actions that depart from cultural expectations or definitions of what is situationally appropriate" (Stokes & Hewitt, 1976, p.838, emphasis in original). Criticising symbolic interactionist approaches for their failure to provide an adequate account of culture (cf. also Giddens, 1979,p.254ff) these authors offer a possible and plausible conceptualization of the interface between culture and conduct. Alignment in its second usage by these authors refers to situations where there exists a perceived discrepancy between what is socially and normatively expected and what has actually taken place.In this context they use the term culture to refer to "...objects, actions and meanings that are 'ideal' in one of several senses: they are felt to be normatively appropriate or required, typical and/or probable with respect to the people and situations involved, technically correct in the sense that people know how to act toward certain objects, and recognizable in that they can be designated linguistically in terms that those who 'have' a given culture can understand..." (Stokes & Hewitt, 1976, p.843). It is in this sense that an anticipation or recognition of fractured social interaction is an anticipation or recognition of a 'misalignment' between culture and conduct. The social practices that people engage in, in attempts to avoid or repair such situations, are practices which are employed in reinstating culture, and thus in imposing social order.

The interface between culture and conduct, and between social order and orderly behaviour is founded upon the pervasive feature of human action that we have elaborated upon in Chapter 1: reflexivity. This refers to the continuous monitoring of action with regard to its accountability, not only in terms of one's own conduct but also that of others. The criteria guiding the evaluation of action are to be found in the general social expectations, norms, conventions, and guidelines which are deemed appropriate within the definitions of given situations. Obviously, analytic examinations of strictures upon behaviour and their violation, such as that presented here, are historically bound in particular respects, since the conventions governing appropriate or competent conduct in cultures are subject to change over time. For example, the outstanding work of Norbert Elias

(1977) on the evolution of manners and civilization from the middle ages onwards demonstrates the dramatic changes that social conventions pertaining to such behaviours as eating, drinking, dressing, sex and forms of address have undergone in European society. This clearly indicates that the particular types of customs prevailing in a given society or its subcultures are subject to historical change. Indeed, Gergen's (1973) argument concerning the scientific status of social psychological knowledge leads one to conclude that psychological analyses of accounting and accountability are generally confined to particular social contexts and that the accounting practices which are identified as prevailing in such situations will be nothing but historical documentations within broader temporal conceptions of science. It is therefore apparent that an attempt to outline the precise *criteria* guiding judgments of action competence or incompetence can only be valid for a temporal or cultural location. Furthermore, the repertoire of social practices referred to in the preceding chapters as facework, motive talk, responsibility ascription, etc., may alter as a function of time. New social practices will be added, some old ones will become obselete, still others will be modified and so on. *However, the pervasive aspect of the accountability of social conduct as a general feature of social existence is that it is an essential and undismissable desideratum for orderly social interaction at any level.* As we have argued in the preceding section, accountability of conduct is a necessary condition for the ontological foundation of social order. Without the accountability of social conduct, it is impossible to conceive of a society resembling an organized interlocking of individual actions, or for that matter maintaining sociality and intersubjectivity. However, this is not to say that individuals are held accountable for *each and every* aspect of their social conduct. Indeed, such a state of affairs would hamper rather than enable orderly social interaction, a point made eloquently by the Victorian novelist and essayist William Makepeace Thackeray in his essay 'On Being Found Out':

> Just picture to yourself everybody who does wrong being found out, and punished accordingly. Fancy all the boys in all the schools being whipped; and then the assistants, and then the headmaster....Fancy the provost-marshal being tied up, having previously superintended the correction of the whole army...After the clergymen has cried his peccavi, suppose we hoist up a bishop, and give him a couple of dozen:(I see my Lord Bishop of Double-Gloucester sitting in a very uneasy posture on

his right reverend bench). After we have cast off the bishop, what are we to say to the Minister who has appointed him?...The butchery is too horrible. The hand drops powerless, appalled at the quantity of birch it must cut and brandish. I am glad we are not all found out.

Accountability of social conduct, then, cannot be total. Furthermore, just as the degree to which persons are held accountable for their conduct may vary within social groups and within cultures, so it may vary between them. Nevertheless, all groups and cultures reflect the fact that individuals are held accountable for their conduct, in so far as that conduct is expected to be consistent with local or cultural norms and/or internally consistent. Given a plurality of social groupings, it follows that different codes of conduct will obtain across those groupings. What is central to our present considerations is that accountability of conduct is an essential feature of human life, however diversified group allegiances and memberships may be, and is a *general feature of social coexistence* in that it cuts across the boundaries of group memberships. In our view, this means that the social psychological processes which are responsible for the maintenance of established forms of culture are *transhistorical* and *transcultural*.

Indeed, an example illustrating the present type of social psychological approach to the question of social order is provided in the classic work by Evans-Pritchard (1940) on the Nuer. Characteristic of this society is the following: "The ordered anarchy in which they live accords well with their character, for it is impossible to live among Nuer and conceive of rulers ruling over them. The Nuer is a product of hard and egalitarian upbringing, is deeply democratic, and is easily roused to violence. His turbulent spirit finds any restraint irksome and no man recognizes a superior...That every Nuer considers himself as good as his neighbour is evident in their every movement"(Evans-Pritchard, 1940,pp.181-182). In this society, where there is no political system manifest in the institutionalized forms familiar to Western societies, social order is maintained "within the system of thought" as Douglas (1980) puts it. '(The Nuer's) commitment to a theory of sin and of its consequences is the ontological anchorage for the control mechanism of Nuer political life...The Nuer theory of sin is the touchstone of reality to which all their elaborate legal fictions relate" (Douglas, 1980,p.71). In fact, in Douglas' (1980) assessment of this work the possibility of social order is obtained by the fact that

"The Nuer hold others totally accountable; they must be prepared to die and prepared to kill. They expect themselves to be held equally accountable"(p.71). Because the reality of Nuer society presents an unusual and totally absorbing perspective on social control that contrasts sharply with forms of thought fostered and developed in Western societies since Hobbes, if not earlier, it provides a good illustration of our argument. Social order and social control rest largely on the accountability of conduct, and irrespective of the particular socio-historical or cross-cultural conventions and rules for behaviour, accountability of conduct remains a transhistorical and transcultural feature of human sociality.

5.3.3. THE PLACE OF ACCOUNTABILITY IN EVERYDAY LIFE

From the general argument advanced so far one can derive more specific and detailed implications for order and control in everyday life and how they are obtained. The order and regularity found in the social life of any community are based upon some understanding and consensual agreement about how the activities of everyday life are to be coordinated and arranged. Thus, it is impossible to conceive of any social coexistence without mutually shared rules and conventions which provide the guidelines that define conduct as acceptable or unacceptable, comprehensible or incomprehensible. These guidelines obviously need not be explicitly available to the members of the community. Nevertheless, they provide the foundations of an orderly social life, enabling the predictability and sensibility of human action as well as establishing the possibility of an 'objectively shared social reality', that is a reality shared by everyone in the community. "In the absence of such shared assumptions, enabling A to predict how B should behave in familiar circumstances and how A's own actions ought to be received, social life could scarcely exist" (Roberts, 1979, p.31). Such guidelines also provide cultural criteria for when and how members who deviate from these guidelines are to be held answerable and accountable for their conduct. They also provide recipes for interpreting and dealing with such deviations or transgressions, as we have seen in the previous three chapters. Thus, the rules and conventions of human communities, themselves human artifacts, are essential to the maintenance of order and continuity in everyday life and are universal to the human species (Roberts, 1979) as long as they live in communities, which is in itself an inevitable condition of human existence. Thus, the ontological foundation of accountability, and therefore social order and control, are to be found in the malleability of human nature, and the dependence of humans on conspecifics for survival, which together result in an elaborate 'social technology',in the form of rules and conventions that regulate human coexistence and endow human communities with an *historically determinate quality* which is of their own making.

Through the creation of historically determinate worlds, and thus the creation of continuity and regularity for interpersonal relationships, the human species is able to reach beyond the undulate nature of subjective realities to an objectivated reality shared by everybody, and thereby provide the possibility of social coexistence. The social technologies that have been developed by humans to regulate interpersonal and intergroup relations from the simple to the complex forms of social existence can be regarded as intricate forms of social 'engineering'.However, there is at least one aspect of such social engineering which distinguishes it from the rest of what is generally understood to be engineering. This is the fact that rules and conventions governing social conduct have not been planned and applied deliberately, but rather have evolved as a consequence of the needs to coordinate social action, defuse disputes and conflict, and regulate social interaction. The deliberate application of design and planning to the regulation of human relationships is a relatively novel and largely unsuccessful enterprise and as such it occupies the position of poor relation to the engineering of mechanical systems. The regulative procedures which we have evolved for our everyday lives have not kept pace with our technological advancement, in that the possibilities developed through innovations in technology have not been complemented by an increase in the moral and cultural advancement of society in general. Mostly, such social engineering as there is has emerged out of need rather than a conscious demand for the peaceful and creative regulation of our social coexistence in order to prevent further conflict.

Whatever the limitations imposed by this mismatch between our social 'engineering'. However, there is at least one aspect of such social advancement, an inevitable condition for any human community is the need to develop mutually shared conventions and rules in order to conduct an orderly and well coordinated social coexistence. The presence of such regulative social guidelines also means that all societies must have accounting practices, which enable people to keep a check on each other's conduct. The use of rules, conventions and accountability can therefore be seen as social performances by members of the societies in question.

Accounting practices will obviously take on different forms in different cultures, as we acknowledged earlier. However, "[d]espite the wide range of organizational forms which may be found in small-scale societies, the mechanism for maintaining continuity and handling disputes tend almost universally to be directly embedded in everyday life, unsupported by a differentiated legal system" (Roberts, 1979, p.27). Indeed, even the presence of legal institutions does not guarantee order and continuity in everyday life. If social control and order were only enforced by third parties then they would not be maintained for long.

5.4. Conclusions: the epistemological status of accountability of conduct

Having elaborated upon the ontological foundations of accountability of conduct in relation to human reflexivity and having derived more specific arguments about the transcultural and transhistorical aspects of accountability as a limiting factor on human forms of existence and coexistence, we now return to our counterargument to Gergen's contention that social psychological knowledge is historically bound.

The purpose here is to develop a general case which, in our view, places the impermanence argument (cf. also Gergen 1978, 1980) in a broader but integrative perspective. As we have seen, some attempts to resolve this problem (e.g. Triandis, 1978) seek to identify formulations of social behaviour which have generality beyond cultural and historical confines. Other attempts have tried to achieve the same objective by employing analytic distinctions (e.g. content - process distinctions: Manis, 1975; Semin & Manstead, 1979) but these contain the same shortcomings, chiefly because these formulations still subscribe to a literal interpretation of empirical methodology as bound by experimentation and measurement, and are therefore ethno- and chronocentric. However useful these types of empirical approaches may be, they do not enable comparability of constructs as long as they are wedded to observational constructs. This problem is also one of the major arguments of Gergen's more recent (1980, pp.239-246) thesis.

Indeed, the general problem of the contextual definitions of constructs or concepts is not a new one, for in different guises it has
occupied cognitive psychologists (e.g., Bransford & Franks, 1974;
Franks, 1974) linguists (Labov, 1973), philosophers (Bar-Hillel,
1954; Pierce, 1933; Russell, 1940), ethnomethodologists (e.g. Garfinkel & Sachs, 1970), cognitive sociologists (e.g. Douglas, 1971), and
philsophers of science (e.g. Hanson, 1958; Hooker, 1973; Keat &
Urry, 1975) . Incorporating what is regarded as the debate on the
theory neutrality of observations (cf. Keat & Urry, 1975) into social
psychological investigations has nevertheless provided the impetus
for the contention that the claims of positivistic approaches in social
psychology to provide universally valid knowledge should be rejected,
and that such approaches should instead be regarded as yielding
'historical documentations' (cf. Gergen, 1978, 1980). The argument is
then extended to a central proposition which is that knowledge in
social psychology and society stand in a dialectical relationship. The
cultural relativism argument is thereby obtained (e.g. Buss, 1975,
1979; Gergen, 1978, 1980). In fact, this thesis has been present within
social psychology for a long time, for it constitutes a fundamental
tenet of Meadian social psychology. Peter Berger (1966) draws
attention to this in a much neglected article. Here he outlines what he
terms a "sociology of psychology" (p.110), a concept which was later
to be rediscovered as a new idea in psychology (e.g. Buss, 1975). As
Berger describes it, "...The sociology of knowledge has an interest not
only in various theories *about* psychological phenomena (what one
may call a sociology of psychology) but in these phenomena
themselves (what one may then, perhaps impertinently, call a
sociological psychology)" (Berger, 1966, p.110, emphasis in the
original). Berger suggests that since any particular psychological
reality is basically attached to an identity which is socially defined, it
therefore follows that such psychological realities must be located in a
socially constructed world. This type of perspective has far-reaching
consequences for the status of psychological theories. Every socially
constructed world contains psychological models. Such models
change as a function of the historical and cultural trends of the
respective societies. Thus, models which involve witchcraft or
demonology are rejected in present-day society, whereas a psychoanalytic model is not. In short, there is a dialectical relationship
between social constructions of the world and psychological realities.
As Berger argues:

Just as the individual can verify his socially assigned identity by introspection, so the psychological theoretician can verify his model by 'empirical research'. If the model corresponds to the psychological reality as socially defined and produced, it will quite naturally be verified by empirical investigation of this reality. This is not quite the same as saying that psychology is self-verifying. It rather says that the data discovered by a particular psychology belong to the same socially constructed world that has also produced that psychology.

Once more, the relationship between psychological reality and psychological model is a dialectic one. The psychological reality produces the psychological model, insofar as the model is an empirically verifiable representation of the reality. Once formed, however, the psychological model can act back upon the psychological reality. The model has *realizing* potency, that is, it can create psychological reality as a 'self-fulfilling prophecy'. In a society in which demonology is socially established, cases of demon possession will empirically multiply. A society in which psychoanalysis is institutionalized as 'science' will become populated by people who, in fact, evince the processes that have been theoretically attributed to them"(Berger, 1966, p.114).

This incisive analysis provided by Berger has found echoes in some of the more reflective examples of recent critical appraisal of social psychology (e.g. Buss, 1975, 1979; Gergen, 1978, 1980). The emergence of this view has inevitably been shaped by the historical circumstances and the 'state of the art' of social psychology in the late 1960s, and early 1970s. This rather more reflective stance is therefore itself an historical product, probably arising from one particular type of reflection that emerged from the discipline's manifest signs of anxiety with respect to its progress as these were articulated in numerous papers on the so-called crisis in social psychology (cf. Armistead, 1974; Elms, 1975; Harré & Secord, 1972; Israel & Tajfel, 1972; McGuire, 1973; Ring, 1967; *inter alia*). A number of theories were undergoing the fate that Meehl (1978) notes: "Most of them suffer the fate that General McArthur ascribed to old generals. They never die, they just slowly fade away" (p. 807). A number of experimental phenomena were discovered to be unstable and unreplicable, and the 'social psychology of the psychological experiment' encouraged the process of uncomfortable introspection. These within-paradigmatic (cf. Gadlin & Ingle, 1975) criticisms were undoubtedly important in preparing the ground for the possibility of a 'here today, gone tomorrow' argument, because the discipline of social psychology had by then accumulated sufficient history to provide a vantage point from which a new dogma could be launched. In this sense it is no coincidence that the relativist critique is located historically in the 1970s. Indeed, this contention is further supported by the fact that a number of papers published in the 1930s (e.g. Bentley, 1929, 1937; Rosenzweig, 1933) addressing the same issues which were to become topical in the debate on the 'social psychology of the psychological experiment' passed unnoticed, both by their contemporaries and by later generations. That these critiques had no impact on contemporary social psychology is due, in our view, to the fact that the social psychology of the 1930s had not accumulated a sufficient body of data. By contrast, the social psychology of the 1970s had collated a large body of data which enabled and encouraged the adoption a 'reflective stance' towards the procedural paradigms that had been employed in psychology in general and in social psychology in particular.It is rather remarkable that an outstanding contribution such as Berger's (1966) paper should also have passed unnoticed, because it articulates most eloquently the arguments that have recently been developed by theorists such as Buss (1975).* The invisibility of earlier critiques of the conventional paradigm in social psychology and statements concerning the dialectic between psychology and society become understandable if one regards the debate initiated by Gergen (1973, 1976, 1978, 1980) as itself being an historical product. It has been possible to engage in this debate in the light of the 'accumulated wisdom' of approximately eighty years of social psychology, and mainly from a particular cultural viewpoint, namely North American, although the role of European thinkers in this contribution has been substantial. What we wish to argue here is that it has only been possible to develop the relativist critique for a set of reasons which are themselves historically located and conditioned. The notion that social psychological knowledge is historically and culturally relative is just *one* step that can be taken in the *process of detached evaluation of what is possible and not possible in appraising human social behaviour*, and it is in this light that it should be seen. The development of this notion is still a reflection of concerns within the confines of one culture, leading to a cultural relativism 'metaphor'

---

* The difference between Berger's (1966) paper and the recent debate in social psychology is mainly one of the tone that is adopted towards social psychology as a discipline. It must be noted, however, that Berger was exclusively concerned with Meadian social psychology in writing his paper and was therefore more positive in his appraisal of the contributions that social psychology had made, whereas the recent debate focuses on experimental social psychology.

or myth, with its attendant logical problems. However valuable its contribution to social psychology has been, Gergen's thesis that social psychological knowledge is historically bound remains, in our view, a restricted approach to the problem, because it takes only one step out of several possible steps of detachment. This, in turn, is because it has remained primarily an introspectively orientated development within social psychology. If one were to define the boundaries of debate in other than intradisciplinary terms and therefore adopted a more open view of the contributions made by other disciplinary activities to the understanding of human behaviour in general, and social behaviour in particular, then other steps of detachment would become possible.For whatever reasons, this willingness to consider perspectives developed outside the discipline has not been especially popular in social psychological thinking and yet the scope that such perspectives offer is considerable. Consider, for example, additional steps to the detachment that has been brought about by the cultural and historical boundedness argument such as the introduction of a cross-cultural perspective, the addition of a social-anthropological perspective, a socio-history of cultures perspective, a biological perspective, an ethnographic perspective. These additional perspectives enable the re-evaluation of knowledge beyond that afforded by the historical distancing produced within the relatively sheltered confines of social psychology. They also provide more detailed information concerning what is involved in the forms of expression that human existence can take.

A cross-cultural perspective on cognitive psychology has for example, resulted in Rosch's seminal work on colour coding (Rosch, 1975, 1977). She suggests that: "In so far as psychology is to be a science whose statements are of some interest and beauty, it must attempt to formulate principles of the mental and behavioural functions of humans which are general and universal. That is not to say that theory must focus on the ways in which humans are the same; rather, the universality of theory comes from its ability to encompass and predict differences as well as universals in human thought and behaviour... Such an ideal can be better approached, I believe, if cross-cultural investigations and general experimental psychology became more closely integrated. Without the guidance of general psychological theory, cross-cultural psychology can only continue to amass miscellaneous facts, or pursue its own autonomously developed research traditions — such as the inherently inconclusive comparison of the performance of Western and traditional peoples on standard psychometric measures. Equally strong is the need for experimental psychology to take into account cross-cultural diversity. Laboratory studies can also evolve into autonomous research traditions in which specialized and atypical sets of stimuli become the exclusive domain of investigation and the problem-solving strategies of particular subject populations are taken for general psychological laws" (Rosch, 1977, p.3)

One disturbing fact that confronts culturally relativist views which propagate "theoretical audacity" in social psychology (cf. Gergen, 1980) is that despite the existence of considerable variation in cultural forms of human social behaviour, this variation is not completely random. However, the introverted quality of unidisciplinary approaches to the study of human behaviour can blind us to this fact. By contrast, making use of the insights afforded by other disciplinary approaches to similar problems enables one to appreciate such problems in better perspective. The adoption of such a "multiple-distancing" allows one to distinguish between those aspects of social existence which are integral and those concomitant forms of social relationships and behaviours which vary across cultures.

In applying a multiple distancing approach to the issue of accountability (Section 5.3, above), it was apparent that such an approach is concerned with the examination of 'fundamental limiting notions'. Let us now elaborate on what is meant by our use of the term fundamental limiting notions. These notions are revealed in the expressions that human knowledge can and does take as a consequence of relatively invariant ecological, existential, material and biological conditions. They can be founded on the ontological conditions of human coexistence, as was argued in connection with accountability, but also on other limiting notions such as birth, death, motherhood, fatherhood, etc. One feature of such fundamental limiting notions is that their cultural manifestations may be variable, as is maintained by the historico-cultural relativist point of view. Such notions do not predetermine a particular expression of social behaviours and knowledge across cultural and historical boundaries. In that sense the present approach is not predictive or deterministic. Let us illustrate the relationship between fundamental limiting notions and cultural expressions by means of an example other than accountability, namely procreation. It may appear at first that human knowledge concerning procreation is universal, constrained as it is by the invariant relationship between procreation and sex. In certain societies, however, such as some Australian aboriginies (Roth, 1903), and Trobriand islanders (cf. Malinowski, 1913, 1932), "...knowledge of impregnation, of the man's share in creating a new life in the mother's womb is a fact of which the natives have not even the slightest glimpse" (Malinowski, 1913). Indeed, Bakan argues in a somewhat different context that "...the Bible is a document which both expresses and depicts the crisis in paternalization. The crisis is both historical and ontogenic. As historical, it corresponds to a period in history when the role of the male in conception was discovered and, more importantly, *socially* assimilated" (Bakan, 1974, p.206). Regardless of the anthropological controversy surrounding the issue of 'virgin birth' (cf. *Man*, 1969-1976) the important point is that the sex-procreation relationship is a fundamental limiting notion. Even if the concept of fatherhood is not available in a particular culture, procreation has to be socially reckoned with and structures not only the knowledge but also the social relationships between members of the community. Furthermore, the assimilation into society of the knowledge that a male is necessarily involved in the act of procreation has limiting implications for the types of relationships that can exist between members of that society. However, much recent pharmaceutical and surgical developments have enabled humans to circumvent biological restrictions, and have thereby enabled the elaboration of different forms of social relationships between females, males and their offspring, the fundamental limiting notion of the sex-procreation relationship remains a central feature of social relationships, in that it imposes structure and does not allow a random permutation of relationships, myths and metaphors. In other words, however much the sex-procreation relationship may be be modified by knowledge or technology, it is still the source of a set of stipulations, which have their expression in the creation of human social institutions. This will continue to be the case as long as human life forms exist. It is in this sense that the sex-procreation relationship is a fundamentally limiting notion. It has to be socially assimilated and reckoned with, irrespective of time and location, and thereby imposes structure on human social existence. One further aspect of considerable importance should be noted. This concerns the types of limitations entailed by such notions. They impose constraints irrespective of whether or not they are culturally available. Thus, if the sex-procreation concept or the accountability notion are not available as objectified knowledge in a

culture they nevertheless impose structure on human coexistence .
Their cultural availability may modify the conditions and
limitations that are imposed, but these conditions and limitations
cannot be escaped or negated completely. This means that these
limiting notions still impose structure.

This is true not only of the biological conditions of human existence
but also of material and ecological conditions. For example, human
time conceptions will and do vary from society to society, and
from one era to another. However, an examination of the various time
conceptions that humans have evolved suggests that: "In the matter of
the indication and reckoning of time...we have not to do with a number
of conceptions which may be supposed to be as numerous and as
various as we please. At the basis lies an accurately determined and
limited and indeed small number of phenomena, which are the same
for all peoples all over the globe, and can be combined only in a certain
quite small number of ways" (Nilsson, 1920, p.2). The interpretations
placed upon these phenomena and the relative social significances that
are attached to them may and do vary from culture to culture, but the
invariant existence of these phenomena constitutes a fundamental
limiting notion.

We are not concerned here to establish a fully developed framework
for analysing the variant and invariant features of human social
existence and behaviour. Rather, we are concerned simply to make
two propositions. The first is that there are a number of ways in which
one can detach knowledge of human social behaviour from its
historical and cultural contexts. One of these ways is by establishing
the relativity of this knowledge as it develops within a given
community. This type of detachment has been fostered and developed
in recent critical treatments of social psychology, beginning with
Gergen's (1973) argument. However, this is just *one* way of distancing
oneself from knowledge of social behaviour. The present form of the
relativism argument (Gergen, 1978, 1980) recommends the establishment of a 'generative social psychology', in which human social
action is regarded as infinitely malleable. Such a recommendation
contains within it a logical contradiction for, as we have argued it
represents a position of 'absolute relativism'. Another possibility, the
one suggested here, is to engage in alternative steps of detachment
from the social and historical constraints on knowledge of human
social behaviour. This can be achieved by construing the problems
surrounding human social behaviour from a variety of perspectives

thereby enabling the identification of fundamental limiting notions. This leads us to the second proposition. Human life forms and social behaviours are not random; they are bound by a structure. The present argument is that the examination of human forms of existence must attend to the structural impositions that are contained in the physical, biological and psychological environment. If these are not ascertained then there is no limit to the generation of alternative myths in the pursuit of forms of social existence and behaviour, its reasons and its artifacts. This basically means that without an understanding of fundamental limiting conditions it is impossible to appreciate the limits to human social coexistence, the modifications and varieties that their expressions can take, and also whether or not particular theories about social behaviour can claim to have transhistorical and trans-cultural validity.

References

Allen, V. A. Situational factors in conformity. In L. Berkowitz (Ed.), *Advances in Experimental Social Psychology*, Vol. 2. New York: Academic Press, 1965.

Antaki, C. *The Psychology of Ordinary Explanations of Social Behaviour*. London: Academic Press, 1981.

Apsler, R. Effects of embarrassment on behaviour towards others. *Journal of Personality and Social Psychology*, 1975, **32**, 145-153.

Archibald, W. P. & Cohen, R. L. Self-presentation, embarrassment and facework as a function of self-evaluation, conditions of self-presentation and feedback from others. *Journal of Personality and Social Psychology*, 1971, **20**, 287-297.

Arkkelin, D., Oakley, T. & Mynatt, C. Effects of controllable versus uncontrollable factors on responsibility attributions: A single-subject approach. *Journal of Personality and Social Psychology*, 1979, **37**, 110-115.

Armistead, N. *Reconstructing Social Psychology*. Harmondsworth: Penguin, 1974.

Asch, S. Studies of independence and conformity: A minority of one against a unanimous majority. *Psychological Monographs*, 1956, **70**, (Whole No. 416).

Austin, J. L. A plea for excuses. In J. D. Urmson & G. Warnock (Eds.), *Philosophical Papers*. Oxford: Clarendon Press, 1961.

Ausubel, D. P. Relationships between shame and guilt in the socializing process. *Psychological Review*, 1955, **62**, 378-390.

Badcock, C. R. *The Psychoanalysis of Culture*. Oxford: Basil Blackwell, 1981.

Bakan, D. Paternity in the Judeo-Christian tradition. In A. W. Eister (Ed.), *Changing Perspectives in the Scientific Study of Religion*. New York: Wiley, 1974.

Bar-Hillel, Y. Indexical expressions. *Mind*, 1954, **63**, 359-374.

Bartlett, F. C. *Remembering*. London: Cambridge University Press, 1932.

Batchelor, J. *The Ainu of Japan*. London: The Religious Tract Society, 1892.

Bentley, M. 'Observer' and 'subject'. *American Journal of Psychology*, 1929, **41**, 682-683.

Bentley, M. The nature and uses of experiment in psychology. *American Journal of Psychology*, 1937, **50**, 452-469.

Berger, P. Identity as a problem in the sociology of knowledge. *Archives Européennes de Sociologie*, 1966, **7**, 105-115.

Berger, P. & Luckmann, T. *The Social Construction of Reality*. London: Allen Lane, 1966.

Black, M. *Models and Metaphors*. (Studies in language and philosophy). Ithaca: Cornell University Press, 1962.

Black, M. *The Labyrinth of Language*. London: Pall Mall, 1968.

Blum, A. & Mchugh, P. The social ascription of motives. *American Sociological Review*, 1971, **36**, 98-109.

Blumer, H. Society as symbolic interaction. In A. M. Rose (Ed.), *Human Behaviour and Social Processes*. Chicago: Houghton Mifflin Co., 1962.

Blumer, H. Sociological implications of the thought of George Herbert Mead. *The American Journal of Sociology*, 1966, **71**, 535-544.

Blumer, H. Action vs. interaction. *Society*, 1972, **9**, 50-53.

Blumstein, P. W. The honouring of accounts. *American Sociological Review*, 1974, **39**, 551-566.

Bocock, R. *Freud and Modern Society*. Southampton: Thomas Nelson and Sons Ltd., 1976.

Bower, G. H., Black, J. B. & Turner, T. J. Scripts in memory for text. *Cognitive Psychology*, 1979, **11**, 177-220.

Bransford, J. D. & Franks, J. J. Toward a framework for understanding learning. In W. B. Weimer & D. S. Palermo (Eds.), *Cognition and the Symbolic Processes*. Hillsdale, N. J.: Erlbaum, 1974.

Brown, B. R. The effects of need to maintain face on interpersonal bargaining. *Journal of Experimental Social Psychology*, 1968, **4**, 107-122.

Brown, B. R. Face-saving following experimentally induced embarrassment. *Journal of Experimental Social Psychology*, 1970, **6**, 255-271.

Brown, B. R. & Garland, H. The effects of incompetency, audience acquaintanceship, and anticipated evaluative feedback on face-saving behaviour. *Journal of Experimental Social Psychology*, 1971, **7**, 490-502.

Brown, N. O. *Life Against Death*. London: Routledge & Kegan Paul, 1959.

Burger, J. M. Motivational biases in the attribution of responsibility for an accident: A meta-analysis of the defensive-attribution hypothesis. *Psychological Bulletin*, 1981, **90**, 496-512.

Buytendijk, F. J. J. The phenomenological approach to the problem of feelings and emotions. In M. I. Reymert (Ed.), *Feelings and Emotions*. New York: McGraw Hill, 1950.

Buytendijk, F. J. J. *Mensch und Tier*. Hamburg: Rohwolt, 1958.

Buss, A. R. The emerging field of the sociology of knowledge. *American Psychologist*, 1975, **30**, 988-1002.

Buss, A. R. Causes and reasons in attribution theory: A conceptual critique. *Journal of Personality and Social Psychology*, 1978, **36**, 1311-1321.

Buss, A. R. (Ed.), *Psychology in Social Context*. New York: Irvington Publishers, Inc., 1979.

Cantor, N. & Mischel, W. Prototypes in person perception. In L. Berkowitz (Ed.), *Advances in Experimental Social Psychology*, Vol. 12. New York: Academic Press, 1979.

Chaikin, A. & Darley, J. Victim or perpetrator: Defensive attribution of responsibility and the need for order and justice. *Journal of Personality and Social Psychology*, 1973, **25**, 268-275.

Cheal, D. Rule governed behaviour. *Philosophy of the Social Sciences*, 1980, **10**, 39-49.

Crook, J. H. *The Evolution of Human Consciousness*. Oxford: Clarendon Press, 1980.

Darby, B. W. & Schlenker, B. R. Children's reactions to apologies, *Journal of Personality and Social Psychology*, 1982, **43**, 742-753.

Darwin, C. *The Expression of the Emotions in Man and Animals*. London: Murray, 1872.

Deutsch, M. & Krauss, R. The effects of threat on interpersonal bargaining. *Journal of Abnormal and Social Psychology*, 1960, **61**, 181-189.

Dewey, J. *Human Nature and Conduct*. New York: Holt, 1922.

Douglas, J. *Understanding Everyday Life*. London: Routledge & Kegan Paul, 1971.

Douglas, M. *Evans-Pritchard*. London: Fontana, 1980.

Durkheim, E. *The Rules of Sociological Method*. Glencoe, Ill.: Free Press, 1958 (Originally published 1895).

Elias, N. *Ueber den Prozess der Zivilisation*. Vols. 1 & 2. Frankfurt a. M.: Suhrkamp, 1977.

Elms, A. C. The crisis of confidence in social psychology. *American Psychologist*, 1975, **30**, 967-976.

Emerson, J. Behaviour in private places: Sustaining definitions of reality in gynecological examinations. In H.P. Dreitzel (Ed.), *Recent Sociology*, No. 2. New York: Macmillan, 1970.

Emler, N. P. & Hogan, R. Developing attitudes to law and justice: An integrative review. In S. Brehm, S. M. Kassin & F. X. Gibbons (Eds.), *Developmental Social Psychology*. New York: Oxford University Press, 1981.

Evans-Pritchard, E. E. *Witchcraft, Oracles and Magic Among the Azande*. Oxford: Clarendon Press, 1937.

Evans-Pritchard, E. E. *The Nuer: A Description of the Modes of Livelihood and Practical Institutions of the Nilatic People*. Oxford: Clarendon Press, 1940.

Fauconnet, P. *La Responsibilité*. (2nd. Ed.) Paris: Alcan, 1928.

Feinberg, J. Action and responsibility. In A. R. White (Ed.), *The Philosophy of Action*. Oxford: Oxford University Press, 1969.

Felson, R. B. & Ribner, S. A. An attributional approach to accounts and sanctions for criminal violence. *Social Psychological Quarterly*, 1981, **44**, 137-142.

Feyerabend, P. K. Explanation, reduction and empiricism. In H. Feigl & G. Maxwell (Eds.), *Minnesota Studies in the Philosophy of Science*. Minneapolis: University of Minnesota Press, 1962.

Feyerabend, P. K. *Against Method*. London: NLB, 1972.

Fincham, F. D. & Jaspars, J. M. Attribution of responsibility to self and other in children and adults. *Journal of Personality and Social Psychology*, 1979, **37**, 1589-1602.

Fincham, F. D. & Jaspars, J. M. Attribution of responsibility: From man-the-scientist to man-as-lawyer. In L. Berkowitz (Ed.), *Advances in Experimental Social Psychology*, Vol. 13. New York: Academic Press, 1980.

Fishbein, M. & Ajzen, I. Attribution of responsibility: A theoretical note. *Journal of Experimental Social Psychology*, 1973, **9**, 148-153.

Fortes, M. Custom and science in anthropological perspective. *International Review of Psychoanalysis*, 1977, **4**, 127-154.

Franks, J. J. Toward understanding understanding. In W. B. Weimer & D. S. Palermo (Eds.), *Cognition and the Symbolic Processes*. Hillsdale, N. J.: Erlbaum, 1974.

Freud, S. *Das Unbehagen in der Kultur*. Wien: Internationaler Psychoanalytischer Verlag, 1930.

Freud, S. *Fragen der Gesellschaft, Ursprunge der Religion*. Siegmund Freud Sonderausgabe, Band IX. Frankfurt a. M.: Fischer, 1974.

Fromm, E. & Xiram, R. *The Nature of Man*. New York: Macmillan, 1968.

Gadlin, H. & Ingle, G. Through the one-way mirror: The limits to experimental self-reflection. *American Psychologist*, 1975, **30**, 1003-1009.

Garfinkel, H. *Studies in Ethnomethodology*. Englewood-Cliffs, N. J.: Prentice-Hall, 1967.

Garfinkel, H. The origins of the term ethnomethodology. In R. Turner (Ed.), *Ethnomethodology*. Harmondsworth: Penguin, 1974.

Garfinkel, H. & Sacks, H. The formal properties of practical actions. In J. C. McKinney & E. A. Tiryakian (Eds.), *Theoretical Sociology*. New York: Appleton-Century-Crofts, 1970.

Garland, H. & Brown, B. R. Face-saving as affected by subjects' sex, audience's sex and audience expertise. *Sociometry*, 1972, **35**, 280-289.

Gasking, D. Mathematics and the world. In A. Flew (Ed.), *Logic and Language*. Garden City, N. Y.: Doubleday & Co., 1955.

Gauld, A. & Shotter, J. *Human Action and its Psychological Investigation*. London: Routledge & Kegan Paul, 1977.

Gehlen, A. Die Entwicklung der Anthropologie von der Philosophie zur Erfahrungswissenschaft. *Hessische Hochschulen fuer Staatswissenschaftliche Fortbildung*, Vol. 17. Bad Homburg, 1957 (Revised version: Zur Geschichte der Anthropologie. In A. Gehlen, *Anthropologische Forschung*. Hamburg: Rohwolt, 1961).

Gergen, K. J. Social psychology as history. *Journal of Personality and Social Psychology*, 1973, **26**, 309-320.

Gergen, K. J. Social psychology, science and history. *Personality and Social Psychology Bulletin*, 1976, **2**, 373-383.

Gergen, K. J. Toward generative theory. *Journal of Personality and Social Psychology*, 1978, **36**, 1344-1360.

Gergen, K. J. Toward intellectual audacity in social psychology. In R. Gilmour & S. Duck (Eds.), *The Development of Social Psychology*. London: Academic Press, 1980.

Giddens, A. *Positivism and Sociology*. London: Heinemann, 1974.

Giddens, A. *New Rules of Sociological Method*. London: Hutchinson, 1976.

Giddens, A. *Central Problems in Social Theory*. London: Macmillan, 1979.

Goffman, E. On face-work: An analysis of ritual elements in social interaction. *Psychiatry: Journal for the Study of Interpersonal Processes*, 1955, **18**, 213-231.

Goffman, E. Embarrassment and social organization. *American Journal of Sociology*, 1956, **62**, 264-274.

Goffman, E. *The Presentation of Self In Everyday Life*. New York: Doubleday, 1959.

Goffman, E. *Encounters*. Indianapolis, Ind.: Bobbs-Merrill, 1961.

Goffman, E. *Relations in Public: Micro-Studies of the Public Order*. Harmondsworth: Penguin, 1971.

Gross, E. & Stone, G. P. Embarrassment and the analysis of role requirements. *American Journal of Sociology*, 1964, **70**, 1-15.

Gurwitsch, A. The common-sense world as social reality. *Social Research*, 1962, **29**, 50-72.

Hamilton V. L. Who is responsible? Toward a *social* psychology of responsibility attribution. *Social Psychology*, 1978, **41**, 316-328.

Hanson, N. R. *Patterns of Discovery*. London: Cambridge Unversity Press, 1958.

Harré, R. *The Principles of Scientific Thinking*. London: Macmillan, 1970.

Harré, R. Blueprint for a new science. In N. Armistead (Ed.), *Reconstructing Social Psychology*. Harmondsworth: Penguin, 1974.

Harré, R. The ethogenic approach: Theory and practice. In L. Berkowitz (Ed.), *Advances in Experimental Social Psychology*, Vol. 10. New York: Academic

Press, 1977.

Harré, R. & Secord, P. *The Explanation of Social Behaviour*. Oxford: Basil Blackwell, 1972.

Harris, B. Developmental differences in the attribution of responsibility. *Developmental Psychology*, 1977, **13**, 257-265.

Harris, J. W. *Law and Legal Science*. Oxford: Clarendon Press, 1979.

Harris, M. *Cannibals and Kings: The Origins of Cultures*. London: Fontana, 1978.

Harvey, J. H. & Smith, W.P. *Social Psychology: An Attributional Approach*. Saint Louis: Mosby, 1977.

Harvey, J. H. & Weary, G. *Perspectives on Attributional Processes*. Dubuque, Iowa: Wm. C. Brown, 1981.

Harvey, J. H., Ickes, W. J. & Kidd, R. F. (Eds.), *New Directions in Attribution Research*, Vol. 1. Hillsdale, N.J.: LEA, 1976.

Harvey, J. H., Ickes, W. J. & Kidd, R. F. (Eds.), *New Directions in Attribution Research*, Vol. 2. Hillsdale, N.J.: LEA, 1978.

Harvey, J. H., Ickes, W. J. & Kidd, R. F. (Eds.), *New Directions in Attribution Research*, Vol. 3. Hillsdale, N.J.: LEA, 1981.

Hart, H. L. A. The ascription of responsibility and rights. *Proceedings of the Aristotelian Society*, 1948/1949, **49**, 171-194.

Hart, H. L. A. *Punishment and Responsibility*. Oxford: Clarendon Press, 1968.

Hart, H. L. A. & Honoré, A. M. *Causation in the Law*. Oxford: Clarendon Press, 1959.

Heider, F. Social perception and phenomenal causality. *Psychological Review*, 1944, **51**, 358-374.

Heider, F. *The Psychology of Interpersonal Relations*. New York: Wiley, 1958.

Hempel, C. G. The theoretician's dilemma: A study in the logic of theory construction. In H. Feigl, M. Scriven & G. Maxwell (Eds.), *Minnesota Studies in the Philosophy of Science*, Vol. 2. University of Minnesota Press, 1958.

Henchy, T. & Glass, D. C. Evaluation apprehension and the social facilitation of dominant and subordinate responses. *Journal of Personality and Social Psychology*, 1968, **10**, 446-454.

Hewitt, J. P. *Self and Society: A Symbolic Interactionist Social Psychology*. Boston: Allyn & Bacon, 1976.

Hewitt, J. P. & Hall, P. M. Social problems, problematic situations, and quasi-theories. *American Sociological Review*, 1973, **38**, 367-374.

Hewitt, J. P. & Stokes, R. Disclaimers. *American Sociological Review*, 1975, **40**, 1-11.

Hobbes, T. *Leviathan*. New York: McMillan, 1962 (Originally published 1651).

Hochschild, A. R. Emotion work, feeling rules, and social structure. *American Journal of Sociology*, 1979, **85**, 551-575.

Holzkamp, K. *Kritische Psychologie*. Frankfurt a. M.: Fischer, 1973.

Hooker, C. A. Empiricism, perception and conceptual change. *Canadian Journal of Philosophy*, 1973, **3**, 59-75.

Husserl, E. *Ideas: General Introduction to Pure Phenomenology*. New York: Collier Books, 1962.

Israel, J. & Tajfel, H. *The Context of Social Psychology*. London: Academic Press, 1972.

Jahoda, M., Lazarsfeld, P. L. & Zeisel, H. *Die Arbeitslosen von Marienthal: Ein Soziograpischer Versuch mit einem Anhang zur Geschichte der Soziographie*. Allensbach: Verlag fur Demoskopie, 1960 (Originally published 1933).

Jones, E. E. How do people perceive the causes of behaviour? In I. L. Janis, (Ed.), *Current Trends in Psychology: Readings from American Scientist*. Los Altos, Calif.: Kaufmann, 1977.

Jones, E. E. & Davis, K. E. From acts to dispositions: The attribution process in person perception. In L. Berkowitz (Ed.), *Advances in Experimental Social Psychology*, Vol. 2. New York: Academic Press, 1965.

Jones, E. E., Gergen, K. J. & Davis, K. E. Some determinants of reactions to being approved or disapproved as a person. *Psychological Monographs*, 1962, **76**, (2, Whole No. 521).

Jones, E.E., Kanouse, D. E., Kelley, H. H., Nisbett, R. E., Valins, S. & Weiner, B. *Attribution: Perceiving the Causes of Behaviour*. Morristown: General Learning Press, 1972.

Jones, E. E. & McGillis, D. Correspondent inferences and the attribution cube: A comparative appraisal. In J. H. Harvey, W. J. Ickes & R. F. Kidd (Eds.), *New Directions in Attribution Research*, Vol. 1. Hillsdale, N. J.: Erlbaum, 1976.

Keat, R. & Urry, J. *Social Theory as Science*. London: Routledge & Kegan Paul, 1975.

Kelley, H. H. Attribution theory in social psychology. In D. Levine (Ed.), *Nebraska Symposium on Motivation*, Vol. 15. Lincoln, Nebraska: Nebraska University Press, 1967.

Kelley, H.H. Attribution in social interaction. In E. E. Jones et al. (Eds.), *Attribution: Perceiving the Causes of Behaviour*. Morristown: General Learning Press, 1972a.

Kelley, H.H. Causal schemata and the attribution process. In E. E. Jones et al. (Eds.), *Attribution: Perceiving the Causes of Behaviour*. Morristown: General Learning Press, 1972b.

Kelley, H. H. The process of causal attribution. *American Psychologist*, 1973, **28**, 107-128.

Kelley, H. H. & Michaela, J. L. Attribution theory and research. *Annual Review of Psychology*, 1980, **31**, 457-502.

Kelly, G. *The Psychology of Personal Constructs*, Vols. 1 and 2. New York: Norton, 1955.

Kohlberg, L. Stage and sequence: The cognitive-developmental approach to socialization. In D. A. Goslin (Ed.), *Handbook of Socialization Theory and Research*. Chicago: Rand McNally, 1969.

Kohlberg, L. Moral stages and moralization: The cognitive-developmental approach. In T. Lickona (Ed.), *Moral Development and Behavior: Theory, Research, and Social Issues*. New York: Holt, Rinehart & Winston, 1976.

Kreilkamp, T. *The Corrosion of the Self: Society's Effect on People*. New York: New York University Press, 1976.

Kruglanski, A. W. The endogenous-exogenous partition in attribution theory. *Psychological Review*, 1975, **82**, 387-406.

Labov, W. The boundaries of words and their meanings. In C. N. Bailey & R. W. Shuy (Eds.), *New Ways of Analysing Variation in English*. Washington D. C.: Georgetown University Press, 1973.

Lakatos, I. Falsification and the methodology of scientific research programmes. In I. Lakatos & A. Musgrave (Eds.),, *Criticism and the Growth of Knowledge*. Cambridge: Cambridge University Press, 1970.

Landy, D. & Aronson, E. The influence of the character of the criminal and his victim on the decisions of simulated jurors. *Journal of Experimental Social Psychology*, 1969, **5**, 141-152.

Langer, E. J. Rethinking the role of thought in social interaction. In J. H. Harvey, W. J. Ickes & R. F. Kidd (Eds.), *New Directions in Attribution Research*, Vol. 2. Hillsdale, N.J.: Erlbaum, 1978.

Langer, E., Blank, A. & Chanowitz, B. The mindlessness of ostensibly thoughtful action: The role of "placebic" information in interpersonal interaction. *Journal of*

Personality and Social Psychology, 1978, **36**, 635-642.

Langford, G. *Human Action.* New York : Doubleday, 1971.

Lerner, M. J. & Miller, D. T. Just world research and the attribution process: Looking back and ahead. *Psychological Bulletin,* 1978, **46**, 176-189.

Lowe, C. A. & Medway, C. A. Effects of valence, severity, and relevance on responsibility and dispositional attribution. *Journal of Personality,* 1976, **44**, 518-538.

Lyman, S. M. & Scott, M. B. *Sociology of the Absurd.* New York: Appleton-Century-Crofts, 1970.

McGuire, W. J. The yin and yang of progress in social psychology: Seven koan. *Journal of Personality and Social Psychology,* 1973, **26**, 446-456.

McHugh, P. *Defining the Situation.* Indianapolis: The Bobbs-Merrill Co., 1968.

McKillip, J. & Posovac, E. J. Attribution of responsibility for an accident: Effects of similarity to the victim and severity of consequences. *Proceeedings of the 80th Annual Convention of the American Psychological Association,* 1972, **7**, 181-182.

McKillip, J. & Posavac, E. J. Judgments of responsibility for an accident. *Journal of Personality,* 1975, **43**, 248-265.

McMartin, J. A. & Shaw, J. I. An attributional analysis of responsibility for an happy accident: Effects of ability, intention, and effort. *Human Relations,* 1977, **30**, 899-918.

Malinowski, B. *The Family Among the Australian Aboriginies.* London: London University Press, 1913.

Malinowski, B. *The Sexual Life of Savages in North Western Melanesia.* (3rd Edition with special foreword). London: Routledge & Kegan Paul, 1932.

Manis, M. Comments on Gergen's 'Social psychology as history'. *Personality and Social Psychology Bulletin,* 1975, **1**, 450-455.

Manstead, A. S. R. & Semin, G. R. Social transgressions, social perspectives, and social emotionality. *Motivation and Emotion,* 1981, **5**, 249-261.

Markus, H. Self-schemata and processing information about the self. *Journal of Personality and Social Psychology,* 1977, **35**, 63-78.

Marsh, P., Rosser, E. & Harré, R. *The Rules of Disorder.* London: Routledege & Kegan Paul, 1978.

Mead, G. H. *The Philosophy of the Present.* Chicago: Chicago University Press, 1932.

Mead, G. H. *Mind, Self and Society.* Chicago: Chicago University Press, 1934.

Medway, F. J. & Lowe, C. A. Effects of outcome valence and severity on responsibility attribution. *Psychological Reports,* 1975, **36**, 239-246.

Meehl, P. E. Theoretical risks and tabular asterisks: Sir Karl, Sir Ronald, and the slow progress of soft psychology. *Journal of Consulting and Clinical Psychology,* 1978, **26**, 806-834.

Mehan, H. & Wood, H. *The Reality of Ethnomethodology.* New York: Wiley, 1975.

Mehrabian, A. Substitute for apology: Manipulation of cognitions to reduce negative attitude toward self. *Psychological Reports,* 1967, **20**, 687-692.

Milgram, S. *The Individual in a Social World: Essays and Experiments.* Reading, Mass.: Addison-Wesley, 1977.

Mill, J. S. *A System of Logic: Ratiocinative and Inductive* (2 Vols., 1843). London, 1868.

Mills, C. W. Situated actions and vocabularies of motive. *American Sociological Review,* 1940, **5**, 904-913.

Modigliani, A. Embarrassment, facework, and eye contact: Testing a theory of embarrassment. *Journal of Personality and Social Psychology,* 1971, **17**, 15-24.

Monson, T. C. & Snyder, M. Actors, observers, and the attribution process: Towards a reconceptualization. *Journal of Experimental Social Psychology,* 1977, **13**,

89-11.

Moscovici, S. Preface. In C. Herzlich, *Health and Illness: A Social Psychological Analysis*. London: Academic Press, 1973.

Much, N. C. & Shweder, R. A. Speaking of rules: The analysis of culture in breach. In W. Damon (Ed.), *Moral Development* (New Directions for Child Development, No. 2). San Francisco: Jossey-Bass, 1978.

Natanson, M. *Literature, Philosophy, and the Social Sciences*. The Hague: M. Nijhoff, 1962.

Natanson, M. Introduction. In A. Schutz, *Collected Works*, Vol. 1. (*The Problem of Social Reality*). The Hague: M. Nijhoff, 1973.

Natanson, M. Phenomenology and typification: A study in the philosophy of Alfred Schutz. *Social Research*, 1970, **37**, 1-22.

Neisser, U. *Cognition and Reality*. San Francisco: Freeman, 1976.

Nillson, M. P. *Primitive Time Reckoning*. Oxford: University Press, 1920.

Nisbett, R. E. & Ross, L. *Human Inference: Strategies and Shortcomings of Social Judgment*. Englewood Cliffs.,N.J.: Prentice Hall, 1980.

Nisbett, R. E. & Wilson, T. D. Telling more than we can know: Verbal reports on mental processes. *Psychological Review*, 1977, **84**, 231-259.

Orne, M. T. On the social psychology of the psychological experiment with particular reference to demand characteristics and their implications. *American Psychologist*, 1962, **17**, 776-783.

Orne, M. T. Hypnosis, motivation, and the ecological validity of the psychological experiment. In W. J. Arnold & M. M. Page (Eds.), *Nebraska Symposium on Motivation*. Lincoln: University of Nebraska Press, 1970.

Parsons, T. *The Social System*. Glencoe, Ill.: Free Press, 1951.

Parsons, T. The superego and the theory of social systems. *Psychiatry*, 1952, **15**, 15-24.

Perrin, S. & Spencer, C. Independence or conformity in the Asch experiment as a reflection of cultural and situational factors. *British Journal of Social Psychology*, 1981, **20**, 205-209.

Peters, R. S. *The Concept of Motivation*. London: Routledge & Kegan Paul, 1958.

Peters, R.S. Motivation, emotion, and the conceptual schemes of common sense. T. Mischel (Ed.), *Human Action: Conceptual and Empirical Issues*. New York: Academic Press, 1969.

Pierce, C. S. *Collected Papers*. Cambridge: Harvard University Press, 1933.

Pliner, P. & Cappell, H. Drinking, driving, and the attribution of responsibility. *Journal of Studies on Alcohol*, 1977, **38**, 593-602.

Polanyi, M. *The Tacit Dimension*. Garden City, N. Y.: Doubleday & Co. , 1966.

Pollner, M. Mundane reasoning. *Philosophy of Social Sciences*, 1974, **4**, 35-54.

Portmann, A. *Biologische Fragmente zu einer Lehre von Menschen*. 2nd. Ed., Basel, 1951.

Portmann, A. *Zoologie und das neue Bild des Menschen-Biologische Fragmente zu einer Lehre des Menschen*. Hamburg: Rohwolt, 1962.

Pyszczynski, T. A. & Greenberg, J. Role of disconfirmed expectancies in the instigation of attributional processing. *Journal of Personality and Social Psychology*, 1981, **40**, 31-38.

Reisman, S. R. & Schopler, J. An analysis of attribution process and an application to determinants of responsibility. *Journal of Personality and Social Psychology*, 1973, **25**, 361-368.

Regan, D. T., Williams, M. & Sparling, S. Voluntary expiation of guilt: A field experiment. *Journal of Personality and Social Psychology*, 1972, **24**, 42-45.

Riecken, H. W. A program for research on experiments in social psychology. In N. F.

Washburn (Ed.), *Decisions, Values, and Groups,* Vol. 2. New York: Macmillan, 1962.

Ring, K. Experimental social psychology: Some sober questions about some frivolous values. *Journal of Experimental Social Psychology,* 1967, **3**, 113-123.

Roberts, S. *Order and Dispute: An Introduction to Legal Anthropology.* Harmondsworth: Penguin, 1979.

Rosch, E. The nature of mental codes for color categories. *Journal of Experimental Psychology: Human Perception and Performance,* 1975, **1**, 303-322.

Rosch, E. Human categorization. In N. Warren (Ed.), *Studies in Cross-Cultural Psychology,* Vol. 1. London: Academic Press.

Rosenthal, R. & Rosnow, R. L. *Artifact in Behavioural Research.* New York: Academic Press, 1969.

Rosenzweig, S. The experimental situation as a psychological problem. *Psychological Review,* 1933, **40**, 337-354.

Ross, A. *On Guilt, Responsibility and Punishment.* Berkeley and Los Angeles: University of California Press, 1975.

Ross, L. The intuitive psychologist and his shortcomings: Distortions in the attribution process. In L. Berkowitz (Ed.), *Advances in Experimental Social Psychology,* Vol. 10. New York: Academic Press, 1977.

Ross, L. Some afterthoughts on the intuitive psychologist. In L. Berkowitz (Ed.), *Cognitive Theories in Social Psychology.* New York: Academic Press, 1978.

Roth, W. E. Superstition, magic and medicine. *New Queensland Ethnographic Bulletin,* 1903, 5.

Rummelhart, D. E. & Ortony, A. The representation of knowledge in memory. In R. C. Anderson, J. J. Spiro & W. E. Montague (Eds.), *Schooling and the Acquisition of Knowledge.* Hillsdale, N. J.: Erlbaum, 1977.

Russell, B. *Inquiry Into Meaning and Truth.* New York: W. W. Norton & Co., 1940.

Ryle, G. *The Concept of Mind.* London: Hutchinson, 1944.

Sattler, J. M. Embarrassment and blushing: A theoretical review. *Journal of Psychology,* 1966, **69**, 117-133.

Schank, R. C. & Abelson, R. *Scripts, Plans, Goals and Understanding.* Hillsdale, N. J.: Erlbaum, 1977.

Scheff, T. J. Negotiating reality: Notes on power in the assessment of responsibility. *Social Problems,* 1968, 16, 3-17.

Scheler, M. *Die Stellung des Menschen im Kosmos.* Darmstadt, 1928.

Schlenker, B. R. Social psychology and science. *Journal of Personality and Social Psychology,* 1974, **29**, 1-15.

Schlenker, B. R. Social psychology and science: Another look. *Personality and Social Psychology Bulletin,* 1976, **2**, 384-390.

Schlenker, B. R. *Impression Management: The Self-Concept, Social Identity, and Interpersonal Relations.* Monterey, Calif.: Brooks/Cole, 1980.

Schlenker, B. R. & Darby, B. W. The use of apologies in social predicaments. *Social Psychology Quarterly,* 1981, **44**, 271-278.

Schneider, D. J., Hastorf, A. H. & Ellsworth, P. C. *Person Perception.* Reading, Mass.: Addison-Wesley, 1979 (2nd. Edn.).

Schönbach, P. A category system for account phases. *European Journal of Social Psychology,* 1980, **10**, 195-200.

Schutz, A. Common-sense and scientific interpretation of human action. *Philosophy and Phenomenological Research,* 1953, **14**, 1-37.

Schutz, A. *The Phenomenology of the Social World.* London: Heinemann, 1972.

Schutz, A. *Collected Papers,* Vol. 1. (*The Problem of Social Reality*). The Hague: M. Nijhoff, 1973.

Schutz, A. *Collected Papers*, Vol. 2. (*Studies in Social Theory*). The Hague: M. Nijhoff, 1964.

Schutz, A. & Luckmann, T. *The Structures of the Life World*. London: Heinemann, 1974.

Scott, M. B. & Lyman, S. Accounts. *American Sociological Review*, 1968, **33**, 46-62.

Sedlak, A. J. Developmental differences in understanding plans and evaluating actors. *Child Development*, 1979, **50**, 536-560.

Semin, G. R. A gloss on attribution theory. *British Journal of Social and Clinical Psychology*, 1980, **19**, 291-300.

Semin,, G. R. Strictures upon strictures. *British Journal of Social Psychology*, 1981, **20**, 304-306 (a).

Semin, G. R. Peinlich, peinlich: Aber warum eigentlich? *Psychologie Heute*, 1981, **12**, 22-28 (b).

Semin, G. R. The transparency of the sinner. *European Journal of Social Psychology*, 1982, **12**, 173-180

Semin, G. R. & Manstead, A. S. R. Social psychology: Social or psychological? *British Journal of Social and Clinical Psychology*, 1979, **18**, 191-202.

Semin, G. R. & Manstead, A. S. R. The beholder beheld: A study of social emotionality. *European Journal of Social Psychology*, 1981, **11**, 253-265.

Semin, G. R. & Manstead, A. S. R. The social consequences of embarrassment displays and restitution behaviour. *European Journal of Social Psychology*, 1982, **12**, 367-377.

Semin, G. R, Rosch, E. & Chassein, J. A comparison of the common-sense and 'scientific' conceptions of extraversion-introversion. *European Journal of Social Psychology*. 1981, **11**, 77-86

Semin, G. R., Rosch, E. & Krolage, J. 'Scientific' models of personality as social representations. Unpublished manuscript, University of Sussex, 1982.

Semin, G. R., Rosch, E., Krolage, J. & Chassein, J. Alltagswissen als implizite Basis fuer wissenschaftliche Persoenlichkeitstheorien. *Zeitschrift Fuer Sozialpsychologie*, 1981, **12**, 233-242.

Shaver, K. G. Redress and conscientiousness in the attribution of responsibility for accidents. *Journal of Experimental Social Psychology*, 1970, **6**, 100-110 (a).

Shaver, K. G. Defensive attribution: Effects of severity and relevance on the responsibility assigned for an accident. *Journal of Personality and Social Psychology*, 1970, **14**, 101-113 (b).

Shaver, K. G. *An Introduction to Attribution Processes*. Cambridge, Mass.: Winthrop, 1975.

Shaver, K.G. & Carroll, A. B. Effects of severity and sex of perpetrator in the attribution of responsibility. Paper presented at the Eastern Psychological Association Convention, Atlantic City, N. J., April, 1970.

Shaw, J. I. & McMartin, J. A. Perpetrator or victim: Effects of who suffers in an automobile accident on judgmental strictness. *Social Behaviour and Personality*, 1975, **3**, 5-12.

Shaw, J. I. & McMartin, J. A. Personal and situational determinants of the attribution of responsibility for an accident. *Human Relations*, 1977, **30**, 95-107.

Shaw, J. I. & Skolnick, P. Attribution of responsibility for a happy accident. *Journal of Personality and Social Psychology*, 1971, **18**, 380-383.

Shaw, M. E. & Reitan, H. T. Attribution of responsibility as a basis for sanctioning behaviour. *British Journal of Social and Clinical Psychology*, 1969, **8**, 217-226.

Shaw, M. E. & Sulzer, J. L. An empirical test of Heider's levels in attribution of responsibility. *Journal of Abnormal and Social Psychology*, 1964, **69**, 39-46.

Shepard, J. W. & Bagley, A. J. The effects of biographic information and order of presentation on the judgment of an aggressive action. *British Journal of Social and Clinical Psychology*, 1970, **9**, 177-179.

Shott, S. Emotion and social life: A symbolic interactionist analysis. *American Journal of Sociology*, 1979, **84**, 1317-1334.

Shotter, J. Vico, moral worlds, accountability and personhood. In P. Heelas & A. Lock (Eds.), *Indigenous Psychologies (The Anthropology of the Self)*. London: Academic Press, 1981.

Smith, D. Theorizing as ideology. In R. Turner (Ed.), *Ethnomethodology*. Harmondsworth: Penguin, 1974.

Staub, E. *Positive Social Behavior and Morality*. Vol. 1 (*Social and Personal Influences*). New York: Academic Press, 1978.

Staub, E. *Positive Social Behavior and Morality*. Vol. 2 (*Socialization and Development*). New York: Academic Press, 1979.

Stebbins, R. Role distance, role distance behaviour and jazz musicians. *British Journal of Sociology*, 1969, **20**, 406-415.

Stokes, R. & Hewitt, J. P. Aligning actions. *American Sociological Review*, 1976, **41**, 838-849.

Stone, G. P. Appearance and the self. In A. Rose (Ed.), *Human Behaviour and Social Processes*. Boston: Houghton-Mifflin, 1962.

Storch, O. *Die Sonderstellung des Menschen in Lebensabspiel und Vererbung*. Wien, 1948.

Sykes, G. M. & Matza, D. Techniques of neutralization: A theory of delinquency. *American Sociological Review*, 1957, **22**, 664-670.

Tajfel, H. Experiments in a vacuum. In J. Israel & H. Tajfel (Eds.), *The Context of Social Psychology: A Critical Assessment*. London: Academic Press, 1972.

Taylor, S. E. & Crocker, J. Schematic bases of social information processing. In E. T. Higgins, C. P. Herman & M. P. Zanna (Eds.), *The Ontario Symposium on Personality and Social Psychology*, Vol. 1. Hillsdale, N. J. : Erlbaum, 1980.

Tedeschi, J. T. & Riess, M. Verbal strategies in impression management. In C. Antaki (Ed.), *The Psychology of Ordinary Explanations of Social Behaviour*. London: Academic Press, 1981.

Thorngate, W. Process invariance: Another red herring. *Personality and Social Psychology Bulletin*, 1975, **1**, 485-488.

Triandis, H. C. Some universals of social behavior. *Personality and Social Psychology Bulletin*, 1978, **4**, 1-16.

Trigg, R. *Reason and Commitment*. Cambridge: Cambridge University Press, 1973.

Von Uexküll, J. *Umwelt und Innenwelt der Tierre*. Berlin, 1921.

Von Uexküll, J. *Streifzuege durch die Umwelten von Tieren und Menschen*. Hamburg: Rohwolt, 1958.

Ungar, S. The effects of status and excuse on interpersonal reactions to deviant behaviour. *Social Psychology Quarterly*, 1981, **44**, 260-263.

Vidmar, N. & Crinklaw, L. D. Attributing responsibility for an accident: A methodological and conceptual critique. *Canadian Journal of Behavioural Sciences*, 1974, **6**, 113-129.

Walster, E. Assignment of responsibility for an accident. *Journal of Personality and Social Psychology*, 1966, **3**, 73-79.

Walster, E. "Second-guessing" important events. *Human Relations*, 1967, **20**, 239-250.

Weber, M. *The Theory of Social and Economic Organization*. New York: Oxford University Press, 1947.

Winch, P. *The Idea of a Social Science and its Relation to Philosophy*. London: Routledge & Kegan Paul, 1958.

Winch, P. Understanding a primitive society. *American Philosophical Quarterly*, 1964, **1**, 307-324. Reprinted in B. Wilson (Ed.), *Rationality*. Oxford: Basil Blackwell, 1970 (Page references in present volume refer to reprinted version).

Woolbert, C. H. The audience. *Psychological Monographs*, 1916, **21**, 37-54.

Wortman, C. B. & Linder, D. E. Attribution of responsibility for an outcome as a function of its likelihood. *Proceedings of the 81st Annual Convention of the American Psychological Association*, 1973, **8**, 52-55.

Author index

Wortman, C. B. 140
Xiram, R. 168
Zeisel, H. 170

Subject index